IGNORANCE

IGNORANCE

EVERYTHING YOU NEED TO KNOW ABOUT NOT KNOWING

ROBERT GRAEF

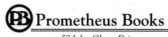

Prometheus Books

59 John Glenn Drive
Amherst, New York 14228

Published 2017 by Prometheus Books

Cover design by Jacqueline Nasso Cooke
Cover image © Superstock/Masterfile
Cover design © Prometheus Books

Trademarked names appear throughout this book. Prometheus Books recognizes all registered trademarks, trademarks, and service marks mentioned in the text.

The Internet addresses listed in the text were accurate at the time of publication. The inclusion of a website does not indicate an endorsement by the author(s) or by Prometheus Books, and Prometheus Books does not guarantee the accuracy of the information presented at these sites.

Every attempt has been made to trace accurate ownership of copyrighted material in this book. Errors and omissions will be corrected in subsequent editions, provided that notification is sent to the publisher.

Inquiries should be addressed to
Prometheus Books
59 John Glenn Drive
Amherst, New York 14228
VOICE: 716–691–0133 • FAX: 716–691–0137
WWW.PROMETHEUSBOOKS.COM

21 20 19 18 17   5 4 3 2 1

Library of Congress Cataloging-in-Publication Data

Names: Graef, Robert, author.
Title: Ignorance : everything you need to know about not knowing / by Robert Graef.
Description: Amherst : Prometheus Books, 2017. | Includes bibliographical references and index.
Identifiers: LCCN 2017027284 (print) | LCCN 2017042068 (ebook) | ISBN 9781633883222 (ebook) | ISBN 9781633883215 (pbk.)
Subjects: LCSH: Ignorance (Theory of knowledge)
Classification: LCC BD221 (ebook) | LCC BD221 .G73 2017 (print) | DDC 121—dc23
LC record available at https://lccn.loc.gov/2017027284

Printed in the United States of America

CONTENTS

ACKNOWLEDGMENTS

A work of nonfiction cannot be written without help. I am indebted to a corps of friends who were frank in pointing out problems with the text. Thanks for encouragement and advice go out to Earnest Pihl, Martha Smith, Emily Davis, Gary Fye, Bruce O'Neill, and Cheryl Bela. To Charles Davis and Michael Dorsey, much gratitude for your technical help.

Special thanks to the dedicated reference librarians of the Sno-Isle Regional Library System who fill their days by helping people like me to ferret out hidden information. Our public libraries serve branches of the world's most democratically enlightening institutions, and their work enriches the substance and spirit of their society.

Many thanks to the Prometheus team; to Editor in Chief Steven L. Mitchell who dared to take a chance with *Ignorance*; to copyeditor and world-class nitpicker Jeffrey Curry who taught me that my idea of "clean copy" needs some work; to Editorial Assistant Hanna Etu who kept things moving on all fronts; to Mark Hall who, among other things, assembled outstanding back cover copy; to publicist Cheryl Quimba who let the book world know about *Ignorance*; and to Jacqueline Nasso Cooke for her provocative cover design.

Additional thanks to Mathieu Roy whose editorial skills whipped the manuscript into shape. And thanks to the patient baristas at Marysville's Eighty-Eighth Street Starbucks where the price of a tall brew-of-the-day rented the workstation where the daily background of coffee shop din helped me to put the project together.

Finally, and because its role in nonfiction literature isn't properly appreciated, credit is due to *Wikipedia*, that broad-based global network of individuals, organizations, clubs, and communities that work together to create the people's encyclopedia. As the most powerful example of volunteer collaboration and open content sharing in the world, *Wikipedia*'s contributions to societal knowledge and reduction of ignorance stand above critics' nit-picking discoveries of its imperfections. Thanks to all who work to provide open, accurate, and unbiased information.

INTRODUCTION

The recipe for perpetual ignorance is: Be satisfied with your opinions and content with your knowledge.

—Elbert Hubbard

U p and down, light and dark, yin and yang—it seems that so many concepts are split between polar opposites that one might imagine the book of Genesis's metaphoric tree of knowledge of good and evil set opposite to a tree of ignorance of good and evil. God commanded Adam and Eve, "You may freely eat the fruit of every tree in the garden—except the tree of the knowledge of good and evil. If you eat its fruit, you are sure to die."[1] They disobeyed, but instead of death their sentence was commuted to a life of hard labor and suffering. Their choice was between that of accepting the status quo of the garden's ample ecosystem and that of following wherever their minds led them. Biting into the symbolic fruit gave the couple the freedom to pursue and try whatever occurred to them—to compose symphonies, spread pornography, or build printing presses or atom bombs. God's good-and-evil pairing was very much like the juxtaposition of A and Z in that it included all of the positions between the poles, in the same way that the Bible's pairing of east and west included all the territory between. The metaphorical distance between abject ignorance and openness to knowledge encompasses everyone's intellectual position, from knowing bits of this and that to reaching for great hunks of knowledge, whether good or evil. Although interpretations of the Genesis passage vary, no one disputes the importance of the difference between knowing and not knowing or the dangers of knowing the wrong stuff.

The Bible story offers a thumbnail clue of how we got where we are. Along the way, brave souls pioneered new paths of knowledge, following them wherever they led, discovering that their routes traced narrow lines through the untracked terrain of ignorance. Stepping off the path invites both threats and adventures, just as swimming beyond the reef puts us perilously within the food chain. While ignorance poses real threats to comfort, safety, security, health, and contentment, knowledge is one of our best means of assuring positive outcomes. Experience confirms that the rewards of pursuing the right knowledge are sufficient to justify a lifetime of learning, especially when they include learning how to avoid and combat ignorance. It begins with learning how to identify ignorance for what it is and does, and this is not a simple task. If the tree of ignorance may be thought of as situated at one pole and the knowledge tree at the other, then all of our growth toward the knowledge tree increases our distance from the tree of ignorance and erodes the remaining distance, all of which carries the name of ignorance.

There you have it, a definition. But like all definitions it has an upside and a downside, for every definition is a clarifying trap. While definitions seek to explain, they also put limits on concepts by locking ideas within tidy, rigid boundaries. Thoughts on ignorance shouldn't be so limited because it takes light from many sources to expose how its constraints set people and their ideas against harmony, progress, and each other. Because definitions lack what it takes to complete Big Pictures, they are assisted by airy metaphors herein. In this book, I will draw on a variety of sources, including allegory, theology, myth, folkways, science, literature, and other images of reality, since there is no corner of human history that is free of the fingerprints of ignorance.

Since there is so much more that is unknown than is known, ignorance will always cover more territory than knowledge. With the totality of human thought having touched only bits of the cosmic whole, we are left with a vast and enticing mystery that begs to be explored. Yet the unknown is every bit as real as the known, which means that poorly understood forces and dynamics account for much of what we experience, including weather, disease, seismic events, and sun spots. When a tornado touches down or an El Nino event in the Pacific scrambles weather patterns, mystified people write off their effects with exclamations of "How odd!" or "Stuff happens!"

Put yourself in the picture as we explore a mental model that compares the known with the unknown:

You are clutching the top rung of a very tall ladder, so tall that you cannot see its bottom. It leans against a limitless canvas on which you mark a prominent spot with a broad-tipped carpenter's pencil. The infinite canvas reaches beyond your sight in all directions, and the total pictured on its height and breadth is meant to represent every fact, function, and thing in the universe, while your pencil spot covers the small portion of reality with which you have had some contact. The rest of the canvas is unknown to you, terra incognita, an infinite testament to the insignificance of anyone's grasp on all there is to know.

Zooming in, you see that the penciled spot is made up of thousands of tiny flakes of graphite that metaphorically represent all the information in your personal knowledge base, just as every other person's knowledge might be represented by the substance and flakes of other pencil spots. We live, think, and dream in our own small spots, surrounded by the unknown, but it is how we handle our situations that makes all the difference. Some of us use our flakes of graphite as building blocks to wall ourselves off from imagined threats lurking in the unknown, like the fearsome sea monsters drawn on uncharted regions of early maritime maps. Others use the same flakes to build roads and bridges to access whatever wonders the unknown might offer. Building walls instead of bridges is the essence of ignorance. To limit life by living within intellectual confinement is to earn and accept the imprisonment of human spirit.

Little lights pop on and off across near reaches of the Big Picture to signal where researchers are grasping for clues that point the way toward yet-to-be-discovered knowledge. Whereas that landscape was largely dark in past centuries, it glows more brightly with time as newly discovered knowledge drives wedges between those who embrace its novelty and traditionalists who don't. The divide widens with people's differing inclinations to understand new data and their significance. Some grasp the challenge and strive to keep pace while others hold to outmoded or disproved facts and beliefs that set them against the ever-changing world that is.

The evolution of digital technology sets the pace for acquisition of new data and, along with it, knowledge. In 1981, Apple offered the first mass-memory device for home offices, the Corvus hard drive, a desktop memory that boasted a then unheard-of capacity of 5.65 megabytes. The Corvus drive was stage one in the evolution of bigger, faster digital memory options, culminating with the Cloud. Cloud capacity is measured in petabytes, each of which equals more than a million of the Corvus era's megabytes. But that is just the beginning. A collection of 1,024 petabytes of memory equals one exabyte. Multiply exabytes by 1,024 to convert them to zellabytes. Do the same to 1,024 zellabytes to get one yollabyte. Science can foresee a need for such numbers, but, given the short time it took for that level of data storage to arrive, it was impossible for growth in analytic human understanding to keep pace with the technology.

Faster computers with bigger memories enable researchers to connect dots as never before. The system feeds on growth like a ramjet feeds on speed: growth stimulates more growth to reach farther faster. Results have been generally good but sometimes not so good because our capacity for distinguishing good from bad, useful from wasteful, and positive from negative has not developed as quickly. The Big Data concept of great institutions ramped up the three V's of information handling: huge Volumes, dizzying Velocities, and limitless Variety, with the NSA's population-wide collection of personal information serving as a prime example. While devices become quicker and storage greater, the imbalance between information overload and human analytic capacity imposes a wedge between the curious who try to make sense of it and the incurious who find comfort in ignoring mind-bending change.

If for no other reason, ignorance deserves increased attention because so much more is unknown than known. Ignorance is the root of waste, discord, tension, and conflict. Whether we admit it or not, ignorance—not knowing—is everyone's unacknowledged companion, aided by those who, in pursuit of power and profit, make it their business to hold others ignorant. History is filled with accounts of political and commercial powers managing knowledge to control popular beliefs and behavior. Exposing the roles that agents of ignorance play in our lives cannot help but advance efforts to improve rather than aggravate problems faced around the world. The remainder of this book is dedicated to this task.

As I near the end of a life of study I am struck by the discomforting reality that a tech-savvy fourteen-year-old has a greater informational reach than I do. If, as they say, knowledge is power, then it is somewhat frightening to think of that baton passing to the young. Although young people are skilled at inventing and offending, are they better at *knowing*? Amid the confusion of digital static does the stuff they access reveal its deeper meanings to them? I choose to believe that in my time, a kinder and gentler era, we knew things that today's kids don't understand, just as they know (thank God!) how to solve their grandparents' cell phone and computer problems. The best I can come up with to allay this discomfort is that, just possibly, neither generation is, on balance, less knowledgeable than the other. It is also significant that there are different things that different generations *don't know*. Kids cannot know my historical perspective. I cannot be a "digital native." In our more generous moments, we might look across generational divides to find that we are complementarily ignorant.

The unfortunate shortage of generous moments of that sort produces differing schools of thought or non-thought that mark and separate us into tribes. It invites people to live unnaturally small lives, using the little they know to insulate themselves against what they don't know. Ironically, ignorance leaves good people unaware of how deeply it biases their political and economic attitudes against their own best interests. When Christians are more likely to let politics dictate their place of worship than for worship to influence their politics, ignorance of what matters runs deep.

In a verbal society, knowledge is transmitted from sender to receiver in a code known as language. Without it, we would be ignorant of much of what we know because words serve as hooks on which to hang meanings. Henry Hazlitt wrote, "A man with a scant vocabulary will almost certainly be a weak thinker. The richer and more copious one's vocabulary and the greater one's awareness of fine distinctions and subtle nuances of meaning, the more fertile and precise is likely to be one's thinking. Knowledge of things and knowledge of the words for them grow together. If you do not know the words, you can hardly know the thing."[2]

Words are like baseballs. As there are speakers and hearers, so there are pitchers and batters. And just as a word is a word, a baseball is a baseball though what both might do after being launched widens their definitions. An author's use of a word will carry interesting nuances that, depending upon the mood and direction of a paragraph, might curve or dodge one way or another. Any batter's record would improve if only he knew the "stuff" a pitcher was putting on a ball—a slider, a curve, a changeup, a fastball, or a duster. Likewise, readers are advantaged when they know the "stuff" a writer puts on his words, which makes the appendix's explanation of terms an important part of this text. Its intent is to so clarify the many aspects of ignorance so that ignorance of ignorance may be brought to light and dealt with.

We learn through words and examples. Knowledge is cast in words. Words encapsulate meaning to form little packages of concept that, when opened, yield images of apple, cloud, grass, or cougar. Words can be as unruly as dogs referred to pet psychologists. Just as trainers can train dogs to attack and subdue, there are word trainers who cast happy words into dark contexts to reduce their happiness, or lift the mood of dark words by smothering them in love and light. Even a word as blighted as "war." War isn't bad; it is good because it protects us from foreign aggression, terrorists' threats, and loss of liberty and freedom. War restores the position of the United States as a leader of nations. War is good because it bonds us as a people against foreign enemies instead of leaving us to bicker among ourselves. War is good and will remain so because wordsmiths shape it to be perceived as good, largely by keeping the nation ignorant of its negative aspects. Efforts are made to decouple war from casualties, blood, body counts, collateral damage, environmental havoc, and financial cost. Better to cast war in terms of the heroes who carry the promise of liberty and freedom to oppressed peoples, the protection of our homeland, and the sacrifice of young people who put their lives at risk. Wordsmiths shape wars to be admirable efforts that deserve unquestioning support and respect.

While definitions in older dictionaries were fashioned from linguistic roots, the new *Urban Dictionary* adds gritty new concepts to old words. The new usages don't always connect with words' literal origins: ball and air, for instance, are combined as airball to describe a clean miss. An apple is a phone. A cloud is remote digital storage. Grass is now legal to smoke. A cougar is a sexually aggressive older female. These changes illustrate that much of the battle against ignorance is simply keeping up with change. But the rest, forces that promote ignorance by corrupting and restricting knowledge, must be brought to light and opposed zealously, for they erode at the soul of the nation.

CHAPTER 1

WHAT IS IGNORANCE?

I say there is no darkness but ignorance.
—William Shakespeare, *Twelfth Night*

Ignorance invades a mind whenever an observer sees something new and, by giving it a name, believes it has gained some knowledge of it. At best, this will be shallow knowledge because, like rare bird sightings, we often get only one look, though in situations where we can look as much as we please we often don't look closely enough, use a properly educated eye, or make a bias-free record of the sightings. Imagine that two observers, at different times and places in the Amazon Basin, spot never-seen-before birds, one flying toward observer A, the other flying away from observer B. They each recorded the birds' observable markings so that they may each separately announce their discoveries to the world. But since discovery is the stuff from which reputations are made, neither was eager to suggest that their separate observations might have been of opposite ends of the same bird. This fictitious example is offered as an illustration of how ego and a hundred other pitfalls stand ready to promote faulty knowledge. Incomplete or inaccurate information yields flawed understandings, which, when taken for more than they are worth, pollute knowledge. Humility, not certitude or exclusivity, is necessary because we can't know it all. We are all ignorant.

You will find metaphors overworked here, but it can't be helped. Because ignorance alludes to that great body of stuff that's "out there" but not known, we work with a shortage of descriptions, dimensions, or properties to reference to help us understand what it is or might be. Until a bit of knowledge is wrested from the unknown it can't exist even as mystery, for a good mystery exists because it has dropped clues to its existence that tease us to wonder toward it, if not into it. Although the achievements of our brains lead to the conceit that we *know*, for the most part we can only know slivers of the universe's facts and functions. We are ignorant, wholly or in part, of almost all that there is to know, and we always will be. It has always been this way, and metaphor has been the best means of addressing ideas that are too big or mysterious to get our minds around them. It's especially useful because metaphor opens up ideas while descriptors limit them.

Whether you're studying a bird in an Amazonian jungle or reading the book of Genesis, it pays to look again, and again, and again until the knowledge we collect morphs into understanding. So we return to the Garden of Eden to see whether considerations springing from another look might add anything to the first: the great metaphor of God forbidding Adam and Eve to eat of the fruit of the tree of knowledge of good and evil. The metaphor set their choice of eating or not eating the forbidden fruit as a cause of the future course for humanity. The death penalty for disobedience was commuted to exile from Eden's idyllic square one where Homo sapiens lived in harmony with nature, accepted things the way they were, and took no more from nature than they needed. Their choice had been (a) to eat the metaphorical fruit of the tree of knowledge of good and evil—that is, to lose primitive simplicity—or (b) to avoid the fruit, and the disobedience it stood for, forever. Choosing plan A led to always looking for a better way, weighing alternatives, inventing a better mousetrap, and scheming to claim the lion's share of whatever gains might be achieved—plus skimming a bit of profit to appease the thinkers' greed and ego. But under plan A, things can fall apart, fortunes and reputations may come crashing down in career-ending bad publicity, and even death is possible. Or one could choose plan B and trudge blamelessly through a life punctuated by blessings from a loving but sometimes harsh God. By following that plan, they would have left no evidence of their existence other than scrawlings on the walls of caves. The book of Genesis laid it out as a choice but one that fell on account of humanity's default setting for plan A. It was and is the choice of every upwardly mobile culture that contests with less competitive cultures using arrogance, ambition, and power seeking to satisfy the god they collectively created, whose name is More.

Additional visits to the Garden Story would likely turn up different insights. For instance, the choice of plan A, our plan, works so long as everything expands—increased GDP, more housing starts, children who have it better than their parents, advertisers' promises of "all-new" cars with more bells and whistles, longer life spans, and technology's splashier special effects, all driven by a growing base of knowledge. It has been a long time since a few leather-bound tomes could contain the entire science of medicine. A doctor in the year 1900 was ignorant of all but a fraction of what the average general practitioner of 2016 knows, and much of what he did know would have to be unlearned to function in today's medical world. But faced with change of that magnitude, people who worry that education isn't keeping pace with change aren't worried enough to get serious about taking steps to cope with it. It takes willful ignorance to avoid knowing that education needs attention, that other nations are overtaking us, and that to the winners will go the spoils.

The arrival of the digital age heralded a switch from an intellectual polarity of knowledge vs. ignorance to one of known vs. unknown, leaving notions of stupidity and empty-headedness as minor players in the realm of not knowing. The revised way of thinking acknowledges an unknown realm that impacts lives at least as much as that which is known. Visitations from the unknown that traditionalists write off as inexplicable good or bad luck are becoming better understood as the effects of things that we are not yet able to explain.

I was once fully qualified to teach physics and work in the field, but now, unless a hobbyist is curious about the history of vacuum tube electronics, I am useless to the needs of twenty-first-century technology. My kind of professional ignorance is a small part of the picture. Greater problems arise from lack of knowledge about what makes other people tick, the senselessness of one "ism" persecuting another, and how the arrogant insensitivity of ascendant cultures tramples less aggressive cultures into oblivion. In short, the social world is perpetually in crisis due to ignorance. American arrogance on the international scene, which some refer to as American exceptionalism, reflects an uninformed insensitivity that produces embarrassing errors such as Hollywood's ill-advised film *The Interview*, a "comedy" based on a fictional plan to assassinate North Korea's dictator Kim Jong Un.[1] Had the US Department of State been working back channels to ramp down tensions with that nation, Hollywood's error certainly torpedoed that. Yet the film's producers' insensitivity to blowback was matched by the media's failure to point out that the film was a bad idea, in poor taste, and more than potentially destructive of progress in international relations. Hopefully, the fiasco will serve as a cautionary example of how ignorance of global forces and counterforces leads Americans into doomed adventures. There was a time when naïve imperialists, missionaries, and colonial governments could get away with that sort of thing, but that time is gone, remembered best and documented most accurately by those who suffered under it.

Some, like newly arrived immigrants to America, take the need to be better informed seriously, while a greater number of native-born citizens drift through life with the passivity of pelagic sea organisms that move only because currents carry them. That drifting may be partly due to the sea of impermanence that moves wage earners through an average of eleven jobs and seven mini-careers over a typical working lifetime, or tenuous marriages and relationships that last as long as convenient for lack of the glue that once wove lives into stable communities (I recall a wedding where the bride and groom's homemade vows bound them "as long as love shall last"). The doubt that accompanies impermanence roils visions of tomorrow, confining the clarity of vision to questions of the moment, such as, Should I do it? How long will it take? How much will it cost? What about financing? The future is seen through a haze of doubt born of change and loss of tradition. People long for reason to sing, "On a clear day you can see forever," but impermanence and doubt about their purpose have bound them into a dispiriting cloud of not knowing.

THE DIGITAL REVOLUTION

While younger people grow up as digital natives, the older generation runs the country with smatterings of computer skills. While they may have rudimentary user skills, their thinking is still rooted in snail mail and landlines. That age, call it Technology 1.0, has been swallowed into history and is never coming back. Digital calculating, imaging, analyzing, projecting, archiving, communicating, creating, and entertaining have evolved through stages that might be thought of as 2.0, 2.7, 3.3, and so on. In terms that society understands better, information technology has grown to become a $3.4 trillion industry.[2]

Once the firewalls protecting governmental secrecy were proved vulnerable, Ariana Huffington said, "WikiLeaks was inevitable. It was bound to happen . . . what WikiLeaks showed us was that there is a huge discrepancy between what government claims is happening and what actually goes on."[3] Or as writer and thinker Stewart Brand said, "To some extent, excessive secrecy has been analyzed as the effort of an organism to hide its pathologies from itself."[4] The downside is that the justifiable amount of secrecy that protects individuals' privacy, businesses' proprietary information, and grandma's secret recipes has proved to be porous. The call for absolute transparency from WikiLeaks and friends won't be answered because that level of openness is too idealistically overreaching for our cynical and hypercompetitive world.

IGNORANCE IN THE NEW CENTURY

The United States is in the midst of moving from one characterizing national mind-set to another. The 9/11 mind-set was one of outrage and revenge that cast about for ways to respond to the disaster. The nation's leaders were caught bewildered by an amorphous, stateless, well-endowed, technically proficient, and uncompromising army of avowed enemies. Their confusion was born, in part, of ignorance about what motivates people to hate us, and that ignorance helped shape misguided efforts to deal with the problem. It is bad enough that we knew so little about our enemies. It is worse that we know so little about ourselves that we are blind to what makes much of the world view us with concern.[5]

Superpatriots who have read this far will be thinking that if this is how I feel, I should live somewhere else. Superpatriots who share in the ignorance of "if it's American it must be right" cannot understand that there is nothing unpatriotic about criticism and that expressing concern about America's actions helps keep the Ship of State from running aground. To do otherwise would be irresponsible, for, if ours is truly a democracy ruled by a government of the people, doing what we can to question and correct our government's errors is not an option—it's a responsibility. First, citizens need to *know*. For instance, when an ISIS spokesman says, "We intend to rid the world of democracy," is he speaking for all of Islam or only his bloodthirsty sect? As we continue to export the American Way, are we willing to accept that other nations may not be entranced by the priorities and actions of US government and culture? Might we come to understand that Congress, the Supreme Court, and the CIA are not always seen as attractive models for governmental reform elsewhere? Do we understand why nations on the receiving end of US international policy hold varying views of America's intentions?

A slice of the American population has been drawn into the tunnel-visioned ignorance of the "true believer," an unthinking ideology that supports the interests of a corporatocracy that uses government as a cash cow while simultaneously vilifying it as a hindrance to profitability. Others act from uninformed decision making and the kinds of attitude that breed shortsighted polarization: "I know what I know, and that's good enough for me." Conservatives rightly believe in personal responsibility while liberals cast their votes for social responsibility. But when conservatives control the levers of government, scant attention is given to social responsibility in fear that liberal concessions will break the bank while corrupting public morals. Each side trusts the other to unbalance the socioeconomic scales while both sides are, more or less, caught up in ideological myopia.

A different analysis contrasts purposeful with willful ignorance. Purposeful ignorance comes into play when movers and shakers decide what knowledge should be kept hidden to advance their interests, while willful ignorance occurs when someone identifies with scraps of intellectual turf and defends them against all counter-arguments. Either way, ignorance corrupts affairs whenever people so intensely commit their thoughts to a chosen direction that all else loses importance. A few examples:

Political ideologues oppose whatever the other party proposes with all the emotional unreason of Manchester United soccer fans. Locked-in dedication to one-dimensional interests is capable of imprisoning the minds of rabid quilters, bodybuilders, and social media addicts. Tunnel vision disqualifies otherwise good citizens from Great Debates, leaving them to defend scraps of opinion with insufficient knowledge. Overly focused specialists are ignorant by means of knowing too narrowly. They may be savants of the academic world who care for nothing aside from following their chosen star. The ignorance of the hopelessly gullible is punctuated by trusting the next too-good-to-be-true Nigerian opportunity, even before their memories of having been swindled before have faded.

STUPIDITY IS NOT IGNORANCE

By their actions, some mark themselves as stupid, and there is not much to be done about that. Stupidity (not to be confused with ignorance) is a state of non-thought whose sufferers shut down receptors when it appears that incoming information might be discomforting, leaving them open to little but random fascinations. The truly stupid are more likely to be shorter on native brainpower than the ignorant. *Webster's New World Dictionary of the American Language* has this to say about the state of being stupid:

> Stupid, adj. [L. stupidus < supere, to be stunned or amazed], 1. In a state of stupor; dazed; stunned; stupefied. 2. Lacking normal intelligence or understanding; slow-witted; dull. 3. Showing or resulting from a lack of normal intelligence; foolish, irrational . . . implies such a lack of intelligence or incapacity for perceiving, learning, etc. as might be shown by one in a mental stupor.[6]

Because truly stupid people share space with thoughtful citizens, they have a capacity for messing up human affairs. If their day-to-day activities are benign they are no more a hindrance than bumpers in pinball machines—obstacles that can be avoided with a little practice. But they own the citizen's right to vote, dissent, react, raise the NIMBY flag, and oppose change for the unreasoning reason that change changes things. A wonderful example of societal stupidity was cited in a *Washington Post* column by Christopher Ingraham:[7]

> Thirty-seven percent of Americans think the news media should be required to get government approval before reporting on national security issues.

Let that sink in for a moment. Ingraham was quoting from an Annenberg Public Policy Center poll that measured Americans' lack of knowledge of the structure and functions of government. Only one-third of respondents could name all three branches of government. Another third couldn't name any.[8] This lack of knowledge helps to explain why nearly four of every ten Americans think Congress should pass a law (as reported in the quotation above) in direct contradiction of the First Amendment. Because Americans trust Congress even less than the media, there is some cognitive dissonance in their desire to give Congress the authority to decide what does and does not get printed in the papers. The Annenberg poll also pointed out that civic ignorance is fed by closed-minded leadership that, through distraction and obstruction, works to keep pertinent knowledge from the masses. While much of society's ignorance results from the self-serving agendas of powerful knowledge manipulators, the potential for informational mischief by careless actors large and small can be diminished only with an across-the-board reduction of the anti-intellectual cynicism that reaches back as far as Ben Franklin's writings.

> *He was so learned that he could name a horse in nine languages. So ignorant that he bought a cow to ride on.*
> —*Poor Richard's Almanac*, 1752

EVOLVING IGNORANCE

At least two generations have grown up in a society in which ancestral traditions waned significantly. Family land fell into the hands of corporate farmers. Three mobile generations moved away from the influence of family, churches, and neighbors, leaving them free to believe or not believe, to do or not to do. With their social relationships weakened, they hunger for the comfort of tradition, which likely accounts for the brisk market in antiques, retro décor, and old hand tools displayed on den walls. Though a surplus of studies have sought to prove that Boomers and Millennials think differently than their grandparents, no science is needed to confirm a breaking down of community. Trending issues in marriage, parenting, personal finance, and voting patterns strongly suggest that people now think and view the future with less confidence than their parents, a phenomenon that appears to be directly related to how outlooks and expectations have changed from previous generations.

In *Amusing Ourselves to Death*, Neil Postman observed that society was, at the time of its publication in 1985, into its second digital generation, the first having grown up during the last decades of the twentieth century when digitization secured footholds in world culture.[9] Now, digitized communication and entertainment *are* culture and technology has become ideology. They have changed us at least as much as our ancestors were changed by the arrival of the automobile age when everything from social patterns to sexual expression was redefined in ways that society was unprepared for. To be unaware of how we are changed by wholesale adoption of a new technology or to think that technological change is always our friend is to be ignorant of information technology's effects on society. Moreover, it takes a truly insensitive person not to recognize that preoccupation with an ideologically managed informational diet might lead to further polarization.

The effects of digitization are no less profound than those that followed the invention of the printing press. Two twentieth-century shake-ups followed the introduction of radio and television, devices that delivered speed-of-light transmission of information and entertainment. We found ourselves changed without having been given the opportunity to critique the change because that's how technological innovation operates. It insinuates itself into lives, beginning as fascinating novelties and, like air conditioners in cars, quickly become necessities. It needs only one thing to win us over: a population that believes in technological progress. Unless we come to the unlikely judgment that computers and smartphones are not good for us, calls to rid society of them would fall on deaf ears. They have won us over. They own us. They fill us with a quantity of infotainment that often overshadows information, opening doors to forces that seize advantage by shunting real information to the side by obscuring it with trivia. This is a great challenge for the human mind to deal with, but not too much for thinkers who know enough of the right stuff to understand what is at risk.

The uncritical belief that science can fix anything has, in fact, created problems that threaten natural balances. Bill Vitek, Wes Jackson, and a growing army of concerned like-minded thinkers have linked the parade of record-breaking environmental disasters with cause-and-effect data that defies refutation.[10] They reject the common belief that science and technology are above criticism as servants of society, citing a surprising paradox. It appears that knowledge often accumulates fastest in minds that hold small worldviews and that the record of actions guided by their knowledge-based worldviews shows them to be, on balance, dangerously experimental. Like the pills touted in "ask your doctor today" TV ads, science encourages quick fix technologists to load nature with potent variables without thoroughly understanding how they will interact with the biosphere's precious balances.

CHANGE AND CREDIBILITY

Credibility is the first victim of change. A merchant seaman of the 1850s might have returned home to tell his son about Shanghai. When that son sailed the Pacific in 1865, he found that Dad was right. When the son's son visited Shanghai eighteen years later, three generations could share stories as though they had walked the same Shanghai streets together. Compare that with a recent visit my wife and I made to the Washington State University campus where we both earned degrees. Fifty years had so changed that campus that we became lost and had to ask for directions. Change causes doubt, and doubt causes confusion that dims the public's ability to constructively question the status quo. Change causes thinkers to burn more time and energy maintaining intellectual balance than their predecessors spent doing so.

We need better tools to cope with change, especially when prioritizing and directing searches for knowledge. Science offers some ideas about which areas might, with least risk and cost, remain unexplored for the time being and which options offer the best opportunities for opening doors to further discovery. It is a matter of picking battles as wisely as possible, which is an uncertain art. Research managers find that the task of separating what needs to be known from what can be left unknown is complex and inexact. For instance, the best choices between paths of inquiry are seldom picked by taking a simple either/or approach because while science must consider the advantages and disadvantages of conquering some aspect of ignorance, it also must guestimate the cost of remaining ignorant and set priorities accordingly.

The reasons for falling into ignorance, or accepting being coaxed into that void, or willfully electing to shut down receptors deserve study. Daniel Kahneman's groundbreaking tour of the mind, *Thinking, Fast and Slow,* provides insights into the ways people are set up to deal with such decisions. Kahneman proposes two systems that steer the ways we think. System 1 is fast, intuitive, and emotional. System 2 is slower, more deliberative, and logical.[11] Ignorance, whether general or selective, is more common to System 1 thinkers, who are more susceptible to bias than the more highly vigilant System 2 thinkers.

Kahneman was fascinated by how the "unawareness manifestation" of ignorance affects thought. He cited a classic experiment conducted by Christopher Chabris and Daniel Simons in which they filmed two teams, one clad in black and one in white, passing basketballs back and forth.[12] The subjects were instructed to count the number of passes completed by the white team only. Halfway through the test, a woman in a gorilla suit crossed the court, thumped her chest, and moved on. Of the thousands of people who viewed the film, more than half didn't report seeing anything unusual. The instructions and selective focus on the white team left observers largely blind to anything else. If people can be conditioned to ignore something that happens right before them, think of the political potency of this phenomenon should a political party or other special interest want to sneak a shady issue under the public's radar.

Because the Powers That Be routinely do just that, discriminating thinkers have become justifiably cynical of what is said and written. Are fine-sounding broadcast messages crafted to help or victimize us? Their effect may work to bring about a resolve to vote against the public's best interests or to approve national and international initiatives that, in the end, will erode at one's pride of citizenship. A nudge toward ignorance may take the form of the sanitized history so common in children's textbooks that renders youngsters ignorant of how the United States is regarded by other nations. It may take the form of consumer choices that work against our health, safety, or financial stability. Although the Powers That Be would not agree, fullness of knowing, unbounded from commercial or political propagandists, is necessary to protect against ignorance. Walter Wink popularized the term "the powers that be" as a label for webs of movers and shakers whose transcendent power defies control.[13] As European governments were once beholden to the Hanseatic League, America's policies are ruled by a corporatocracy that, by means of moneyed influence over Congress and the media, calls the shots.

Learning one's way out of ignorance can be pretty disturbing as I found out when I met with sufferers of Hansen's Disease, or leprosy. I had read about Hansen's Disease, but my understanding was limited to scholarly descriptions. Then a friend took me on a tour of a West African residential Hansen's Disease hospital that was modeled after Father Damien's facility on the island of Molokai. After the white-coated staff introduced themselves and explained their work, they left us to wander about. We stopped to talk with patients who were missing fingers, noses, lips, and were otherwise disfigured by damp sores. They were generally in good spirits and felt no pain because the disease kills sensory nerves. They wanted to touch and be touched, and when one gentleman reached out to me I recalled how our guide had mentioned that caregivers don't pick up the disease by contact, so, with great trepidation, I let him take my hand in his oozing hand that was missing a finger. That disturbing encounter with an unfortunate human who was likely sentenced to life in that hospital ward shook me. He held my hand as we talked. Afterward, I washed—oh, how I washed! For some months afterward I would look at the hand as though it was different from the hand that hung from my other arm. That contact between our two hands jarred me into understanding Hansen's Disease on an affective level. Losing ignorance can be discomforting when it entails shedding the insulating comfort of not knowing.

CHAPTER 2

THE SIZE OF PERSONAL UNIVERSES

*There are far more things in Heaven and Earth, Horatio,
than are dreamt of in your philosophy.*
                                    —William Shakespeare, *Hamlet*

Before one casts one's mind loose to get a sense of how it fits into the great scheme of things, it would be a good idea to first find out where that mind is rooted. The seventeenth-century French philosopher, mathematician, and scientist Rene Descartes puzzled over that issue, asking himself, "What is it that makes me tick?" Not "what do I do for a living?" and not "what do others expect me to do when the pressure is on?" He was obsessed with knowing more about his nature and what floated his boat. For lesser minds, that kind of introspection might be no more than high-level navel-gazing, but Descartes, a gifted mathematician, was into deeper analysis. He stripped away the trivia that fills most humans' attention until he was left only with that which would keep him going if he found himself stuck in, say, solitary confinement. He summarized all that was left, the only thing that he could be certain of, with his famous proclamation: "I think, therefore I am."

There is a bit of that in all of us. In fact, most people can't not think when faced with a compelling problem. It's automatic for healthy minds to shift from sizing up problems to figuring out ways to get through them, and it is how we handle those situations that define our intellects. Some might resort to knee-jerk reactions, do a quick inventory of available tools, or act out the old couplet, "When confused or in doubt, run in circles, scream and shout." Others might seek help and settle down in teams to think through challenges. Whatever success each manages to bring about reflects two things: the appropriateness of whatever problem-solving knowledge they possess and the effects of crippling ignorance that act as malware on thought. Since ignorance is typically at the root of bias, prejudice, failed plans, discord, and conflict, it pays to focus more attention on how the effects of small personal universes reduce our chances of success.

ME-MY-HERE-NOW

Personal universes may be measured against at least four scales: personal, material, spatial, and temporal. In the worst-case scenario, the personal is me; the material, mine; the spatial, here; and the temporal, now. The egocentric *me* has trouble recognizing the needs, desires, or ambitions of others. Things have value by benefitting *me*. Whatever comes to *me* is measured against scales of personal comfort, satisfaction, and gain. *Us* is an unwelcome foreign concept that wants a share of what the egocentric *me* claims, posing a competitive challenge to *me*. *Me* dwells in a small intellectual cocoon.

The first person possessive pronoun "my" labels one's real and imagined deeds to ownership of every kind: cars, clothes, real estate, friends, thoughts, and dreams. Early evidence of *my* is documented in children's preschool progress reports that read, "Needs to work on sharing toys with others." Those children grow up to be adults who seldom share their home with guests, loan books or tools, and commute solo when carpooling would be the more sensible option. In choosing *my* over *ours*, their intellectual world remains small.

The problem of *here* cripples ballot issues aimed at supporting infrastructure when small thinkers refuse to accept social responsibility for anything that lies beyond their property limits. Empty nesters don't understand why everyone should pay school taxes. Federal legislators with limited international experience don't recognize the interconnectedness of global relations. Small-minded thinkers' personal geographical universes pull inward so that, like farmers minding their acreages, their intellects aren't vitally concerned about what happens on the other side of the fence.

As for *now*, matters of the moment become so dominant that, aside from undercurrents of abiding worry, they shove aside preparation for the future and learning from the past. Spending trumps budgeting. Short-term profit taking trumps maintenance. Cravings for rich food trumps long-term maintenance of healthy bodies. Moment-by-moment avoidance of child-rearing issues ensures future challenges to both child and parent. Lives that are locked into *me, my, here,* and *now* can't help but be confined to small universes that adversely affect not only themselves but their surrounding world.

THE PROBLEM OF FRAMES

Anyone who feels, as Descartes did, that they *are* because they think has a nature that opposes restrictions on thought. These restrictions might be in the form of limiting frames that corral thoughts like wild ponies, forgetting that fences work both ways by not only keeping things from leaving but also from entering. Frames are necessary because it is easier to deal with issues when they are set in defining contexts. Frames play dual roles. They give shape to captive bodies of thought while filtering out new information that fails to resonate with old information. Recognizing the way frames cripple thinking by limiting acceptance of new content alerts thinkers to make them wonder what it is that specifically limits the size, direction, and range of their thoughts. Given that brains are the sharpest tools on any research jobsite, that might well be the most important question. Stuart Firestein, professor of neuroscience at Columbia University, lives that question as he studies how tradition and frames limit our access to a reality that feeds us a million or so times more information than what each of us knows.[1]

Research that is limited to reshuffling old information offers the satisfaction of producing somewhat predictable results, whereas probes into the mysteries of the universe deliver a mix of failure and surprise. That explains why a disproportionate amount of money and energy is usefully spent on dredging through data, reprocessing familiar terrain to discover needed corrections and creative extrapolations. Firestein enjoys this because the information that fills textbooks and technical manuals is, to a considerable degree, suspect insofar as some facts will always be found to have "exceeded their shelf-lives." He also knows firsthand that researchers gain almost as much trophy-hunter satisfaction from knocking cherished "facts" from pedestals as they do from pulling in new understandings from the great unknown.

As an experienced researcher, Firestein understands the limits of the scientific method, that procedure of questioning, constructing, testing, and accepting or rejecting hypotheses. He chuckles at the imprecision of so-called precise science and happily welcomes the foggy notion of imagination into his kit of intellectual tools. He would be delighted to watch a bunch of bright teenagers equipped with safety training, tools, and welding torches turned loose in a junkyard with the instruction to "make something." Firestein keeps certainty at arm's length, understanding that probes into the great unknown yield unexpected results. With the amount of scientific data doubling every ten to twelve years, he rejects the possibility that one mind might fully comprehend even a corner of it when the best minds can't help but be ignorant of facts and relationships inhabiting hidden niches within their specialties.

EXPANDED PERSONAL UNIVERSES

While stick-in-the-mud lifestyles offer the comfort of relatively stable personal universes, intellectual wanderers find stimulation in the excitement of expanding their personal universes. But the many who bask in the peace and comfort of yesterday's social insularity find themselves shaken by the impact of immigrants from far-off places. Storefront signs in foreign languages, bulletins written in English and Spanish—PISO MOJADO, the chatter of Somalis, Russians, Syrians, Koreans, and Guatemalans in grocery stores—what are they talking about? Main Street shops filled with skin tones from vanilla to chocolate look and sound more like the United Nations than "traditional" America. Most immigrants spoke at least two languages when they arrived and are learning another: English. While the personal universes of native-born Americans of immigrant stock seek stability, those of new immigrants expand at a feverish pace. Should home-grown American parents need to prod listless children into better performance in school, they might say, "Learn like an immigrant. Adopt their conviction that education is a lifeline to a worthwhile future." Lacking the comfort of cultural security, immigrant children seize on education as their portal to a better life. Their exceptional parents had the daring to cast off dead-end futures, hunger, and poverty for a chance at opportunity. "Immigrant" is too mild a description for who they are and what they do. Call them "exiles," for they are cut off from perilous pasts. Immigrant or exile, they are aggressive expanders of personal universes.

The "stranger in a strange land" experience peaked in 1969 when Neil Armstrong and Buzz Aldrin set foot on the moon. The knowledge universe of all humanity underwent a seismic shift when their pictures came back to show our habitat as Spaceship Earth, a blue-and-white orb turning in space. Seeing it as a finite environment stirred us to think for a time, though not long enough, that our global home is a shared and finite biosphere. All the resources we'll ever have are in our care. Or mess it up and we die, giving it over to tested survivor species, like cockroaches and horseshoe crabs. We have lived the Genesis commandment to a conscienceless fault: "Be fruitful and increase in number; fill the earth and subdue it. Rule over the fish of the sea and the birds of the air and over every living creature that moves on the ground."[2]

Charles Mann wrote in the introduction to Peter Menzel's *Material World*, "In effect, the human race has entered into a great wager. We are, so to speak, betting the planet."[3] We do this though we are profoundly ignorant of the rules of nature's game. Does climate change incrementally with global warming creeping up by tenths of degrees or will global temperatures reach some threshold where heat-sensitive species and processes go off the tracks and the whole system crashes? We don't know. The plural we-don't-know translates to Latin as "ignoramus." The Big Ignoramus includes global warming deniers, the Lord-will-provide Christians, fossil fuel advocates, destructive exploiters of land and sea, uber-consumers, and that great segment of society that goes along because it can't be bothered with the discomfort of knowing and changing.

LOOKING AHEAD

The world's population has increased by more than five times since my father's birth in 1903, causing the global population curve to rise so vertically that, according to conservative estimates, one in every sixteen humans who ever lived is alive today.[4] More disturbing is that the planet's plague of people, unlike more benign species, has developed methods of forcefully impacting whatever it wishes to control. Charles Mann's great wager breaks the bet with the planet into two aspects: (1) the environmental consequences of producing everything from Levi's 501s to iPads, where adverse effects aren't predicted as carefully as profits, and (2) the effects of human activity on interrelated planetary resources and systems that are insufficiently understood and keep us guessing.[5] Thus far, human responses to environmental issues are such that even the most far-reaching and insightful schemes reach no further than proposing attempts at management, not restoration.

Environmental watchdogs' reports describe how willful ignorance of the anthropocentricity and insular *me*-ness of small personal universes upset natural balances. Homo sapiens' dedication to comfort and abundance has yet to take into account the interdependence between humans and other species. That interdependence, however, cuts only one way because, while we cannot get by without the rest of nature, the rest of nature could do very well without us. The anthropocentric mind-set, coupled with the power to do anything we want, has resulted in a damning operational definition of what constitutes wildlife habitat:[6] "Wildlife habitat is the remaining areas of land and sea that offer no opportunity for human development or exploitation." Here is a definition that has yet to be effectively countered by environmentalists' call for big thoughts and personal action: "Think globally, act locally."

People have always lived most comfortably within existing knowledge, imagining the realm beyond informational horizons as terra incognita populated by monsters. Living on the firm ground of the Knowledge World works well for people who believe that what they don't know can't hurt them. A new but not yet dominant perspective recognizes that the world can no longer turn blind eyes and deaf ears to whatever lies beyond understanding. We look at knowledge as an asset, like cash in the bank, tallied and deposited. Whatever value might be accorded to the mysterious content of the unknown goes unrated because our value system requires precise quantification. But because understanding of the known world isn't as precise as we'd like it to be, we run into problems. Some of them are born of using our imprecise perceptions as standards for measuring whatever we encounter. Having named, measured, and cataloged all that we "know," we deem ourselves knowledgeable, regardless of how poorly we understand the nature of what we measure.

We know little about the far reaches of outer space. The dimensions of the universe are so vast that science must invent names for the never-before-needed magnitudes used to estimate them. In closer-to-home measures, our little solar system's volume is about two cubic light-years, of which we've "explored" a mere speck. Zooming out, the observable universe has a volume of something like 400,000,000,000,000,000,000,000,000,000,000 cubic light-years. Or so we think. The area that humans have probed with telescopes may only amount to two percent of that, reduced by pushing the decimal point thirty zeroes to the left. Though it is so far distant that humankind may never have direct contact with most of it, the universal laws of astrophysics, the universal sameness of elements and rocks, and the way things interact remain constant throughout space.

Zooming back in to fill the screen with Planet Earth, there is more unlearned about its oceans than has yet been discovered, and even if we discover it all, discovery is a far cry from understanding. It seems that with each discovery, nature throws surprises at the discoverers to remind them that there will always be more left shrouded in mystery in our terrestrial world than we can ever know.

The unknown impacts lives and events more than the known. It can't be otherwise because there is so much more of it. Our body of knowledge is to the Unknown as a mountain pass highway is to the total of the mountain range it cuts: insignificant. We work to broaden that swath of knowledge, probing outward from known routes using what we know to meaningfully connect dots. We've accumulated so much knowledge that preparation for working with it had to change from juggling memorized and printed knowledge to skillfully navigating within digital archives. The last great change spanned more than a century over which the knowledge contained in libraries was sliced and diced into the ever-finer specialties that divide the Dewey Decimal System's subject divisions into areas as small as ten-thousandth parts.

STRAINS ON THE DEWEY DECIMAL SYSTEM

Changes in library collections measure how Western thinking grows in some fields while shrinking in others. In 1873, Melville Dewey devised a one-thousand division system for cataloguing all nonfiction works. The first tenth, numbered 000 to 099, once contained pure-thought topics plus spin-offs about knowledge and thinking. It was titled "Information and General Works."[7] By the mid-twentieth century, the 000–099 section that had once been a tenth of all nonfiction had shrunk to occupy only a few partially filled shelves and would have remained small had computer geeks not claimed much of its empty space for their specialty. A look at the numerically tiny 796 section, a hundredth part of the 700–799 section for arts and recreation, tells a different story. While the 796s numerically represent only one one-hundredth of the 700s section, they have grown to occupy whole aisles of books, ranging from works on how to fletch an arrow shaft to water-color techniques. The overgrown section on self-help (158.1) barely existed seventy-five years ago but is now stuffed and overflowing, suggesting something about the way humanity's collective intellectual universe flexes with trends, whims, needs, and fears.

Humans specialize, invent, and speculate. In trying to achieve some sense of purpose they now and then ask, "Why are we here?" They busy themselves making mechanical and electronic gadgets that draw them into increasingly sophisticated games of "what if?" What if they were on the moon? What if they had cameras small enough to pass through minor arteries? What if there were ways to carry them beyond the stars? Ignorance of realms they have yet to understand tugs at them, stirring scientists and sci-fi writers to push at conceptual frontiers that they speak of as the Realm of the Possible.

There may be no better spokesperson for unknown realms than Brian Greene. In his 2011 national bestseller, *The Hidden Reality*, Greene led readers on a mind-bending romp through conceptual descriptions of not just a universe but a multiverse that exists differently but together with its member universes.[8] To explain what happens when minds lay themselves open to revolutionizing inspiration, he offered a much-quoted *aha* moment he experienced as a child. It had to do with the way his closet mirror could reflect another mirror on the opposite wall of his bedroom. One mirror reflected the other reflecting the other reflecting the other in ever-diminishing images that appeared to recede to a distant point. He remembered,

Sometimes I would imagine an irreverent me (in the image) who refused to fall into place down the line, disrupting the steady progression and creating a new reality that informed the ones that followed. During lulls at school I would sometimes think about the light I had shed that morning, still endlessly bouncing between the mirrors, and I'd join one of my reflected selves, entering an imaginary parallel world constructed of light and driven by fantasy.[9]

Greene is an unusual thinker who was born to experience *aha* moments. Like early explorers who set off without the benefit of charts, it is his nature to cast himself loose from the constraints of conventional thinking to expand the reach of his perception. The zeal to expand our reach is as old as history. Michelangelo expressed it on the Sistine Chapel's ceiling by picturing Adam's hand stretching to touch the mystical hand of God but unable to bridge the enigmatic gap that kept him from reaching it. As Robert Browning observed, "Man's reach should exceed his grasp, or what's a heaven for?"[10] Striving against ignorance is acted out in kitchens by creative cooks, in research labs, in teachers' lesson plans, and especially on remote farms where farmers have nothing to depend on for keeping things running but their own wits; healthy minds do the courageous best they can with what they have to work with. Greene wrote,

> I don't know how things will turn out. No one does. But it is only through fearless engagement that we can learn our own limits. It's only through the rational pursuit of theories, even those that whisk us into strange and unfamiliar domains that we stand a chance of revealing the expanse of reality.[11]

THE LURE OF THE UNKNOWN

People are understandably cautious about stepping into the unknown. Better the devil they know than the devil they don't. Fear of poorly understood wilderness threats leaves me unwilling to camp out in the Yukon. Poorly understood market variables keep me from investing in certain stocks. Not knowing the limits of my endurance, I choose not to climb Mt. Rainier. In each case, ignorance of specifics ignites fear or suspicion but only within persons thinking of participating in particular endeavors. Ignorance explains why ancient mariners decorated the unexplored far corners of their maps with fearsome creatures. Fearsome, indeed, for if there is one word that describes how early navigators felt about the unknown, it is "fear."

Thanks to science, that fearsome unknown keeps getting bigger. While we continue to learn, the total of what we know diminishes in comparison to everything that is. This is a difficult pill to swallow for a species set apart by its egocentricity. I once dined at the top of Seattle's Space Needle, where its rotating restaurant gave views of Seattle's workforce's taillights streaming toward the suburbs. At the wheel of every car was an unapologetic center of a personal universe. A few thinkers of ancient times managed to break from that limitation to consider that it was not one's patch of known geography but the entire planet that was the center of the universe. That understanding held sway even after Nikolaus Kopernik (Copernicus) tracked planets to prove that the sun, not the earth, was the center of everything. Galileo was forced to recant his belief in a heliocentric solar system. "Impossible and blasphemous," said his ignorant inquisitors, "for the book of Genesis clearly states that the Earth has primacy, being made by God before He created the sun." But even the Church could not halt truth. Brian Greene described the ignorance-dispelling revolution that followed:

> Nicolaus Copernicus' heliocentric model of the solar system is acknowledged as the first convincing scientific demonstration that we humans are not the focal point of the cosmos. Modern discoveries have reinforced the lesson with a vengeance. We now realize that Copernicus' result is but one of a series of nested demotions overthrowing long-held assumptions regarding humanity's special status: we're not located at the center of the solar system, we're not located at the center of the galaxy, we're not located at the center of the universe.... Such cosmic downgrading from headliner

to extra . . . [and] . . . everything we know points toward human beings not occupying a privileged position.[12]

Efforts by curious minds to grasp some kind of order in the unknown have yielded wonder and frustration as discovery after discovery opened windows to the mysteries of an ever-bigger universe. After curious thinkers found that the rules of classical physics couldn't perfectly explain the ever-unfolding reality, mysteries solved pointed to deeper mysteries. Things really opened up when it was found that subsequent findings could be pursued only by setting aside the concept of a *uni*-verse and replacing it with a many-layered *multi*-verse. Having been repeatedly in the position of the curious person who, after hearing barking from a doghouse, thumped on the roof to drive out a dozen cats, we have learned to expect whatever comes. The results of cutting-edge inquiry remind us that the one constant outcome of probing the unknown is surprise, a common element in science fiction plots. Sci-fi is a venue where speculative thinkers conduct alpha testing on ideas and where seminal thoughts that might become knowledge are planted. The Fremen of Frank Herbert's *Dune* could not have existed on the planet Arrakis without still-suits that may well become concept prototypes for Mars explorers' survival suits.[13] Sci-fi attracts the imagination: "We've never been there so let's go. It's never been done so let's see if we can make it happen."

IGNORANCE VS. THE OPEN MIND

The science fiction genre illustrates what happens when ignorance of the unknown is mated with knowledge and imagination. The genre throws inadequate knowledge into new situations and puts it to the test. Can its possessors survive engagement with strange adversaries and environments? In the laboratory of the mind, sci-fi offers technological dry runs that set the stage for real-world scientific adventures.

To Herbert, putting a sci-fi plot together was to play a grown-up game of "what if?" in which thought explorations might possibly serve as precursors to real exploration. Though few sci-fi readers hope to become actual space travelers, the unexplored unknown that sci-fi inhabits actually does come to visit our here and now in the form of meteor strikes, supernovae, and deep-space discoveries.

There will always be arguments over the value of science fiction. Nuts-and-bolts thinkers who dismiss everything not cast in documented cause and effect have little respect for it, deeming it speculative storytelling (which it is). To be fair, if our body of knowledge were to swallow the "what if?" situations of sci-fi whole, the knowledge base of astrophysics would become a shaky foundation on which to build. Conservative critics, though, go too far in rejecting sci-fi's way of thinking outside the box. They are mistaken in thinking that knowledge has to grow straight ahead when it might grow sideways or invert itself. Or they can face the truth that unpredictability is predictable.

OPEN MINDS AND LITERATURE

Open minds recognize that wherever houses are built, pieces of construction debris might be dragged off into the woods by children with dreams of building camps, forts, or lunar landers in alien settings. Unconnected bits of thought, like plywood trimmings, should not be written off as purposeless by people with no notion of how dreams might be fulfilled when our minds are free to pursue them. Leo Szilard,[14] a wildly inventive physicist of the early twentieth century, was shadowed by his students, for he had a habit of sketching radical ideas on paper and dropping them in wastebaskets.[15] Scientific careers—and possibly a few sci-fi plots—were based on his castoffs. Like sci-fi writers, Szilard's mind knew no confines. He probed the universe of yet-undefined things and occurrences with an informed looseness that defied convention and broke rules. His universe knew no bounds.

The lure of the unknown is with us from birth. Witness a three-year-old boy in the waiting room of a medical clinic that presents itself as unexplored newness. Before the boy-child's mother can restrain him, he has unscrewed knobs from drawers and explored the "cave" under a coffee table. He can't help it. It is his nature, and, unless adults press him into conformity, he will grow to push envelopes and color outside the lines throughout life. His is the curiosity that spurred the age of exploration and the Renaissance. When Columbus first thought of sailing beyond sight of land his dream was no more adventurous than the generation of children who, after reading Jules Verne's *From the Earth to the Moon*, dreamed of becoming astronauts. Young minds in the early 1900s soared off to otherworldly places under the spell of Edgar Rice Burroughs, just as previous ages were uprooted from their here and now by Jonathan Swift, Voltaire, and Homer. When the confusion of the time becomes too chaotic or confining to serve as a storyteller's backdrop, sci-fi steps in, offering blank-slate backgrounds against which writers' messages achieve a clarity that would be impossible to attain if set against the mundane muddle of everyday life. As with other fictional genres, the best sci-fi functions as society's superego, that hovering part of awareness felt as conscience, buyers' remorse, or guilt. Sci-fi offers a way for insightful writers to hold up mirrors before the society they write to. Beyond offering adventurous romps, the genre is capable of illustrating real-world issues that earthly knowledge controllers would have us dodge. Herbert's Dune trilogy is a masterful example of how ignorance-dispelling thought springs from informed imagination. Amie Kaufman and Meagan Spooner of the *Huffington Post* put it differently:

> Real science fiction is as close to an intense discussion of philosophy as you can get while still reading fast-paced, page-turning fiction. And it doesn't always give us the answers. Sometimes it leaves us to answer the questions ourselves, and that discussion is one readers of all stripes relish.[16]

THE CASE FOR SPECULATIVE FICTION

Sci-fi's questions are like those of grown-up teenagers: Are we alone? Do I matter? What could happen if people became other than human? If there is one thing that growing youngsters are concerned about, it's the future, even if that future is no more distant than tomorrow. Of course teens are preoccupied with how they look in the moment and what friends say about them behind their backs, but they are also caught up in deeper thoughts and questions that take them beyond the here and now. For proof, look at what your children are reading. If they read nothing, look out: ignorance is taking root.

Like other conscientious people, sci-fi authors get up each morning and ask themselves, "Is what I do for a living meaningful? Is there purpose in the words I write? Do my efforts help to open minds?" A number of published authors offer explanations of what science fiction means to them:

Brian Aldiss: "Science fiction is the search for a definition of man and his status in the universe which will stand in our advanced but confused state of knowledge."[17]

Greg Bear: "The simplest solution of all is in fact quite profound—that the real difficulty lies not in understanding what is alien, but in understanding what is self. We are all aliens to each other, all different and divided."[18]

Ray Bradbury: "Science fiction is the most important literature in the history of the world because it's the history of ideas, the history of our civilization birthing itself."[19]

Kurt Vonnegut: "I have been a sore-headed occupant of a drawer labeled 'Science Fiction' ever since, and I would like to point that out, particularly since so many serious critics mistake the drawer for a urinal."[20]

William Wilson (1851): "Fiction in poetry is not the reverse of truth, but her soft and enchanting resemblance. Now this applies especially to Science Fiction, in which the revealed truths of science may be given, interwoven with a pleasing story which may itself be poetical and true."[21]

Authors of the genre leverage current knowledge to envision yet-to-be-experienced real-world adventures. To bring that off, they put us in a position similar to that of fifteenth-century sailors, when to be out of sight of land was to be at the mercy of the unknown in all its fearsome mystery. The difference is that sci-fi gives its characters just enough tools and creativity to cope if they keep their wits about them. The recipe calls for some knowledge, some hardware, and enough informed ignorance to effectively question whatever might lie out there. It is not too different from children carting scrap lumber into the woods to give shape to their dreams.

IGNORANCE IS VERY AMERICAN

No one puts human nature's efforts at pushing the boundaries separating the known from the unknown into proper perspective until they learn to say, "I don't know," when unsure. And they will be certain to be unsure when pushing boundaries. Not everyone possesses the humility to do that, and among those who do, not all have the passion and patience to wrestle with the great unknown until, at length, something falls into place. Those who stand aside from this identify themselves with intolerance of change and difference and other forms of blindness that hold mysteries at a distance. Hardcore intellectual recluses inhabit the extreme, and as a teacher I met a few of these in remedial math classes during what should have been their formative school years. They greeted me with sullen stares that said, "Go ahead, try to teach me something. I dare you."

I kept a table stocked with magazines at the back of the room where nonfunctioning nonstudents idled until they realized that learning was where the real action was and rejoined the class. Over the course of a semester, the class gained some and lost some, but, on balance, it worked because they were left to choose their own path. Whether they are children or adults, non-learners should not be allowed to steal energy from learners. As long as they choose to stay in their shells, non-learners dwell in small universes where they become lost to themselves and society. The best that can be done is to figure out what makes them that way and what society can do to keep from losing more of its people to intellectual darkness.

Ignorance as an American issue isn't new. In 1837, Ralph Waldo Emerson wrote, "The mind of this country, taught to aim at low objects, eats upon itself."[22] A harsh judgment. Was Emerson on to something or had he picked up his pen on a bad day? Either way, the trend in numbers of closed-minded citizens who spend energy acting out against change indicates that society might be losing hard-won intellectual gains to hostile reactionaries who view change as a threat. They may be found everywhere, from remote cabins with No Trespassing—Violators Will Be Shot signs posted on gates to seats in Congress.

Critics point to public school test scores as an indicator of decline in intellectual activity. According to their "mature" opinion, it is because video and digital media have triumphed over print culture, and, to be fair, something of value has indeed been lost in that transaction. It has yet to be determined how much has been gained. During the course of change from print media to digitized communication, an odd arrogance developed among anti-intellectuals who took pride in distancing themselves from the bookish behaviors of "eggheads." Considering that a National Science Foundation study found that one in four Americans still thinks that the sun revolves around the earth, thinking people should be alarmed that so many believe that they don't need to know the truth about such things and that knowledge doesn't matter.[23]

Reasonable people wonder why it is that, in the face of reason, many cling to outdated social freedoms that don't fit life in the twenty-first century. It may just be that it is harder to give up something dear than to acquire something new. Society generally frowns on shooting guns in urban environments and dumping trash wherever convenient, which points to certain freedoms of the frontier myth that need adjustment. Nevertheless, it has proved easier to discourage abuse of land than to promote social codes that govern how people should share space. One problem is that the smaller a personal universe, the more fiercely its inhabitant will defend its turf. Small-universe people might do better to rethink the effects of their positions because the record shows that, in their ignorance, people with small personal universes are easy marks for ignorors.[24]

Propaganda artists angling for profit and power target the small-universe faction because, while they may be resistant to change in some ways, their ignorance leaves them gullibly open to the pitches of propagandists. The Powers That Be gain advantage over them by promoting competition over cooperation and independence over interdependence, positions that sell well to the ignorantly gullible. While the small-universe contingent bristles at interference with their traditions and beliefs, voting records show that they can be swayed into voting against their best interests. Time and time again, they are won over by political messages that undermine cooperation and interdependence. They are made to think that banding together as unions and supporting planetary preservation would damage their interests. Messages are crafted to convince America's rank and file that trickle-down economics benefits workers and that predatory pricing among drug producers are to the benefit of the nation. To bring that off, the Powers That Be must keep citizens ignorant of that which enhances the common good. It is better for them that they keep people ignorant and misinformed for they would lose their advantage if they allowed the ranks to organize for gain.

When personal universes are measured in terms of ownership, they eventually run into trouble. That happened when unrestrained claims to frontier lands ran into limiting conflicts with the end of unpopulated frontiers to settle. As lives began to overlap, cooperation became as important as competing for ownership of land and water rights. Though rational people long ago abandoned the frontier mentality, recent election results show that the masses still vote for competition over cooperation. The difference between the frontier myth and today's reality is explained in Venn diagrams of sixth-grade math books where sets of numbers may be compared with how people interact. Separate circles represent the mythical frontier where each ranch stood separate. Overlapping circles illustrate today's world with zones of overlap representing shared space and non-overlapped areas representing private or unclaimed space. In urban areas, where life circles overlap elaborately like carpets of autumn leaves, there is little private space. As populations become denser, circles of additional lives overlap in increasingly intricate ways, causing the ratio between private and shared space to lean steadily toward the shared and forcing people toward accepting cooperation over competition. The personal spaces of competitive people who cannot agree to share may loom large in mythologies but are small in actuality. Unwilling to change, they feel stress. Reactions against the world as it is develop into hostility toward roommates, neighbors, drivers, and taxing agencies. As with most versions of not knowing, reactions against overlapping physical spaces signal a reluctance to expand and adjust intellectual universes. That reaction is commonly joined with a perverse conceit in which the ignorant hold up their limited views as superior to knowledge. May they live quietly in their small universes.

CHAPTER 3

WHO CONTROLS KNOWLEDGE?

Control of knowledge is something the elite always does,
especially in a despotic form of government. Information,
knowledge, is power. If you can control information, you
can control people.

—Tom Clancy

Inquiry starts with seminal questions that serve as gateways into the unknown. One might be as petty as, "where did I leave the car keys?" Another might be step one in a carefully drawn questioning strategy as farsighted researchers build thought ladders outward, rung by rung. With the car keys, the ladder might be only one rung: "where in the house did I go after I came home?" With deeper issues, identifying seminal questions is a must because important stuff will be stepped around by not methodically charting routes that consider everything in proper order. Good questioning hierarchies reach for results without breaking the carefully structured "chains of custody" of truth.

Footnotes and bibliographies identify the scholars whose borrowed thoughts are entitled to credit, if not profit. But the question of whether someone can own the knowledge that authors borrow from each other when compiling their works is uncertain, given that knowledge is ideally the stuff of the intellectual commons upon which we all graze. The bulk of it cannot be mine or yours, and claims to ownership should be viewed as exceptional. There will always be attempts to "own" knowledge because, as Francis Bacon observed,

"Knowledge is power." Ownership of knowledge worked better for Stone Age high priests and modern cult leaders since, unlike free intellects, followers of cultish ideologies were denied independence of thought and belief.

The Powers That Be continue to try to control knowledge while the collective influence of universal education, public libraries, a somewhat free press, electronic communications, and twenty-first-century transparency challenge their improper ambitions. Of course the advantage of controlling knowledge is that it leads to control of public thought and public opinion. It follows that the promise of considerable rewards for controlling the public's mind ensures a brisk future for the thought-control industry. That discomforting reality steers the debate from faulty notions of ownership of knowledge to the better questions of who controls knowledge and why.

INTELLECTUAL PROPERTY

Knowledge that is locked down by legal ownership rights becomes intellectual property, a term grown heavy with baggage. The issue first came into focus at the 1883 Paris Convention for Intellectual Properties, a gathering that fizzled when inventors refused to display their work for fear of it being copied.[1] Beginning with copyrights and patents, intellectual property protection wormed its way into law until, in 1974, the need was given heightened attention by the founding of WIPO, the World Intellectual Property Organization, a new department within the United Nations. The term "intellectual property" is a problematic label that glosses over serious considerations bearing on the ownership of knowledge, for knowledge is simply too vast and various. Items falling under the heading of "intellectual property" may be thought compositions in any form: text, visual, material, melody, analysis, design, verse, or drawings. Where they may differ from other kinds of properties is that if you live in a house that I own but you don't pay the rent, I can evict you. But if you read a book that I wrote, the plot stays with you after you turn the last page. To some degree, it leaves my control. I can't stop you from rethinking it or discussing it from memory, though the law forbids you to profit from knowledge or use of my book.

The notion of intellectual property remains hazy because certain shadings of exclusivity of ownership may or may not be warranted or even possible. Defenses of intellectual property rights also may face tough sledding against so-called user rights, freedom of speech, and education. Depending on the field of activity or the nature of the knowledge property under consideration, the case for ownership may be strong or weak as conditioned by natural factors and "standard industry practices." The impossible ideal would have no one owning or exclusively possessing knowledge. Instead, one would *host* knowledge when necessary, understanding that whatever the knowledge might be, it might stay or leave or become irrelevant by discovery that it is flawed. And if knowledge stays, it might serve no better purpose than cluttering the memory with trivia, such as the price of a Hershey's chocolate bar being fifteen cents in 1950. Renee Marlin-Bennett's excellent survey, *Knowledge Power*, summarizes the situation by, in effect, following up every claim to control of knowledge with "however."[2]

Ownership of knowledge is a sticky issue even for the attorneys who spend careers sorting it out. If I think I am first to know something that no one else knows, and I document the processes that led up to that thought, does that mean that, once documented, no one else is allowed to have, publish, or act on that thought? And if someone did know it before I did, might I have trespassed on their intellectual turf? How many shades of gray define various property rights in such situations? If I figure out how to stack bricks in a special geometry, should I worry that my particular brick-stacking process might have been patented or copyrighted by someone else and that, armed with registered ownership rights, the person could make me unstack my bricks and pay for unlicensed use of the design? The licensing and ownership control over knowledge will be tested forever as armies of investigators sift through records in search of intellectual entities that lack secure rights of ownership.

The best-known manifestation of this type of search wasn't in the area of intellectual property but in that of mineral rights. Until most of a century ago, it was common for farmers to be so focused on growing crops that they neglected to file for mineral rights to whatever lay underground. While those dedicated tillers of soil were occupied with seed, fertilizers, cultivation, harvest, and market prices, value hunters sorted through land records to sniff out acreages with unsecured mineral rights, or distressed properties whose distressed owners of record might be talked into parting with those rights. Similarly, searchers ferret out unsecured or lapsed copyrights and patents and whatever other unprotected assets profit-hungry opportunists might dig up.

Material and nonmaterial property rights are related in that a widget, like a book's copyright, can receive a patent that, when analyzed, proves to be a unique end result of a jumble of other people's ideas, patented or not, just as heavily researched books are collections of others' thoughts, assembled to produce fresh thoughts. The next update of a cobbled together device won't be invented from scratch either but will be distinguished by adding a new bead to the string to make the widget demonstrably unique. The inventor, of course, must negotiate rights for usage from inventors of earlier beads on the string. Likewise, copyrighted documents like this one are allowed to be compiled largely from the work of others so long as credit is given to each source and quotes don't amount to a gross theft of large blocks of text. As writers explain it, if you copy one source, it is plagiarism; if you copy from many sources, it is research. This illustrates just how murky the intellectual property business can be.

LEGAL PROTECTION FOR PROPRIETARY KNOWLEDGE

Ownership of a bit of knowledge may be recognized and buttressed by professional review societies, editors, publishers, or witnesses that vouch for writers' originating efforts. But aside from originators' rights to royalties, fees for use, or citation in footnotes, some aspects of ownership are difficult to control. If a songwriter writes a song that you hear, and then you perform it in a nightclub, can the composer claim part of your earnings? If I have a thought and write it up and register it, does the fact of registration nullify the rights of others to own the same thought? The entire notion of ownership of intellectual property is fraught with impossible ethical problems, and, given the position of courts, it seems that enforceability may be relative to the clout of the claimant's legal staff.[3] Yet even Starbucks failed to protect its name against Haidabucks, a British Columbia tribal café; the Starbucks-like logo for the Rat City Rollers roller derby team; Stars and Bucks in Ramallah, Palestine; and Star Bock Beer of Texas.[4] Battles to preserve the Lego corporate image have been litigated in thirty separate jurisdictions, while Budweiser fought image encroachment in forty jurisdictions.[5]

Though industry figures are not available for the total cost of protecting intellectual property, Christopher Heath and Anselm Sanders outlined yet-to-be-resolved intellectual property issues in their 2010 book, *Landmark Intellectual Property Cases and Their Legacy*. In it they list the types of issues courts wrestle with (notice that some of the questions are so basic that one must wonder if any real progress has been made in the field):[6]

Who should be master over the reputation, esteem, and legacy of authors and their works: authors and heirs, or subsequent copyright owners?

Should prevention of unfair competition allow one to "reap what one does not sow?"

Should it be considered a tort to use a well-known mark in a way that may dilute its repute and distinctive character?

What kind of monopolies should be protected, if any?

Does the patent system in its current form allow us to question the assumption that technological progress is good per se, and that novel and inventive solutions should thus be protected?

Should extraneous considerations such as public good and

social usefulness be considered at the stages of grant and enforcement of patent rights?

Should we grant patents over living organisms whose workings and reproduction are a long way from being completely understood?

HACKERS AND LEAKERS

Reactions from governments and corporations when hackers penetrate secured files demonstrate a mix of justified outrage and frustration that their security measures don't provide foolproof protection. Hackers who believe that no code is unbreakable and no data storage is secure display a mix of motives. So-called black hat hackers' motivations include extortion, exposure, and theft, while white hat hackers bill themselves as testers of firewalls. They take themselves to be players in the greatest of all digital games in which they vie for bragging rights for penetrating supposedly secure archives. Germany's CCC, or Chaos Computer Club, hacked past the new iPhone's fingerprint password.[7] TESO works out of Austria, near the TeslaTeam of Serbia. Turkey has Redneck; China, the NCPH and Honker Union. The Syria Electronic Army operates on the fringes of chaos, and India has miluOrm. These loose webs of here-today-gone-tomorrow rogues shy from publicity, so they disappear and reappear, going underground and resurfacing rebranded. It's a mistake to assume that even white hat hackers' hands are clean, since they are part of a movement characterized by lawlessness and whose most dangerous hackers we must assume have yet to be identified. The annual cost of industrial cyber espionage to businesses in Germany alone is estimated to have stood near $16 billion since 2013 and approximately $100 billion in the United States. Major General Jonathan Shaw, of the UK, shed light on the nature and magnitude of future costs, saying, "The biggest threat to this country by cyber is not military, it is economic."[8]

In an age when no data can be assumed secure even under the tightest of protections, high-profile data is especially at risk. The hackers' threat of theft or damage is accompanied by a revolutionary philosophy of information custodianship shaped by transparency advocates who work for a more palatable balance between security and utility of information. They challenge justification for securing data and question whether laws ensuring rights to ownership of ideas and knowledge always act in the public's interest. They question enforceability. Does Target own the record of my purchases? Does Toyota own the maintenance record on my car? Of course, Target and Toyota have legitimate interests in inventory control, consumer satisfaction, and quality control, but that knowledge isn't theirs or mine—it is ours, and attempts to secure exclusive control of such records need inspection.

OPENNESS

There are, of course, reasonable exceptions to openness. When privacy or personal safety might be at risk, the federal Freedom of Information Act (FOIA) ensures the government's right to block searches of records that might result in harm. Other than that, releases of once classified government data has worked for the general welfare, though Rand McNally and the Delorme Atlas Company, both publishers of printed maps and atlases, suffered with the FOIA release of satellite photo imagery that gave birth to GPS and Google Maps.[9]

A citizen's FOIA requests may ask for access to any type of information not bound by national security or safety restrictions, which, considering the $11 billion the Department of Homeland Security and public safety agencies will spend on data security by 2022 alone, must still be awesomely wide and deep.[10] Before resorting to a FOIA request, researchers are advised to conduct Internet searches for previously released information.[11] The web is generally the best first point of attack, since other requesters might have already pried the sought-after information loose and published it. A formal FOIA application requires a load of personal data to prove that the searcher and requested data pose no security risks, a body of detail guaranteed to upset the paranoid. And there is the impressive level of rigor required in drafting an application to consider. The applicant must know which of many agencies to address, be incredibly specific and limit the query to one narrow topic. Since every agency has its own set of fees, it is wise to ask beforehand to avoid surprises.

Compared with George Orwell's dim vision of government-held information in his novel *1984*, the Freedom of Information Act offers American citizens a level of openness that contrasts happily with Orwell's gloomy prophesy:

> The party seeks to control everything, past, present and future. Its first effort toward attaining that goal is to control and manipulate every source of information, re-writing and modifying the content of all historical records and other documentary evidence for its own gain. The party forbids its members to keep written records of their lives and mandates that any photographs or documents be destroyed . . . and citizens are soon willing to believe whatever the party informs them.[12]

Excesses and failings of government security agencies come to light now and then to score front-page publicity that professional data hiders would rather avoid. It was in 1997 that Representative David Skaggs quizzed the then head of administrative services of the CIA, asking how much the agency spent each year on classification. "Well," the official said, "that information is classified." Skaggs pushed on. "Why is that?" he asked. The official replied, "I'll have to get back to you on that."[13] Of course, he didn't. The incident in itself was no big deal outside of typifying the government's posture when annoyed by fact seekers.

Until recently, the history of smug rejections of requests for government records had been couched in ill-placed confidence that government security was impenetrable. No one foresaw WikiLeaks—least of all Hillary Clinton, who, seven months prior to Julian Assange's release of a massive trove of classified diplomatic cables to the media, lauded the Internet as "a new nervous system for our planet."[14] In Clinton's defense, few were aware that a half million military and civilian operatives, including Assange's source, Private Bradley Manning, held clearances to rummage about in classified government files. If she had known, she might have injected a note of caution in her proclamation because, given what was found among those files, there was ample reason for an uncompromising conscience like Manning's to be offended.

Copycat hackers line up to gamble their freedom against notoriety, some guided by distaste for what government seals as secret. Others are in it for the sport. If Clinton had known or, for that matter, had anyone responsible for military and US Department of State security inspected the system with the eye of a teenage hacker, they would have predicted that a breach of the system wasn't a matter of if but when. With the clarity of hindsight, John Hamre, former deputy secretary of defense, said, "This was a badly engineered answer to a problem we all knew needed a fix."[15] Hamre pressed for limiting access to a need-to-know basis, a solution that would have cured one problem at the cost of severely crippling the speed of information sharing.

Analysts who examined the WikiLeaks trove are in general agreement that the revelations combed from the heavily redacted dump of documents upset the government not so much because of blood on their hands but egg on their faces.[16] Uncomplimentary references and intemperate language reflected poorly on statesmanship. Details of what should have been career-ending incidents had been classified and tucked away. To their credit, both WikiLeaks and the *New York Times* exercised extreme but humanly imperfect caution to protect assets in the field.

THE WIKILEAKS CHALLENGE

Julian Assange was born on July 3, 1971, in a small town on Australia's northeastern coast.[17] His sometimes idyllic, sometimes haphazard upbringing has been overly inspected for clues that might give reason for what he became and what he did. If there is a consensus, it might be that tensions within his dysfunctional world so possessed him that he lashed back with polished technical expertise and imperfect intellectual balance. The collection of colorful and mystifying details that compose his myth matter little, other than to caution the Powers That Be that he is not unique and that hundreds—if not thousands—of imitators work like military sappers of old to bring down the walls of corporate and government security.

Daniel Ellsberg, leaker of the Pentagon Papers, admiringly described Assange as "the most dangerous man in the world," adding that he had been pursued across three continents by Western intelligence.[18] Ellsberg compared Assange's situation to his own treatment under President Nixon. It was after the media picked up on Nixon's charges against Ellsberg that his myth, like that of Assange, bloomed among the world-weary underground that would evolve to become WikiLeaks and its imitators.

Assange will always wonder whether he will be punished or be free to travel and do more of what he does without fear of retribution from armies of spooks with James Bond–like licenses to kill.[19] That real threat was voiced when knee-jerk reactions to WikiLeaks's revelations called for nothing short of lethal response. Justice Department lawyers invoked the Espionage Act in their attempt to quash the *New York Times*'s announced intent to publish the dump of classified communication. The *Times* had to consider the many ways the government could strike back. With so much at risk, the paper's courageous posture during those perilous days was admirable to all but the security community and those whose privacy they were charged to protect. The *Times* came down on the side of the public's right to know—after redacting every word the paper's legal department deemed potentially damaging to personal safety and vital national interest.[20]

Unauthorized release of classified material is a questionable step toward ensuring that the public is properly informed to judge events for what they are as opposed to what they are painted to be. The alternative is accepting business as usual. In the years since Assange's revelations, a few media voices have moved from uncompromising condemnation of WikiLeaks to grudging acceptance that continuing benefits from WikiLeaks's revelations may exceed the damage done to international relations and the safety and standing of intelligence personnel. Among those questionable benefits is a new reluctance to sweep ill-planned and inappropriate deeds and events that stink of cronyism, high-level screwups, payoffs, and petty or personal conflicts under rugs of secrecy. Another benefit is that the media gained an informal arm, the blogosphere, or, rather, that bloggers seized on an issue that tested and matured their ability to comment on issues from a seemingly infinite number of angles.

Though confusion from bloggers' diversity of viewpoints causes paper-and-ink journalists to question their responsibility, truth is well served when no voices are stilled. There is something akin to the purposeful chaos of nature at work when crosscurrents of undisciplined blogging leave the public looking for central tendencies in discussions of issues. The redeeming factor is that the blogosphere, though many of its persistent contributors are no more than flacks from special interest think tanks, is not as heavily influenced by the Powers That Be as are print and broadcast media. Nicole Belle of the *Crooks and Liars* blog commented,

> I'm of the belief that if this is the price we must pay to show the government that acting as if no one has a right to privacy is a double-edged sword that can hurt them as well, we might as well pay now. If the government thinks it will damage their interests to have their corrupt actions known, perhaps they might not want to participate in them.[21]

There are pros and cons. Few are in the middle on this issue, but multiple voices see all sides. On one hand is the dark realism expressed by Aaron Bady's site, *Zunguzungu*: "simply revealing the specific ways they [US diplomats] are doing these shady things will not be, in and of itself, a necessarily good thing. In some cases, it may be a bad thing, and in many cases, the provisional good it may do will be limited in scope."[22] Bady went on to observe that

> Assange has a clearly articulated vision for how WikiLeaks' activities will "carry us through the mire of politically distorted language, and into a position of clarity," a strategy for how exposing secrets will ultimately impede the production of future secrets. The point of WikiLeaks, Assange argues, is simply to make WikiLeaks unnecessary.[23]

Because international relationships suffered, because revelations caused personal embarrassments, because military and security agencies' misdeeds were brought to light, time will do little to cool the animosities that keep Assange looking over his shoulder wherever he may be. Be that as it may, there is a positive legacy from WikiLeaks that cannot be denied or dismissed. Public knowledge has been served in that the heretofore arbitrary practice of concealment of embarrassing or shady information has suffered a blow.

Mistrust of the custodians of information will not disappear, nor will these custodians voluntarily yield to pressure for more transparency. A related situation simmering in the United Kingdom set citizens' suspicions against a proposal to aggregate digitized health records of patients after extracting every bit of identifying personal information—"anonymizing," they called it.[24] The intent was to amass big data that could be analyzed to improve understanding of the effects of drugs and surgical procedures. In spite of National Health's good intentions and its admirable plan, the scheme fell victim to ignorant mistrust, sparking a flurry of hysterical debate on the relative virtues of secrecy and transparency.

A renewed application of the rules that once governed media markets is needed to regulate the tactics and coverage of knowledge controllers. The history of Big Broadcast Media shows that Powers with the best backing and digital skills determine what information and entertainment the public receives. The same could hold true for the government-military sphere, as pointed out in an April 2009 *New*

York Times article about digital defense. The article revealed that the Pentagon was commissioning contractors to develop a highly classified next generation replica of the Internet for the purpose of providing computer services should adversaries take down the nation's existing systems.[25] In that event, and with a near-absolute concentration of communications in the hands of the Pentagon, it wouldn't take a paranoid critic to envision an Orwellian scenario ensuing.

CHAPTER 4

THE SCOPE OF IGNORANCE

*I am wiser than this man, for neither of us appears to know
anything great and good; but he fancies he knows something, although he knows nothing; whereas I, as I do not
know anything, so I do not fancy I do. In this trifling particular then, I appear to be wiser than he because I do not
fancy I know what I do not know.*

—attributed to Socrates, from Plato's *Apology*

I gnorance can be benign, right up to the point where someone
pretends to know something that he or she does not know: why
a stock rose or fell, why a child is screaming, why Americans carry so
many guns, etc. Explanations rush out of faulty intellects in a type of
attempted communication commonly known as blowing smoke. It
happens when people who fail to take account their level of compe-
tence or incompetence consider themselves more competent than
the people who surround them. That behavior has been labeled the
"Dunning-Kruger Effect" after Cornell researchers David Dunning
and Justin Kruger, who determined that people's lack of awareness
of their limitations limits their ability to critically analyze their own
performance.[1] In other words, they overestimate themselves. More
crudely put, they're too stupid to realize that they're stupid, not
having learned enough about everyone's favorite and most important topic: themselves.

A perpetual question for churches is "who or what is God?"
Those who answer with full confidence that they actually know much

of that which is worth knowing about the Great Deity reach beyond their grasp. They do not know. They cannot know. No one can know, except in part, and even then their knowledge is tainted by the filters of experience. The normal state of not knowing becomes a major problem when the people in control don't know that they don't know. When corporate executives lack understanding of the operations of the businesses they direct, when MBA nonfarmers rule corporate agriculture, when accountants run hospitals, when conglomerates run newspapers, none of those pretenders can be expected to know the ins and outs of the institutions they rule. Dismal histories in banking, agribusiness, mining, Big Pharma, and petrochemicals are replete with disasters orchestrated by unqualified directors. Posing as knowledgeable, they distance themselves from responsibility for negative outcomes by pointing fingers at external forces "beyond their control," thus confirming their ignorance. On the other hand, leaders who accept that they don't know are freed to accept corrective change. Admitting to not knowing opens the door to counsel, which allows accomplishments to rise above random incidents of luck or fate. Acceptance of not knowing can't help but deliver more trustworthy insights and results in decisions that will not be rooted in anything as fallible as one's ego.

THE POWER OF ACKNOWLEDGED IGNORANCE

The positive potential of admitted ignorance is the theme of a successful leadership training program for executives appropriately named, "The Journey of Not Knowing."[2] It takes enrollees on six- to twelve-week courses that move participants' styles of executive action from knowledge actuated to question actuated, a switch that focuses on what must be set right before reaching for new levels of success. Participants develop the understanding that whatever opinion we find ourselves arguing for is simply the hypothesis we happen to be entranced with at the moment. Whatever that might be is proved imperfect under the microscope of objectivity and is revealed as the sort of thing that only shallow thinkers will take for truth. Taylor Hawes, Microsoft general manager of corporate finance and services, said that the program "has gone beyond [expectations] . . . bringing out and developing those we hadn't spotted . . . as well as increasing collaboration and leadership."[3]

Buddhist practice involves interplay between knowing and not knowing. Through Vipassana meditation, Buddhists, on the one hand, emphasize knowing and seeing deeply into experience. Yet, on the other hand, they believe that just as they can develop the capacity to know, so too they can become better at the art of not knowing described as the "Beginner's Mind," which is emptied.[4] This could be a massively significant approach for believers within Christianity or other approaches to the art of living. Whether in farming or neuroscience, experts may know their specialties so deeply that they become blinded to all else by screens of preconceived notions. Not so with beginners who see with fresh, unbiased eyes, which is the thrust of the executive program cited above. It is this "education by stripping away knowledge" that helps to account for the continuing success of the once maligned Maharishi University in Fairfield, Iowa, where Fortune 500 executives happily bunk in vegetarian dorms to share in the experience.[5]

As the opening quotation from Socrates suggests, the posture of not knowing is time-honored. Its essence is found in the annals of every ancient culture where intellect was held in high esteem, as in this Arabic proverb:[6]

> He that knows not
> and knows not that he knows not
> is a fool.
> Shun him.
> He that knows not
> and knows that he knows not
> is a pupil.
> Teach him.

He that knows
and knows not that he knows
is asleep.
Wake him.
He that knows,
and knows that he knows
is a teacher.
Follow him.

Take special note of the last verse. As is often the case in the practice of faith, the teacher is certain in his belief, which might raise a Buddhist's eyebrow, for a person who knows what he knows, no matter how noble his calling, can't help but suffer the intellectual limitation of certitude that, when found among theologians, pollutes humility when he poses as authority of the knowledge of God. It might be wise to add one more verse to the Arabic proverb:

He that knows,
And is content with what he knows
Is closed-minded.
Ignore him.

THE CLOSED MIND OF CERTITUDE

When certitude takes charge early in life, succeeding years become a struggle with reality. Scott Peck identified the problem in his classic work, *The Road Less Traveled*, in which he wrote of people who develop road maps of life early on, then live out their years according to the lines on aging maps when, in reality, the terrain changes over time.[7] As they slip out of tune with what's happening, they fall out of sync with society. Marginalized, they break with old friends who adjust with the flow. They become hostile, distant, and lonely by clinging to outmoded conceptions, all the while certain in their beliefs. As their isolation deepens, their actions become increasingly reactive, hardening against the world around them. They pit what they "know" against current knowledge in an unfair match that defeats them time and time again. They dwell in cocoons of self-deluding righteousness that keep them estranged from a world that just doesn't understand them.

It may seem that the world is full of ignoramus wannabes. Educated folk are observed doing strange things and making illogical decisions that, in spite of their impressive academic credentials, mark them as profoundly ignorant. Which raises the question: is ignorance a matter of how much or how little a person knows, or is it something else? A person may earn the label "ignorant" by displaying reason-defying thoughts, statements, or actions. Or it might be evidenced by the failure to act, speak, or keep silent at appropriate or advantageous times. Smart people with advanced degrees are routinely brought up short because of "ignorance of the law," a deliberate ignorance that, if it can keep one from being prosecuted, may serve as a high roller's fast track to advancement and gain.

Another broad type of ignorance functions not so much through what a person fails to know but through attitudes and perceptions that are so far out of sync with reality that the person cannot recognize problems for what they are. The breadth of behaviors and beliefs that afflict the ignorant is so vast that it would take a lifetime to catalog them. One must be cautious though about judgments of ignorance because even reasonable people known as level-headed thinkers will do or say things that make their observers wonder. Is ignorance an expression of intellectual deficiency? Might ignorance be nothing more than the perceptions of disgruntled people holding strange views? Are there fixed scales of functional knowledge against which ignorance can be measured? Or in an age of specialization, is ignorance simply the knowledge shortcoming one suffers when daring to function outside one's chosen specialties?

Finally, might there be any benefit in pursuing answers to questions such as these, or would it be wiser to accept, given the vastness of the unknown, that not knowing is the natural state of all humanity? And if that's true, might a better course be to not judge who is or isn't ignorant as demonstrated by her actions but how well she humbly and creatively recognizes her relationship with the limitless unknown and makes best use of that recognition?

Minds that stay cooped up within closed patches of intellectual turf end up troubled by the concept of limitlessness. Closed-mindedness requires structure and limits for everything, since whatever manages to enter a rigid mind must have beginnings and ends and resist change over time. They may even have trouble with one-size-fits-all socks because spans of flexibility might be too open a concept. They accept linear cause and effect dynamics and respect mathematics for the fixed equalities of its equations. They ask of infinity, "What or where is the far limit of it? How big is it? Where does it start?"

Theologians once restricted the idea of limitlessness to a property of God but did not extend it to his creation, where people and their limited thoughts had to dwell. God, himself or herself, was infinite, but nothing of his creation was to come close. Depending on what century you were born into, thinking otherwise could get you incinerated, and, if you managed to avoid that ordeal, your books certainly would go up in flames. God and tenets of faith were defined by a church that was bound up in control issues and forbade writing thoughts that strayed outside its permissions. Hence, the people of medieval Europe warmed themselves before book fires in town squares while the authors roasted at the stake.

THEOLOGICAL AND ACADEMIC CERTITUDE

After King Alfonso VI of Castile conquered Toledo in 1085, there was a dustup about whether Iberian Christians should worship according to the Roman Rite or the Mozarabic Rite.[8] A test by fire was proposed, and when a copy of each was tossed into the flames, the Roman Rite was consumed, while the Mozarabic book was only scorched. Anyone who has compared surviving copies of both has reason to suspect that it wasn't God's choice but the industrial-density velum of the Mozarabic that saved it. Beyond sorting rite from wrong, books that dared to propose infinity went straight into the fires. God was infinite—no one and nothing else. God's exclusive position as infinite power and knowledge was symbolized by architectural limits that forbade any building to be taller than the church, which is why, in so many European cities, all but recent structures squat low where land profiles offered no hills upon which to site churches.

The iron grip of church dogma has relaxed, as demonstrated by priests' and pastors' smiling tolerance of bumper stickers reading "My Karma Ran over Your Dogma." Or this wry joke circulating among pastors: a Buddhist stopped at a hot dog stand and said, "Make me one with everything." Infinity and variety are becoming less frightening to the church, and most clerics, even when not entirely grasping the concepts, accept that limitlessness actually resonates better with faith than dogma. Faith can be defined as trust in what you believe, although definitions vary from sect to sect. Dogma, on the other hand, is the body of compulsory belief that members of sects are expected to accept. For instance, Roman Catholics believe in transubstantiation.[9] If you don't, you can't be a Roman Catholic in good standing. Primitive Baptists must accept salvation through faith alone. If you are a Baptist who holds that good works are also necessary, out you go.

Mind-set is basic to worldview and a main determiner of whether one is pessimistic, optimistic, accepting, rejecting, proactive, reactive, forward-looking, or anchored in the past. Mind-set impacts every human activity and colors the results of interpersonal dealings. The open mind heals its own wounds and refrains from wounding others. Its preoccupation with the vastness of possibilities leaves it little time for mischief. It grows, expanding with each venture into the unknown. Open-minded employees are good employees, just as open-minded bosses are good bosses. Both grow with criticism, understanding that whatever they know may not be enough or be perfectly aimed to deal with tomorrow's issues.

Products of closed minds should be accepted with the suspicion that they are less likely to serve the general welfare. One must be cautious not to paint with too broad a brush here. Closed-minded people are capable of generosity and acceptance, just not on the scale or consistency of open-minded folk. Where they get in trouble with themselves and others is in believing that what they know is good enough, an attitude that constricts channels of incoming information. Carol Dweck, a Stanford University psychologist, explored this situation and found three types of bias that limit the range on incoming thought.[10] Bias not only leaves the closed mind deprived of a healthy diet of new information but harbors faulty information in a double whammy that ensures a dangerous level of ignorance of reality. Dweck offers the following list of the origins of bias:

Anchoring bias: getting all of one's information from one source or ideology.

Authority bias: allowing certain commentators or editorialists or "experts" to rule one's thinking.

Confirmation bias: looking for agreement only from inhabitants of one's ideological echo chamber.

Closed-mindedness may be rooted in either nature or nurture. Because nurture is the option that offers the opportunity for change, hope turns toward education where public school teachers accept that stuffing children full of answers is not the way to change minds from closed to open. Closed-mindedness can haunt even multi-degreed scholars who spend their learning years carving out patches of academic turf that they then devote careers defending. To effectively combat closed-minded ignorance, educators have to reverse the time-worn tradition of teachers posing questions for which students are to memorize answers. The reason for placing all our bets on that model is profoundly wrong is that answers terminate curiosity, while questions inflame it. Students infected with important questions become life-long learners who, as intellectual anglers, will troll query lures through oceans of knowledge to hook unexpected answers. Education's revised purpose is not only the filling of student's minds but turning empty minds into open ones.

EFFECTS OF CLOSED-MINDEDNESS

The closed-mindedness of incurious individuals is infectious. Ignorors infect victims with mental malware that interferes the reasoning and weakens or warps the curiosity of the infected. The incurious find themselves ill at ease with knowledge seekers and are easily provoked to act out when sensing that their smaller knowledge bases might be denigrated by what they take to be condescending educated snobs, an attitude that helps to account for the popularity of anti-intellectualism.

They take it personally. They are devastated as others pass them by on ladders of success and contentment. They likely don't understand what causes the lack of fulfillment that poisons their peace of mind. Years of punitive grading by an insensitive system can't help but reinforce other hostile notions toward learning. If Christians, they may have adopted a warped interpretation of "You may freely eat the fruit of every tree in the garden—except the tree of the knowledge of good and evil. If you eat its fruit, you are sure to die."[11] This is a tough issue for theologians who feel bound to God's literal admonition. The metaphorical fact is that Adam and Eve did eat of the fruit, and the rest, as they say, is history, a history of which we are a part. The choice not to eat of the fruit of the tree of knowledge of good and evil might work in a static society with a fixed knowledge base but not in one where change is the one constant feature.[12] To change or not to change is a defining difference that separates conservative and liberal theologies. Furthermore, conservatives' discomfort with changing realities is a major cause of sociopolitical prejudice and bias.

Ignorance is a major cause of the growth of America's economic underclass, since nearly every aspect of American culture has become knowledge-driven, especially employment. Unlike the scene from mythic Western history in which a penniless cowpoke is allowed to sleep in the stable in exchange for shoveling horse poop, getting by in today's world requires a head full of heretofore unnecessary knowledge. Constant learning has become a large part of social overhead that workers ignore at their peril. Ignorance of economics and finance causes tax problems, missed payments, victimization by predatory lenders, bad credit ratings, and missed opportunities. Economic predators who care for their own while conducting rapacious business practices that destroy other families understand this.

Ignorance cripples its hosts, making them poor conversation partners and friends only to whoever might share the misfortune of being similarly afflicted. It becomes broadly dangerous when its hosts are the highly placed and highly educated sociopaths profiled in Paul Babiak and Robert Hare's entertaining book *Snakes in Suits*.[13] Ignorance is not the exclusive province of uneducated minds; it thrives among highly educated, multi-degreed achievers. Like robots designed to perfectly weld body panels, they're the best at what they do. Just don't expect them to relate to or sympathize with needs and agendas outside their self-serving frames.

I once worked with an alto sax player, a graduate of a major conservatory who was an outstanding musical technician. He read music flawlessly but was determinedly ignorant of the nuances that identified the music we played as jazz. For the short time he was with us he rendered pop tunes in a mechanical style while the rest of us worked together as jazz players do to create spontaneous bits of orchestration spiced with punchy rhythm figures and spontaneous ad-lib melodies. Though he worked in a jazz setting, he limited his music to the notes on the sheets while criticizing us for not "honoring the composition." He exemplified the packaging together of orthodoxy, education, and ignorance.

Education and ignorance share space in the narrow minds of certain university honor students who master confined hierarchies of their chosen subject matter while shutting out the rest of reality. Capitalizing on their academic success, they work their way into leadership positions in industry, government, and even education. It happens among leaders in Christianity and possibly other great religions where ignorance-breeding orthodoxies restrain followers from seeking the deeper faith needed for religious relevance in the age they are born into. Church leaders locked into the rigor of ortho-doxy find little comfort outside the canon of their faith. Through predisposition or will, they choose to listen to what God has done and not what he is doing.

The signature of sociopathic ignorance is a lack of remorse for the grief it causes. One tier below, but still among society's informa-tional mischief makers, are rascals whose behaviors mark them as sociopath wannabes. While still possessing the ability to feel remorse, they avoid opportunities to act on it by living walled-off lives that avoid contact with the less fortunate. Executive washrooms, gated communities, Ivy League fraternities, VIP lounges, and exclusive clubs insulate them from exposure to realities that might elicit sym-pathy or guilt. Their defense against the mainstream and its issues produces a finely crafted social ignorance that even holds guilt at bay. As to the gross effect of their not knowing, it is these highly placed ignorati who wrote the book on how to develop an under-class. When bank officers craft policies that bankrupt borrowers by blinding themselves to borrowers' realities, it is beyond willful igno-rance—it is purposeful ignorance. When employers trim staff they haven't bothered to know for no better reason than to strengthen already healthy bottom lines, it is avaricious ignorance.

WHEN MINDS ARE OPENED

A certain young man of my acquaintance attending a nearby uni-versity who is bright enough to succeed in most fields is preparing to teach history in public schools. He spoke to me about his inten-tion to open minds to the social processes and problems that affect society, and, having seen through the masks of disinformation spe-cialists, he is eager to battle the forces of ignorance. His foes know that, while holding a population to an informational disadvantage, they still leave it with the measure of contentment that comes from everyone being in the same boat. If everyone walked with a limp, no one would know what a limp is. If everyone were blind, there would be no concept of blindness. Ignorors know full well that if all people are ignorant, they lose their conception of what ignorance is and does, and that is a frightening thought.

There was a conference held in Kansas in 2004 with the theme, "Toward an Ignorance-Based Worldview."[14] The conference's co-organizer and keynote speaker was Bill Vitek, a professor of philosophy at Clarkson University. Vitek offered these words from Wendell Berry's anthology, *Virtues of Ignorance*:

> If we find the consequences of our arrogant ignorance to be humbling and we are humbled, then we have at hand the first fact of hope: We can change ourselves. We, each of us severally, can remove our minds from the corporate ignorance and arrogance that is leading the world to destruction; we can honestly confront our ignorance and our need, we can take guidance from the knowledge we most authentically possess, from experience, from tradition, and from the inward promptings of affection, conscience, decency, compassion, even inspiration. This change can be called by several names—and it belongs, I think, to all the religions, but I like the practical way it is defined in Ezra Pound's translation of *The Confucian Great Digest*.
>
> "The men of old wanting to clarify and diffuse throughout the empire that light which comes from looking straight into the heart and then acting, first set up good government in their own states; wanting good government in their states, they first established order in their own families; wanting order in the home, they first disciplined themselves; desiring self-discipline, they rectified their own hearts; and wanting to rectify their hearts, they sought precise verbal definitions, of their inarticulate thoughts [the ones given off by the heart]; wishing to attain precise verbal definitions, they set to extend their knowledge to the utmost."[15]

He continues,

> This curriculum does not rule out science—it does not rule out knowledge of any kind—but it begins with recognition of ignorance

and of need, of being in a bad situation. If the ability to change one's self is the first fact of hope, then the second surely must be an honest assessment of the badness of our situation. Our situation is extremely bad, as I have said, and optimism cannot either improve it or make it look better. But there is hope in seeing it as it is. . . . I am trying to follow what T. S. Eliot called "the way of ignorance," for I think Eliot meant us to understand that the way of ignorance is the way recommended by all the great teachers. It was certainly the way recommended by Confucius, "For who but the ignorant would set out to extend their knowledge to the utmost? Who but the knowingly ignorant would know there is an 'utmost' to knowledge?"[16]

Vitek and Berry find themselves in the midst of a historical pattern of thought that co-opts ignorance as a means of rising above intellectual mediocrity. Socrates, Gandhi, T. S. Eliot, and a long list of notable thinkers were part of that. Not one of them was driven toward personal gain or power. All of them had a feel for general welfare and found their center outside the confines of acquisitiveness, greed, position, or power.

Stuart Firestein, professor of neuroscience at Columbia, teaches a class on ignorance. He warns his students that if they aspire to excel in his class they might not want to go public over earning an A in ignorance, which playfully reflects the public's lack of respect for ignorance as a topic worthy of serious study.[17] But when ignorance is laid out on the forensic table, dissected and analyzed, much of interest appears. We find that people whose lives are conditioned by ignorance, which includes all of us, can be separated into two groups—those who, for any number of reasons, apparently happen to be or choose to be ignorant of this or that, and those who make it their business to cause others to be ignorant.

The practice of separating populations into two groups works well in botany, where to identify a flower we first have to determine whether its parts are arranged in sets of threes or in fours or fives. The choice neatly separates monocotyledons that produce flower parts in threes from dicotyledons that are characterized by flower parts in fours or fives. While this dichotomous type of classifying works well with plants, there are no such clear-cut divisions to classify the way people think. This is especially true of how they gain, hold, and process knowledge and ignorance. No one is entirely honest or dishonest, friendly or unfriendly, active or passive, persuasive or gullible. One person might ram a questionable notion down others' throats in the same hour as he falls victim to a slick-talking snake oil salesman. There is a bit of ignoree in every ignoror and vice versa. Ignorors' sense of self requires that they first deceive themselves before they deceive others. It's normal, but not healthy, that so many play the two opposing roles.

FACING UP TO CLOSED-MINDEDNESS

Tensions are thrust upon society by people who reject discomforting changes that the passage of time leaves at their doorsteps. They find themselves caught up in overwhelming fears that their values and freedoms are in danger of being lost amid the change. They want their way of life to remain frozen in time, believing that unbroken cultural continuance is the proper way of the world. According to their unchanging convictions, everything that is truly important is a projection of the past. They live in hallowed yesterdays, struggling to hold time still and negating whatever changes it brings. Marginalized by their conservator's concept of reality and a blanket disenchantment with change, they see their way of life being hunted down by everything they are not. They are not wrong about that. But they are also not right because the changed world that is and the world as it might be are the only choices anyone has.

Nongovernmental organizations (NGOs), missionaries, and nation builders have, at times, shared a different hubris. Too often their zeal to help is shadowed by a combination of social guilt and self-congratulatory pomp for being top dogs. Convinced that their materialistic affluence qualifies them to operate for the betterment of others, they talk themselves into believing that if only they could convert everyone to the culture they treasure, then they and all they stand for would be validated. But cultural conversion deals aren't brought about by exporting theologies and demonstration projects. When a Western power swoops down on a less advanced culture it is usually a case of "ready or not, here we come." Between interventions, imperialists' eyes rove the globe for the next acquisitions. Apart from the many inspiring faith-based and NGO good works, afflicted peoples remember all too well the major powers' record of shouldering into the affairs of other societies to secure natural resources or strategic advantage. Interventionists would be well advised to consider whether their ignorant intrusions might be seen by their targets as paternalistic piracy rather than uplifting charity.

The dizzying pace of change within Western nations is confounding. So much energy is spent keeping pace that it seriously hampers capacity for doing, curing, building, teaching, maintaining, and conducting the great social organism that is us. Two of the darker aspects of change are waste and confusion. Out with the old and in with the new. I recently visited my hometown, Spokane, Washington, hoping for nostalgic walks down memory lanes. It wasn't to be. The valley where I grew up had been scrubbed clean of orienting landmarks: farms, shops, schools, firehouses, and entire neighborhoods had vanished. Discovering that my home, along with a few neighboring homes, still existed struck me as more of a time warp oddity than a warm reminder of what was. Change had robbed me of familiarity with what I once knew well.

If that measure of change left me regretting the loss of my old haunts, then consider change's impact on endangered tribes of the Gobi, North African herders, Kurdish farmers, forest dwellers of the Amazon, or Native Americans as they strive to preserve something of their cultural roots. Aggressive Western culture offers them little in the way of recognition or respect, let alone preservation of what they hold dear. The time is past when misguided missionaries acting as Christian imperialists did their ignorant best to erase culture after culture. Those are gone now, replaced by their betters who live out Jesus's cautionary words: "Whatever you did for the least of these . . . you did for me."[18] Today, the Church's overseas efforts succeed by listening more and talking less, a simple tactic that replaces past institutional ignorance with victories of sensitivity. Faultless NGOs such as the Carter Center, Médecins Sans Frontières, and the Danish Refuge Council now inspire governments that host their services to learn and change. The examples I've chosen succeed because of their rejection of the paternalistic ignorance of their predecessors, not because they learned their way out of it.

The train of time doesn't stand still. Each time we look out one of its windows, the scenery changes. If the train creeps along, we can look ahead to view the future, then see it abreast the train, and see it once again as the past if we turn to look back. Manageable tasks. But if we're aboard a bullet train traveling at more than 150 mph, all is a blur: "Did you see that?"—"What?"—"Oh, never mind, it's gone now." Images and memories of today's happenings must be crafted from split-second impressions or not at all. For the undisturbed herders of the Gobi or remote tribes up the Amazon's tributaries, the train of change barely moves. The scenery is reliably familiar, comfortably unchanging, allowing them to expect that tomorrow will be much the same as yesterday. It is no wonder that primitive peoples bristle at attempts to impose "civilized" ways on them. Yet we call them ignorant, deprived, and in need of all that Amazon.com can provide.

CHAPTER 5

THE MANY BRANCHES OF IGNORANCE

There are as many forms of ignorance as there are causes for not knowing.

—Fr. Joseph McCarthy, SJ

Specialized fields of knowledge are mysteries to the uninitiated, while plumbers and proctologists sleep well knowing that people in need will pay for their special knowledge. In simpler times, tribal populations shared knowledge of how to make and use axes, spears, and fish nets, skills that were more basic to them than the Three Rs are to our culture. Two generations ago, a jack-of-all-trades would build a home without concern for building codes, seismic stresses, hazardous materials, or electrical inspections, but technical progress has taken most building out of the hands of multiskilled craftsmen and passed it on, piecemeal, to specialists. Finish carpenters, roofers, electricians, drywallers, and painters leave all but the highly experienced ignorant of how to properly build an entire house. Of course, there are always ambitious souls who study up on every phase of construction and do it all. In so doing, they may become so focused that much of the nonbuilding world passes them by, leaving them ignorant of political scandals, NFL football, and what a Kardashian is. No one can know it all, nor should they be expected to or want to.

Knowledge and insight grow from the individual experiences that shape our worldviews. If these are narrow, they limit understanding to personal interests. Picture a blacksmith, a miner, a blind person, a cook, a meteorologist, and a musician standing by the tracks as a steam locomotive comes thundering by. Each one comments on the impressive display of heavy metal and power:

The blacksmith says, "The heat in the firebox sure delivers a lot of power."

The miner asks, "How much coal does it burn?"

The cook says, "You could run quite a kitchen with that much steam."

The meteorologist says, "Look at the pollution it's pumping into the atmosphere."

The musician says, "There may be a rhythm to it, but its more noise than music."

The blind person says, "Make it stop. Its noise blots out the rest of the world."

No one understands completely. Experience burdens everyone with filters that equip each with special profiles for knowing and not knowing. Russell Baker warned that even knowledge has its pitfalls: "An educated person is one who has learned that information almost always turns out to be at best incomplete and very often false, misleading, fictitious, mendacious—just dead wrong."[1]

EXPLORING THE PATHWAYS TO IGNORANCE

Trying to know is not the same as being open to everything, in that trying to know is directional while being open is omnidirectional. Conservative critics claim that open-mindedness makes one open to all kinds of evil, and, to a degree, they are right. But being open to everything is not the same as being all accepting. When a possible evil knocks at the door, a person still has the option of sizing it up and pushing it back out onto the street. Not being open to recognizing evil is dangerously close to denying it exists, and that cannot be allowed, since refusing to face up to evil is the first step toward giving it control.

Personal choices of what to accept or reject may reflect pathways to ignorance. For instance, people often choose to reject things simply because they don't know much about them, because they are foreign to them. The opposite side of that coin says that other things might seem more acceptable for no better reason than that they are comfortably familiar. Days are filled with snap decisions based on no more than that. People choose not to join groups or activities because of what friendly sources said about them or because they don't know any members of the group. It's imperfectly normal for people to limit their exposure to newness simply because birds of a feather flock together and they are not part of the flock. Reason plays a minor role in preconditioned choices.

One effective way to block ignorance is to identify causes for the kinds of personal reactions that invite ignorance. In most cases, they will reflect not knowing or ignorance. You didn't join because you didn't know the rules. You reacted to what was said because, well, you just didn't understand. You turned away because something about the scene caused discomfort. If one comes to suspect that she might be caught up in a habit of turning away from new people and experiences, she might want to work up a list of personally insightful questions that point to the roots of the problem. Some samples: Were values involved that I don't agree with? Was my reaction a product of seeing the world through a too-narrow frame? Was I guilty of stereotyping? Did I see something that triggered personal bias or fear? Did the scene contrast too sharply with my image of myself?

All people are ignorant in a number of ways, and if they claim they aren't they prove the point. With personal ignorance being an inescapable condition, deeper understanding of it cannot help but position one at better contact points with knowledge that offers opportunities for action or inaction, like knowing when it is too dangerous to proceed. The absolute best and most constructive thing a person can say when caught short of knowledge is, "I don't know." It takes a disciplined combination of open-mindedness, admitted ignorance, personal security, and knowledge to adopt that attitude and make it work.

The following starter list of types of ignorance suffers the same shortcoming as thrift store jigsaw puzzles—pieces are missing. You will also discover that some of the categories overlap. Another word of caution: please take the categories below as no more than observations from an op-ed journalist who was provoked to set them down by witnessing the negative effects of ignorance in action. Since the list reflects only one person's encounters with ignorance, consider what you could add to it based on your own experiences.

Preknowledge Ignorance

This person lacks experience with, or exposure to, certain information and is, therefore, unqualified to form rational opinions on relevant issues. It is a harmlessly naïve condition so long as one refrains from pretending to understand and resists being drawn into groups where members press their uninformed opinions on others. This type is especially vulnerable to uncritically accepting the pitches of propagandists. It is common for the preknowledge ignorant to defend their meager intellectual turf with rock-hard certitude, a trait that endears them to propagandists. The shallower their knowledge, the more vigorously they defend it.

Post-Knowledge Ignorance

Locked onto early learnings, these unfortunates reject new or changing thoughts as attacks on their trusted body of knowledge. They develop ideological frames early on that reject later input that, if absorbed, would help them on their way. Because their knowledge is limited, they fall victim to the same inflexibility of certitude as the preknowledge ignorant, a condition that encourages them to hold their inflexibility superior to the less fixed convictions of an open intellect. They differ from the preknowledge ignorant insofar as they harden up to defend their obsolete bodies of knowledge, as opposed to being sensitive about their shortage of knowledge.

Ignorance of Self

These are people who go through life continuing to be what they are without being aware of the effects of the positive and negative attributes that make them up. Personal backgrounds and education offer too few opportunities for traits and quirks to be reflected back upon individuals in ways that encourage evaluation and change. They may spend their years with minor speech impediments, not knowing that what they say is not easy to understand. Or they may carry an aggressive habit of cutting others off in midsentence, or be unaware of unpleasant body odor, or be repeatedly victimized for putting unwarranted trust in others. They suffer from not knowing themselves.

Ideological Ignorance

Entire sectors of society are groomed to reject whatever doesn't fit within the frames of their chosen ideological Lords and Masters. Power-seeking ignorors hold them in calculated ignorance, enslaving the gullible and threatening the fearful into submission. It worked for a time for Pol Pot, Adolf Hitler, Idi Amin, and Mussolini, and it is working today for Vladimir Putin and Kim Jong Un. Hitler went so far as to burn unapproved literature and commission the manufacture of radios that could tune only to state-approved stations. A sign of ideological ignorance is when citizens are duped into casting votes against their own best interests.

Ignorance of the Serf

As in days of yore, people still trade independence of thought and action for slavish service to paternalistic lords. Some seem wired to crave subservient positions under the strong, unifying banners of nations, corporations, armies, religions, or special interests. When entering into dependent followership, they adopt entire packages: how to act, how to think, what to like, and what to dislike. The serfs' zealous endorsement of their lords' power positions is matched by their abandonment of interests lying outside the manor's thought perimeters.

Serf-type ignorance takes hold when communities trade locally owned commercial cultures for the distant ownership of big-box retailers. Mimicking the feudal past, Big Boxes draw tribute from locals by shunting profits that once fertilized local economics to distant lords, while also limiting local talent to fewer opportunities to rise into management and ownership. Big Boxes do provide impressive benefits that their emissaries use to obscure what will be lost when they are selling their proposals to local authorities.

Jingoistic Ignorance

I was standing in a group in an observation lounge of a cruise ship watching passengers go ashore for day tours in Costa Rica. The discussion touched on Costa Rica's economy, which is the strongest in Central America, the nation being rated as one of the best places to retire in the entire world.[2] Its citizens enjoy good educations, excellent medical care, longevity, and low infant mortality. And Costa Rica tops all nations in percentage of land dedicated to parks and wildlife reserves.[3] In response to this impressive tally of the country's advantages, one gentleman said, "Yeah, but none of that would've been possible without the backup of the US military."

He was ignorant of the fact that Costa Rica, neighbor to the depressed economies of Nicaragua, Guatemala, Honduras, and El Salvador, is the only nation of the region that hasn't been impacted by US military incursions. Costa Rica does well because it was never "protected" by US forces and chooses not to support an army of its own. Because the critic's generation was taught to fear that the world's nations would fall to Communism like dominoes, and because of clear and present dangers from ISIS, North Korea, and Iran harboring ambitions to threaten us with nuclear weapons, his preoccupation with military action might have masked possible sensitivities to global warming, overfishing, acidification of oceans, overpopulation, air pollution, lack of comprehensive energy policies, fresh water shortages, and inattention to America's burning need for transportation improvements. For more than a century, Americans have been distracted from visions of what could be by military adventures while its citizens were held ignorant of what the battle cry, "In defense of America's interests," actually meant.[4]

Anti-Intellectual Ignorance

There is no accounting for why mistrusting anti-intellectuals throw up barricades against thinkers and thoughts. They don't offer reasons for opposing learning as a way of life; they just shrug it off. To their overly practical way of thinking, intellectuals are effete leftist busybodies who don't produce much of substance. From their point of view, intellectuals occupy publicly funded ivory towers where they dream up utopian schemes that often fail in the real world. Sometimes they're right.

Intellectuals were targets for criticism even before the time of Johnathan Swift's *Gulliver's Travels*, and they always will be. Ecclesiastes 12:12 (New International Version) says, "Of making many books there is no end, and much study wearies the body." Midwest farmers mistrust Ivy Leaguers. Engineers mistrust liberal arts graduates. Practical people, however, do find the broader worldview of intellectuals of some use when dealing with global issues whose scale requires broader outlooks. The biggest flaw in anti-intellectuals' thinking is their certitude. From limited bases of knowledge, they tend to develop inflexible attitudes that defy the corrective process of refining and replacing old knowledge. Their extreme views pop up regularly in letters to the editors of newspapers that say to planners and thinkers, "We'll put our ignorance up against your knowledge any day."

Religious Ignorance

Schools are destroyed in the Middle East for educating girls or teaching from books other than the Koran. Islamic boys sit in street-side circles for memorization and recitation of Koranic verses, their teachers poised to deliver lashes with knotted ropes should anyone nod off.[5] Certain conservative Christians, like conservative Muslims, hold the Bible as not only the base for education but the foundation for knowledge of science and history. No matter that biblical math is flawed, the biblical definition of pi being set at 3.0 in I Kings 7:23, or that biblical chronology is at odds with the geological record. Ultra conservatives hold that study of the world their God created exposes one to the devil's ways and that restricting learning to Holy Scripture positions one closer to God. The terrorists of Nigeria's Boko Haram exemplify this ignorance in that Boko Haram translates from Hausa to English as "Western education is a sin."

History-Morphing Ignorance

Memories age like fine wines, mellowing over time to make uncomfortable past experiences friendlier. For national populations, time's mellowing effect produces palatable national myths by taking the edge off uncomfortable realities. This path becomes a problem when inaccurate memories of past missteps surface to clash with present realities, as when recent attempts at establishing peace in the battle-ravaged Middle East ran headlong into backlash over problems left by past US involvements in the region.[6] Negotiations with Latin American states must dance around a history of issues because Latino histories and memories aren't wiped as clean of American offenses as US history textbooks are.[7] While time and censorship work to ease consciences by burying discomforting facts in shallow graves, they are incapable of erasing reality.

Euphemistic Ignorance

Physical materials are described as natural or synthetic. Natural materials are of nature; synthetic applies to products of lab science. While synthetic products are largely useful and benign, a number of harmful invented products share the innocuous label of synthetic with benign products. Better to know the bad things as unnatural, not synthetic, so that they might more readily be removed from use if necessary. In the political arena, innocent-sounding words hold the public ignorant of unacceptable practices. The Clear Skies Act gave fossil fuel industries permission to pollute the atmosphere. Extreme (extraordinary) Rendition masked the transfer of political prisoners to foreign torture sites.[8] Citizens United betrayed citizens by selling politics to the highest bidders.[9] The euphemizing of bad products and practices not only deceives, but it also corrupts language.

Benign Ignorance

Those who don't bother to inquire deeply and are content to accept the conditions they are born into do little to upset the status quo. Their unquestioning and uncomplicated acceptance of the status quo may allow them to be more in tune with their environments than the habits of climbers and achievers. The Pacific Northwest's Coast Salish Native American way of life boasted an Adam and Eve simplicity that, if practiced around the globe, would have minimized most of the planet's environmental problems. Their culture is remembered in folkways, rituals, carved cedar canoes, lodges, totem poles and clothing, and baskets woven by women from cedar bark, all of them demonstrating an admirably efficient art of living. They made only necessary demands on their physical world while casting the mysteries of nature into meaningful lore that fails to lose fascination over time. That culture was largely erased by white intervention, demonstrating how benign ignorance is the loser in any contest with Western materialism.

Any list of ignorance is incomplete since a unique condition of ignorance exists for every human condition and endeavor. Not all are negative, however, and those that aren't make up for some of the waste and cost of negative ignorance.

Creative Ignorance

This purposeful and potent expression of ignorance enables thinkers to move outward and onward when fixes and futures are stymied for lack of knowledge. It helps poets, dreamers, artists, modern theologians, and, especially, scientists to progress from bases of informed not knowing. This self-acknowledged ignorance cannot be separated from the curiosity, wonder, and awe that impel seekers to follow wherever their investigations lead them. Not knowing is their invitation to new understandings and the polar opposite to how ignorance confines others in the limitations of certitude.

Each of the examples, positive and negative, defines styles of not knowing to illustrate how the many styles of ignorance affect thought. A more useful approach would have individuals from each classification looking inward to discover how their personal ignorance limits the flexibility and reach of their thoughts, an approach that falls on defensively deaf ears when certitude is involved. When individuals define their intellectual stances by what they know, they live a definition of intellectual stagnation that guarantees ignorance.

CHAPTER 6

IGNORORS AND IGNOREES

It is a sign of cultural decay when society's instructors
choose their words to advance personal agendas.

—Herbert Lass

WHAT IS AN IGNOROR?

C ertain people—call them "ignorors"—prey on the gullible to convince them to trade open-mindedness and reason for a shallow sense of belonging. The ignoree's reward is a feeling of social inclusion for being accepted into intellectual dead-end fraternities of ditto-heads. In the process of spreading their beliefs, ignorors reach and pass points where they themselves take on aspects of ignorees, the change taking place as they come to believe their own distortions and lies. Ironically, self-delusion is common among ignorors. Without it, they wouldn't be able to live with making ends justify means. Time spent promoting misinformation causes moral anchors to slip, leading ignorors' personal codes to stray as far from the truth as they would lead ignorees.

Anyone who alters or interrupts the natural flow of information to impact others' behaviors or beliefs is an ignoror. Along with their sponsors, ignorors are agents of ignorance who seem to lack active superegos, that part of subconsciousness that guides behavior toward acceptable ethical standards that reflect Socrates's admonition that the "unexamined life is not worth living." The ignoror's narrow mind-set supports a self-serving disdain of corrective truths that challenge that person's chosen *isms*. If they claim to be Christians, it is a selective claim that ignores the biblical directive, "Thou shall not bear false witness."[1] The flawed mortgage brokers of the early 2000s were classic ignorors who conned gullible home buyers into accepting terms they could not meet. At the same time, some were also Boy Scout leaders and Little League coaches, showing the inconsistency in values that testifies to the disintegrated moral code of the ignoror.

A person who lives an inspected life knows that one can't fully understand one's own position without understanding those it contrasts with. It's the reason travelers choose to study foreign cultures before venturing abroad. It's why sports scouts haunt practice fields to understand rivals' rosters and playbooks. On the dark side, it's why we have spies and corporate espionage. The self-inflicted ignorance of failing to examine all sides is as deficient and disaster-ridden as sailors and pilots who choose not to study the weather. It follows that the willfully ignorant invite disaster when avoiding concern about the cost of their decisions to themselves and others. Nor do they accept responsibility. They can't because for the self-deluder, bad results must always be someone else's fault. This holds true not only for individuals but for members of every tightly defined *ism* or ideology, whether political, religious, or economic, for closed-ended mission statements, oaths, creeds, or other binding or limiting commitments allow only limited pictures of reality.

IGNORORS' DISMAL RECORD

Ignorors' behaviors diminish the power of whatever limited knowledge they hold, for the effects of drafting plans from insufficient knowledge-bases leads to error and waste that mark many of their positions as wrongheaded. The record of ideological ignorance is well described in Jeffrey Sachs's excellent book *The Price of Civiliza-*

tion. Sachs's concern runs deeper than the monetized analyses that portray effects of ignorance in dollars. He fears for the soul of the nation:

> At the root of America's economic crisis lies a moral crisis; the decline of civic virtue among America's political and economic elite. A society of markets, laws and elections is not enough if the rich and powerful fail to behave with respect, honesty and compassion toward the rest of society and toward the rest of the world. America has developed the world's most competitive society but has squandered its virtue along the way. Without restoring an ethos of social responsibility, there can be no meaningful or sustained economic recovery.[2]

Sachs, a clinical economist, holds a holistic view of social problems and imbalances. He points out the willful blindness to the economics of Paul Samuelson that had successfully guided the US economy from the end of WWII through the 1970s.[3] Samuelson's "Great Synthesis" called for market forces to allocate most goods in the economy while calling on the government to perform three essential tasks: redistributing income to protect the poor and unlucky; provide public "goods," such as infrastructure and scientific research; and stabilize the macroeconomy. Ignoring Samuelson's economics could have been justified only by replacing it with a model that offered equal or greater promise, but not the insensitive experimentality of deregulation that delivered advantage to the Powers That Be. The quality of Samuelson's economics is reflected in the longevity of his economics textbook, which was first printed in 1948 and, after selling four million copies over sixty years, is still popular among thinkers and teachers.[4]

Rejection of Samuelson was a signal that predators were on the attack. Reaganomics ignored Samuelson's demonstrably positive economics by (1) fostering a new antipathy toward the government, (2) disdaining the needs of the poor, and (3) setting a tone (trickle-down) that served as blanket permission for the rich to shed moral responsibility. It was a gross abandonment of regulatory safeguards brought about by adherence to an ideological position that, for gain of power and wealth, chose blindness to a philosophy that had served the general welfare of the nation well for decades. From their elite positions, agents of government and corporate power set a course toward a new feudalism, dimly aware that they were creating a rightist authoritarian government that was intolerant of other views, merged corporate interests with the state, was hostile toward socialism, and glorified militarism. According to *The New York Times Guide to Essential Knowledge* and other reputable dictionaries, those are the exact ingredients of Fascism.

Naïve observers might hope that the extreme self-interest that unites the Powers That Be would trigger attacks of conscience that would moderate their excesses, but that hasn't happened. It won't happen because it is the Powers' intent to convince themselves, along with much of the nation, that issues like universal healthcare, early childhood education, social security, efficient mass transportation, cooperation with the international community, a sensible national energy policy, and congressional reform are symptoms of creeping socialism, itself a gateway drug to Communism. Champions of general welfare are written off as wrongheaded, since programs that favor general welfare are seen as providing nanny-state handouts rather than allowing people access to reasonable shares of national prosperity. The Powers' resistance to corrective change requires a compliant citizenry, so care is taken, with media cooperation, to control the public mind by limiting the scope of issues that qualify for national debate.[5] The fact that this happens proves that Huxley was right: "He who controls the past, controls the future, and he who controls the future [expectations] controls the present."[6]

IGNORORS' NATURAL ENEMIES

Scientists' probes into Amazonian forests, deep ocean trenches, and the far reaches of space prove that there will always be more to discover than will be accumulated in digital storehouses. Advances in pure sciences only widen the imbalance between known and unknown. But it is of insufficient concern to the ignorant that the amount we know that we don't know is ever expanding or that the nation's brightest people are at work to expand it even more. Science's discoveries may fascinate the ignorant at some level but not enough to cause them to want to change their outlooks. Disinterest leaves their intellectual comfort zones relatively static, which accounts for the gulf that separates them from open-minded thinkers' active embrace of the unknown. Beyond the social division between ignorors and ignorees, a deeper look into those groups detects differences in how they think. One comparison has scientists enjoying the surprises they draw from the mysteries of the great unknown, while thinkers with small personal universes tending to seek relevance in yesterday's realities. To fixed minds, open-minded searchers' work will always seem a bit odd and wasteful in that it involves what the ignorant see as blind reaching as much as structured pursuit of definable goals.

Attempts to bridge the rift between open-minded and closed-minded thinkers start and end with improved communication that uses language that puts both sides at ease. Education's attempts to close the gap by elevating the intellectual sights of ignorees often fail for not fully understanding the vulnerability of ignorees and the methods of ignorors.

It has to be understood from the beginning that hired manipulators of knowledge cannot be reined in without understanding the tactics of the sponsoring Powers That Be that fund programs of misinformation. It will be found that the Powers and their agents' plans for controlling thoughts begin with scouting the territory before dealing with the inhabitants.[7] They study us. And since variations in how we think and operate set some of us apart as easier marks than others, successful propagandists zero in on the gullible to steer their buying, behaving, and voting. It must work, or the very smart people who pay for it would long ago have quit spending billions on those practices every year.

If specialization limits practitioners' knowledge to corners of their fields, then expanding knowledge within the field of medicine risks increasing ignorance of much that isn't relevant among specialists. When a medical emergency occurs—a broken leg for instance— rather than shouting, "Is there a doctor in the house?" it might serve the injured party better to call out, "Is there an orthopedist in the house?" It would be unwise to expect a proctologist to repair a retina or a podiatrist to deliver babies. No specialized practitioner can know it all. A soldier's MOS (military occupational specialty) slots army personnel into specialized types of duty. Building contractors parcel out jobs to specialist subcontractors. Wherever one looks, specialists so thoroughly fill their thoughts with narrow interests that much of what happens outside their job descriptions passes un-understood, disguised, or hidden. Ignorance is universal and natural.

While natural ignorance of some things may be tolerable, not knowing certain other things may be threatening enough that open-minded scientists and educators devote considerable energy to separate what must be learned soon from what may be left to learn later. Scientists proceed with this task with little guidance, just as educators continue without assurance that there is a best way to prescribe the right knowledge to fit the needs of every student. This and other evidence suggests that it is best that students and planners be equipped with flexible thinking skills that help them adapt to situations as they occur.

CENSORS AND CRITICS

A censor, according to a Scott Foresman dictionary, is "an official who examines material that is about to be released, such as books, movies, art and news and suppresses parts considered obscene, politically unacceptable, or threats to security."[8] Of course, judgments passed on content will be, to some degree, subjective, which means that censors cannot help but slant content toward personal notions of what's right. As the documents leaked by Mark Felt (Deep Throat) and Julian Assange (WikiLeaks) illustrate, exposing hidden information reveals not only the truth behind incidents of history but the motives for hiding them and motives for exposing them. One major motive was found to be the cover-your-behind (CYA) policy of burying incidents that, if known, could decimate support for leaders and their policies. Since exposure must precede change, censorship is an enemy of change. As a foe of investigative journalism, censorship provokes leakers and hackers of conscience to expose wrongdoers before the court of public opinion. Had it not been for the government's excessive and unwarranted censorship, Julian Assange might have targeted corporate records for exposure rather than Department of State records.

Legitimate probes into government records are now more possible than ever, thanks to the Freedom of Information Act. Petitioners receive their requested information with certain passages blacked out by a process called redaction, a form of censorship that holds the public selectively ignorant of sensitive information. But censorship isn't restricted to the political and corporate scenes because published writers of all types may suffer censorship when editors tweak writings to satisfy editorial sensibilities. Ray Bradbury was among the first to publicly criticize editors' unauthorized adjustments of writers' work. It was a censorship movement to "clean up" writing that moved him to choose ideological editing as the theme for his novel *Fahrenheit 451*. Bradbury publicized the trend to change the words of noted authors, saying,

> Every story slenderized, starved, blue-penciled, leeched and bled white, resembled every other story. Twain read like Poe read like Shakespeare read like Dostoevsky read like—in the finale—Edgar Guest. Every word of more than three syllables had been razored.[9]

What Bradbury identified as editorial liberties by misguided nit-pickers was actually the beginnings of a movement to sanitize literature that gained strength until authors were no longer certain that their thoughts would be published as intended. The writers' fear was that manuscripts and their published versions might someday become as dissimilar as printed books and their film versions. For a time, inappropriate editing seemed destined to become the standard for the industry, especially among conservative publishers who felt that by eliminating printed words that conjured up images of bad behaviors, bad behaviors themselves could be reduced.

That well-intentioned thrust into social engineering might have found traction had censors been able to control street-corner conversations, movies, and TV content. Censors' rosy-hued vision of a society free of bad acts and wrongdoers was laudable in intent but profoundly unrealistic—and dangerous. For one thing, it is not social stereotyping to point out that a disproportionate number of antisocial acts are carried out by marginal readers and nonreaders, which pretty much eliminates any chance of cleansing society by cleansing literature.[10] Secondly, when readers look up from sanitized books, they come face-to-face with a reality that mirrors all that was censored from their pages. Still another compelling reason is that negative social issues are less likely to be addressed and solved if censors sweep them under the rug. Readers of all ages deserve opportunities to understand the realities of the world they inhabit.

Bias controllers would have writers describe the perfect neighborhood pickup game of soccer as played by an equal number of boys and girls, representing a perfect balance of races, none of whom use profanity or come from dysfunctional families. Unrealists have to be curbed or there will be two contrasting worlds: the one on paper and the real world. The move to ban language that identifies characters by national or tribal origin, physical characteristics, or behavioral quirks dims the richness of individuality in literary characters. As Brookings Institute scholar Jonathan Rauch wrote, "And what should we do to assuage the feelings of people who have been offended? This and only this: absolutely nothing. Nothing at all."[11] Rauch had this to say of cultural cleansing: "No one has the right to be spared sacrilege—not Jews, not Muslims, not ethnic minorities, not me and not you." His advice on how to respond to those who use offensive language is to ignore them. And to those who feel offended he suggests development of thicker skins. As children of countless generations have put it, "Sticks and stones may break my bones but words will never harm me." This is not to suggest that anyone should accept intemperate language without objection.

Effort spent on silencing spoken or written words without eradicating the thoughts that underlie them is superficial and unproductive. Worse, it leaves holders and writers of antisocial thoughts—and their thoughts—unidentified, a situation that places the rest of society in a dangerous state of ignorance. If we don't know who to fear or why we should fear them, we cannot know why they should be avoided or how to protect ourselves from them. By not knowing the history and complexity of a problem, we can't begin to solve it. Better to let it surface. Although censors believe that hiding ugliness will work to produce a healthier society, hiding ugly realities often worsens issues.

PROFESSIONAL IGNORORS AND THEIR MASTERS

Professional ignorors are tasked with crafting misinformation to support bids for profit and power. When broadcast in clouds of attractive verbiage, their messages need not be factually correct to count if they are repeated again and again with an air of confidence. One study determined that by doubling the amount of money spent on ballot-issue rhetoric, votes will be swayed little more than one percent, which is enough to tip close races.[12] Ignorors' misinformation may be as simple as announcing progress on a number of fronts, which in actuality is Beltway code that disguises not making progress in other areas. Or they may mount a full-court press, as when the fossil fuel industry launched a flood of TV spots identifying oil and coal as the best basis for America's energy future.

Ignorors invade homes when phones ringing at dinnertime signal political polls. Without bothering with the usual "May I have a few minutes of your time?" the caller said to me, "This is a very important survey. Please do not hang up." But nothing is important enough to let my dinner go cold, so I hung up. I have little sympathy for political polls because too many are "push polls" aimed at eliciting predetermined results. Push pollsters can design polls that guarantee a 75 percent result for or against whatever their clients want. For instance, the poll that determined that 75 percent of Americans are categorically against abortion vandalized language and perverted truth, for even the most rabid pro-choice activist is not in favor of abortion. No one is pro-abortion, not even the doctors who perform them. But there are cases of mothers' survival, nonviable fetuses, or rape where the majority endorses abortion.[13] Polls that ask for yes or no votes on contentious issues are usually manipulative and not worthy of a thinking citizen's response. The best response is to get the name of the sponsoring organization, hang up, and check them out.

No huckster, snake oil salesman, or miracle weight-loss promoter distorts truth as much as corporate-funded politicians on the campaign trail. Though many complain about super-rich candidates using their own money to finance opposing campaigns, being beholden to no one allows them to speak from "what you see is what you get" platforms. Although faulted in many ways, Donald Trump enjoys the questionable virtue of being his own man. Meanwhile, mainstream candidates' entrance to the slippery slope of political bondage is buried in the political truism that if you want to make a difference, you first must do what it takes to get elected. How they handle that advice will either exclude principled candidates or compromise the less principled. Politics is gray, not red, white, and blue. As it stands, when office holders' votes reflect sponsors' expectations, it means that personal convictions and constituents' desires go unsupported.

Pollsters' push polls on abortion were as manipulative as the unanswerable question, "Have you stopped beating your wife?" Support of a position is forced by requiring a choice from among four multiple-choice options, three of which are patently unacceptable to everyone, which insures that the outcome is determined before the first call is made. The yes-or-no question, "Are you in favor of abortion?" ignores unfortunate realities that high-minded critics avoid considering to keep their creeds pure.[14] And the question is insensitive to the plight of victims of rape. The highly public question appeals to emotion, not understanding, which leaves society ignorant of the true balance of support for the issue. During the run-ups to recent general elections, emotion-laden charges about abortion served as a smokescreen to keep income disparity, bad big banks, transportation needs, global warming, and campaign finance off the front page. The purpose was political, not moral.

THE MEDIA COMPROMISE

A similar bit of manipulation preceded the Iraq War when media rubber-stamped the war council's charges that critics of the war were unpatriotic. It wasn't enough for home folks to support sons and daughters in uniform; the public was called to a level of loyalty that forbade criticism of the war. Criticism of US Middle East strategy was slammed for dishonoring our troops' effort and commitment. Jingoistic simplicity called for an Orwellian retreat into obedience to the official line that allowed only one viewpoint. News that was contrary to the Pentagon's PR strategy was cut or edited by corporate media editors in accordance with the quasi-partnership between media and government.[15] Since media could not afford to bite the federal hand that doles out tidbits of page-one copy, a certain amount of appeasement was to be expected.

During the 2004 presidential campaign when John Kerry's statements clashed with the conservative mind-set, his military service record was attacked by an odd assortment of patently false charges that had one thing in common: his critics claimed that it was impossible to be a decorated Vietnam hero and a critic of that war. One or the other—a warrior could not be both, which testified to the narrowness of those critics' frames. Kerry was called a waffler and a turncoat because of his correct analysis of the Iraq issue.[16] Kerry was a truth teller, not a waffler. He felt duty bound by patriotism to put an ill-conceived war into perspective by cutting away at veils of ignorance. The media was complicit in the anti-Kerry rhetoric by failing to align itself with the truth and leaving the voting public ignorant of the true nature and military record of Kerry.

Gas-bag pundits weighed in by inflaming gullible veterans and armchair warriors, convincing them that Kerry had dishonored their own sacrifices and service. No matter that Kerry's boots-on-the-ground experience and study confirmed that the Vietnam War was unjust, wrongheaded, and unwinnable, precisely as Secretary of Defense Robert McNamara and President Johnson came to see it. But given the times, and that only one view was allowed when the nation was at war, any deviation from the official line was deemed traitorous, a line that left the public ignorant of all but the administration's misguided will.

CORPORATE IGNORORS

Ignorors abound in corporate America, and nowhere have they been more active than during Big Tobacco's fall from grace. It was in 1953 that Big Tobacco was openly challenged by public awareness that smoking causes cancer. Facing an expanding PR threat, they spent the next two years crafting strategies to counter the evidence of conclusive scientific studies, strategies that would have to be ongoing to keep the death-dealing industry from dying. James Brady, a scientific director for the Council for Tobacco Research, sent a memo to C. C. Little, his superior at the council:

Historically, it would seem that the 1954 emergency was handled effectively. From the experience there arose a realization by the tobacco industry of a public relations problem that must be solved for the self-preservation of the industry.[17]

Strategies evolved to emasculate damning results of studies critical of smoking and to undermine factual information by moving the argument from threats to health to Big Brother dictating lifestyle issues. Robert Proctor, who was in the process of establishing the study of ignorance as the new science of agnotology, used the tobacco issue as his primary case study.[18] Big Tobacco's lying, cover-ups, and distortions generated a wealth of court documents that amounted to a mother lode of information about how industry can hold the public ignorant of facts. Using the tobacco situation as a proving ground for the new science of manufactured ignorance, Proctor set out to expose the methods Big Tobacco used to keep smokers from understanding how smoking affected their health. Along the way, the media's appetite for the tobacco industry's advertising dollars blinded them into complicity with Big Tobacco's defense. In its time of trial, Big Tobacco needed the persuasive power of publishers who buy ink by the barrel, and they got it. The public that depended wholly on corporate media for information was left largely uninformed and misinformed.

ANTI-INTELLECTUALISM

From the beginning there is a cult of anti-intellectualism in the United States. The strain of anti-intellectualism has been a constant thread winding its way through our political and cultural life, nurtured by the false notion that "my ignorance is as good as your knowledge."

—Isaac Asimov

Anti-intellectualism is an old and very American problem. It has been a problem of tragic proportions in China, Russia, Cambodia, and Mexico and was a chronic problem in Argentina and Chile. It occurs where and when leaders become so corrupt and insecure that they fear that reformers might plot their overthrow. When I interviewed a friend with Argentina's equivalent of the EPA, she told me, "We lack leaders. Given our history, potential leaders are reluctant to raise their heads."[1] She was referring to the past government's policy of tossing people with anti-establishment notions into the Atlantic from airplanes. In Argentina and Chile, they are remembered as the Disappeared Ones. They died because their thoughts didn't fit their rulers' narrow frames.

Richard Hofstadter inspected the topic in his book *Anti-Intellectualism in American Life*. If he missed the mark at all, it would be because of his focus on higher education's failure to resonate with intellectual Americans. His criticism indicts media commentators, university administrators, and even the president at the time, exposing them as adherents to what Hofstadter calls the lowest common denominator criterion of thought and technician conformity of lifestyle. It is his opinion that suspicion and hatred of ideas make "American culture as riveting as oatmeal."[2] Hofstadter wrote *Anti-Intellectualism in American Life* after observing with dismay how the GOP and the media managed to write off Adlai Stevenson as an "egghead." The Republican noise machine was able to convince voters that a thinker could not be presidential material because the workings of an impressive mind would be foreign to the thought patterns of common citizens.

THE ANTI-INTELLECTUAL QUEST FOR POWER

Anti-intellectual forces firmed up their ability to affect change when they took over the House of Representatives in 1994. One of their first projects under Newt Gingrich's leadership was to terminate the Office of Technological Assessment (OTA).[3] The OTA had, since its inception in 1972, supplied Congress with objective analysis of scientific and technical issues and had served as a model for technical advice to governments around the world. Termination of the OTA deprived Congress of technological heads-up advice that was essential to America remaining globally competitive in innovation and productivity. There could not have been a worse time to cut Congress off from informed counsel on science. The death of the OTA heralded a Beltway shift from critical thinking to raw political power that provided cover for the programmed reduction in support for general welfare.

It was the beginning of a period characterized by a shortage of imagination and clear-sighted analysis. A glaring example was the reaction to the 9/11 attack, when calls for critical analysis were shouted down as cowardly and replaced with ill-considered, knee-jerk reactions encouraged by right-leaning interests. Not knowing the cost, not knowing how to define or end our involvement, not knowing the people of the land we were about to invade, we went to war in a textbook demonstration of the danger of ignorance in high places.

Politicians hesitated to appear educated in such an anti-intellectual climate. The mood on the street was such that if they appeared or sounded educated they found themselves distanced from a population coached to resent thinkers. So they learned to address the nation with sleeves rolled up and to have a beer with the folks— not citizens, not people, but folks. Obama is anything but a country boy, but he knew full well that flaunting his considerable intelligence would raise charges of "Egghead! Nerd! Fancy-pants shill for the eastern establishment!" When a conservative critic was asked to comment on President Obama's delay in responding to a crisis, he said, "What did you expect? He's an all-things-considered kind of guy." The comment, heard on NPR's *All Things Considered* during the evening commute, reflected the far-rightist view that NPR and its public affairs feature, *All Things Considered*, are Communist egghead propagandists and that linking the president's measured thinking with NPR would tag him with a negative label.

President Bush's election over John Kerry hinged on a choice between Kerry's French cuffs and cuff links vs. Bush's rolled-up sleeves, between a tall, patrician easterner vs. a chainsaw-toting, transplanted Texan. In reality, it was a choice between Kerry, who grew up wealthy, lived in Massachusetts, and went to Yale and Bush, who grew up wealthy, lived in Connecticut, and went to Yale, so it was a wash on wealth, home state, and education. Kerry should have gained points for serving heroically in Vietnam, while Bush should have lost points for going AWOL during mandatory National Guard training sessions. Other than the lies and fabrications of the Swift boat scandal that should have earned red cards for Kerry's critics, the election seemed to have turned on perceptions of the French cuffs vs. rolled-up sleeves issue, an example of how anti-intellectual trivia warps voting patterns.

To cultivate a folksy image, a candidate must not appear smug, aloof, elitist, or deep in thought. The candidate must pose as a mildly educated C student with a limited vocabulary who stumbles over simple grammatical constructions and forgets to zip his fly now and then. Behind-the-scene king makers love this image for three reasons. First, if a candidate stumbles from that position, he is as likely to fall upward as downward. Second, if a candidate is, in truth, not too smart, it means he should be easy to manipulate. Third, the country boy image appeals to a bloc of potential voters that professional ignorors have less trouble manipulating. It leaves thinking voters aghast at the un-presidential candidates set before them as "presidential."

ANTI-INTELLECTUALISM BY THE NUMBERS

Political anti-intellectualism rises from a complex of roots groomed to obscure the purposes and tactics behind an unhealthy share of legislation. Whereas anti-intellectualism was once no more than a limited way of thinking, it has infiltrated government as a bloc that profits from denying science. The potential for profit is such that ignorors pander to the anti-science sympathies of anti-intellectuals to broaden their bases of support. The ignoror opponents of the 2009 Waxman-Markey clean air act, regardless of their educations, assumed the posture of fossil fuel science deniers to scuttle the act because they had been paid $3.22 billion, administered by an army of 807 lobbyists, to do so.[4] They built a good case against Waxman-Markey, citing potential problems with capping and trading the carbon dioxide outputs of plants. It was a spirited debate. Industry must make a profit; the air must be clean. What the public didn't hear was who paid for the opposition to Waxman-Markey and that the reason behind their efforts was purely to ensure healthy bottom lines for the fossil fuel industry.

The sympathies of science-denying anti-intellectualists, like the beliefs and priorities of conservative Christians or retirees, are co-opted when politically expedient. They seldom understand that they will be badly used when politicians cozy up to them and that they are not meant to understand that their cooperation is necessary to "build movements." Movement makers are experts at moving minds into thought-confining corrals that artfully exclude discernment that might reveal their fealty to lords of power and profit. Their movements draw support from mindless consumerism and the mind-numbing effects of social media and other digital distractions. As evidence, in 1982, 82 percent of college graduates read novels or poetry for pleasure. Twenty years later that number had dropped to 67 percent. By 2004, fully 40 percent of Americans under the age of forty-four hadn't read a book of any kind in a year, and the percentage of seventeen-year-olds who read nothing unless required soared.[5] These changes were accomplished largely by the victory of electronics over print media, a change that thinking observers bemoan.

Not all agree. Science writer Steven Johnson, an avowed technophile and apologist for the digital world, filed a counterclaim in his book, *Everything Bad Is Good for You: How Today's Popular Culture Is Actually Making Us Smarter.* He wrote that parents' fear of negative effects from hours of exposure to digital images is unfounded and that kids' hours of rapt and continuous attention develops focus, rather than dulling the mind.[6] The most credible of Johnson's conclusions is that the presence and popularity of digital imagery are here to stay.

The history of our species must be considered. Over 99 percent of our past was spent hunting and gathering. Some graduated to herding, which required months and years of little more than watching animals graze. Although there is no way to track what went on in our distant ancestors' heads, their brains weren't radically different from ours, so they could not have been totally idle. Herders entertained solitary thoughts about the world they knew. No earbuds, no cell phones, no digital downloads—just lone shepherds dealing with hunger, inclement weather, predators, and the well-being of their animals. Thousands of years of that particular life contributed to the evolutionary process that culminated in us. It involved storytelling, standing in awe of nature, simple music, and poetry.

Legends and sagas arising from those times are rich in metaphoric imagery that literal description cannot match. Those illiterate herders exercised imaginative intellect that imbued all nature with character. They composed oral epics that entranced campfire audiences and were passed down from generation to generation as tribal lore. Themes within the Bible may be traced beyond those times until the trails vanish in the mists of prehistory when lore served in place of literacy and myths gathered to form cores of culture.

GENEALOGY OF AMERICAN ANTI-INTELLECTUALISM

America's anti-intellectual bias was carried to the New World by early settlers who suffered persecutions and constraints at the hands of high-born, educated bullies who denied them opportunity to rise. The emigrants were relatively rich in hands-on skills that marked them as separate from the upper classes, whose children populated England's prep schools and universities. Hoover Institute economist Thomas Sowell wrote,

> From its colonial beginnings, American society was a "decapitated" society—largely lacking the topmost social layers of European society. The highest elites and the titled aristocracies had little reason to risk their lives crossing the Atlantic to face the perils of pioneering. Most of the white population of the first decades of the new nation arrived as indentured servants and the black population as slaves. Later waves of immigrants were disproportionately peasants and proletarians, [most] from Western Europe. . . . The rise of American society to pre-eminence as an economic, political and military power was thus the triumph of the common man and a slap across the face to the presumptions of the arrogant, whether an elite of blood or books.[7]

That would change. The Puritans soon found themselves outnumbered by intellectually ambitious settlers who chafed at being looked down upon by Europe's creative thinkers. They craved institutions that could provide their children with the quality of education that had been beyond their reach in England. Though the Puritans held that the Bible was the only book a person needed, their belief failed to stem the colonies' desire for worldly education, as evidenced by the establishment of Harvard in 1636, William and Mary 1693, Yale 1701, College of New Jersey (Princeton) 1746, Kings College (Columbia) 1754, College of Philadelphia (University of Pennsylvania) 1755, Rhode Island College (Brown) 1764, Queens College (Rutgers) 1766, and Dartmouth in 1769.[8]

The mood that dominated the next century defined the image of the ideal American man as one who was practically skilled and successful at his trade. Social standing was earned through the quality of one's work, a respect that carries to this day in the high values TV's *Antiques Roadshow* attaches to handcrafted early-American products. The ideal was the self-made man but, with the exception of doctors and lawyers, not an intellectual one whose knowledge was gained from books. Reverend Bayard Hall wrote about the character of Indiana's men in *The New Purchase, or Seven and a Half Years in the Far West*:

> We always preferred an ignorant bad man to a talented one, and hence, attempts were usually made to ruin the moral character of a smart candidate; since unhappily, smartness and wickedness were supposed to be generally coupled.[9]

It was a mind-set that would prevail through the presidential campaigns of Adlai Stevenson and John Kerry. In the mid-nineteenth century, O. Henry wrote that when "an East Coast university graduate 'gets over' his intellectual vanity—no longer thinks himself better than others—he makes just as good a cowboy as any other young man."[10]

The theme of anti-intellectualism endures as mistrust of intellect and its products, ridicule of education, art, philosophy and literature, and a general reaction against all that takes an extra measure of book study to understand. It stands against workings of the brain, unless connected directly to tools and jobs, with a contempt bordering on hostility. Anti-intellectuals bill themselves as champions of common folk, populists to a fault who espouse a belief that educated people compose a social class that chooses detachment from the masses so they might dominate government and economics at a profit and from a distance. What anti-intellectuals should understand is that their position reflects the same trait that totalitarian dictatorships have used to silence opposition voices. Just as it did in Russia, China, and Cambodia, it poses a danger wherever found.

Thomas Sowell argues that there should be a recognized distinction between reasonable and unreasonable intellectuals. He defines intellectuals as people occupied with ideas, not people who put ideas to work. Sowell's understanding of intellectuals is that, while they are free to generate original ideas, they seldom have to answer for ideas that cause harm, the way doctors or engineers do. Teachers are held suspect for promoting socioeconomic principles that conservative critics generally take as misguided and for dismissing certain "more practical" views, thus steering the formation of opinions before students are, as Sowell sees it, prepared to weigh one view against others.

It is difficult for the man on the street to ignore how his peers see intellectuals as know-it-alls who, by virtue of more years in classrooms, take themselves to be wiser than the average citizen. Historian Paul Johnson wrote, "Beware of intellectuals. Not merely should they be kept well away from the levers of power, they should also be objects of suspicion when they seek to offer collective advice."[11] That over-the-top charge cannot go unanswered.

INTELLECTUALISM, CHALLENGED AT EVERY TURN

Johnson's dim view of thinkers would leave the bean-counting end of mathematics intact while cutting away at theoretical math. Likewise, theoretical physics would suffer while applied physics and engineering would be upheld. Johnson's recipe calls for stagnation of progress and stifling of inquiry that could leave projects such as stem cell research and development of Zika vaccines lacking necessary support. Hope lies in the pattern established by the US Department of Agriculture's work with land grant colleges that brought theorists, researchers, and farmers together, and spin-offs from discoveries within prestigious labs such as Battelle International finding application in Main Street's shops and factories.

Anti-intellectual activists have damaged their targets' careers, removed people from leadership positions, and cost lives. In Argentina, the infamous Night of the Long Batons culminated in President Ongania's purge of intellectuals by dislodging college faculties.[12] Ongania's military spokesman declared, "Our country would be put in order as soon as all the intellectuals who were meddling in the region were expelled."[13] The Khmer Rouge regime in Kampuchea (1975–79) eliminated everyone with more than an elementary education, temporarily reducing Cambodian society to an intellectual stone age. In terms of sheer numbers affected, Mao's Cultural Revolution topped them all when his brutal Red Guards identified and removed the nation's thinkers, academics, technicians, artists, and landowners to camps for "reeducation." Here at home, Joseph McCarthy aimed his anti-Communist witch hunt at intellectuals whose insights embraced social theories outside American commercialism. In recent years, a cabal of anti-intellectuals led by David Horowitz, William Bennett, and Patrick Buchanan actually criticized America's public schools as being "intellectualist."[14] John Searle observed in his book, *The Campus Wars,*

> [T]he two most salient traits of the radical movement are its anti-intellectualism and its hostility to the university as an institution. . . . Intellectuals by definition are people who take ideas seriously for their own sake. . . . But in the radical movement, the intellectual ideal of knowledge for its own sake is rejected. Knowledge is seen as valuable only as a basis for action, and it is not even very valuable there.[15]

No one can be wrong one hundred percent of the time, not even anti-intellectuals. Without doubt, a lot of useless blather is generated by self-styled thinkers who might serve society better by digging ditches or milking cows. Sociologist Stanislav Andreski warned readers of academic books, "Do not be impressed by the imprint of a famous publishing house or the volume of an author's publications. Remember that publishers want to keep the printing presses busy and do not object to nonsense if it can be sold."[16] Certainly, the ranks of constructive thinkers are polluted by the presence of unqualified pretenders, but that should not give critics carte blanche to toss the baby out with the bathwater.

When public figures are labeled intellectual, a ready body of non-thinkers is poised to take them on whether they are rocket scientists, chefs, or musicians. It is a knee-jerk reaction driven by ignorant concerns that intellectuals are behind every nameless threat in the wind. Adlai Stevenson was an intellectual who reckoned that certain topics of his time were of such importance that they deserved the deepest consideration influential people could muster, and it was his dedication to deep thought that separated him from his political opposites and brought him down.

When Stevenson was soundly defeated by Eisenhower in 1952, op-ed columnists, depending on their persuasion, crowed or cried over the results. Most agreed that eggheads had not only taken a beating, but that intellectualism had been defeated at the polls. High-minded debate had bowed to balance sheet analysis. Merchants had bowled over the academics. That this happened in the shadow of McCarthy's witch hunt was surreal. At the time McCarthy was sent packing, one might suppose it was a signal to elevate our intellectual sights a bit, but the nation did just the opposite. The margin that put Eisenhower into office showed that the nation wasn't ready to be led by a thinker. Eisenhower had been a popular leader during WWII and a good man by most measures, plus he had the guts to challenge the establishment. He played a decent game of golf and was a conventional thinker surrounded by businessmen eager to worm their way into federal decision-making circles. In fact, he was a good choice—but the man who was by most objective measures a better candidate for that particular time lost the election.

What separated the parties and their king makers was the old bugaboo, ignorance. The massive power of America's mercantile and industrial titans was guided not by debate over what was best for the nation or its citizens but the bottom lines of Fortune 500 corporations. That posture is a good thing if one is tasked only with maximizing the success of businesses. Yet that myopic focus on profits ignored the health of the socioeconomic engine that generates those profits. It was forgotten that more profit could permit higher wages, which would produce more buying power that would, in turn, generate more profit.

It is difficult to communicate with minds that disdain consideration of all sides, all opinions, or all the facts. What's more troubling is the widespread practice of closing doors to opposing thought to protect ideological comfort zones. This is ignorance in action, the opposite of the open intellect that holds itself receptive to whatever bears on an issue, whether agreeable to one's preferences or not. The open mind's respect for facts and logic runs into the anti-intellectual opposition described by Richard Hofstadter in his book.

Hofstadter cited New Yorker George Plunkitt's assertion that a college education is of no practical use in politics, an opinion that didn't stand against the contributions of educated progressives such as Woodrow Wilson, Teddy Roosevelt, and Henry Cabot Lodge.[17] Though he had little use for higher education, Plunkitt did manage to find anti-intellectual friends in academia in the form of "experts" who, in their support of Plunkitt's machine politics, contradicted academic ethics. Plunkitt's politics depended on support from limited thinkers who could be convinced that they were victimized by intellectuals' corrective work and proposals.

Experts' investment of self in their learnings and beliefs can lock them into intellectual rigidity. Part of graduate education involves defending theses in a process best described as carving out patches of intellectual turf. The role of "defense" of theses in graduate schools sets a tone for what can follow: long-term defense of signature intellectual achievements rather than cooperative reforming and redefining of truth. Note how many times the word "intellectual" was used in describing closed-minded academics. It fits only because ignorati occupy positions similar to those of true intellectuals, not because their thoughts produce much of consequence.

THE ANTI-INTELLECTUAL AGENDA

In 2014, anti-intellectual critics upped their charges that universities were disappointing students by requiring courses that didn't lead to job readiness—courses like civics, music, history, literature, art, and languages.[18] The critics' recommendations for curriculum change were on the mark if the mission was to develop production line robots, but it was deadly for the human spirit. They called for a rebalancing of studies that would leave students ignorant of much of what has enlivened quality of life for as long as our species has walked the earth. The reigning idea that the purpose of an education is to guarantee immediate financial reward is crowding the humanities out of education. Crippling student debt and graduates not finding work in their fields add to the anti-intellectual case. Russell Banks takes a dim view, writing,

> In most countries it's generally thought that literary artists are more likely than members of the governing class to possess the long view and that the long view is rather helpful in obtaining a more or less coherent short view. It's also generally thought that literary artists are less likely than policy makers to be beholden to what we call "special interests." . . . [I]t seems more than unlikely, it seems impossible, for the moral and linguistic clarity of our literary artists to have the slightest influence on the moral and linguistic imaginations of those who rule us.
>
> By and large, our so-called public intellectuals nowadays operate out of think tanks and universities and hold to ideologically determined agendas, financed largely by the military-industrial complex of multinational corporations. They are sociologists and historians, scientists and bureaucrats, scholars and out-of-work journalists and policy wonks, paid to produce papers, articles, and

books that will further the political ambitions of one or the other
of our two political parties and the financial interests of corporate
America.[19]

Banks was focused on the diminished public voice of intellectuals and their replacement by for-hire propagandists who feed
the media's appetite for free content. With suppliers of free editorial material filling pages and airwaves, it is unlikely that corporate
bias will disappear from the media. Meanwhile, the greater part of
America claims to get its news from TV where flavor-of-the-day sensational events rule the airwaves. Video's triumph over print media
caused already cash-strapped investigative newsgathering organizations to reduce staffs of reporters. At the same time, mergers within
print media consolidated newspapers and book publishing under a
shrinking number of mega-publishers. Australian Rupert Murdoch
is developing a publishing empire spanning the English-speaking
world. With footholds in American television (Fox News) and the
publishing houses of HarperCollins and Zondervan, he is amassing
enough coverage clout to affect Western attitudes.

Time Warner entered the big time through mergers made possible by deregulation. It is now possible that editorial instructions
from Time Warner's directors could flood America with one editorial slant should TW choose to promote an official ideology. A Pew
Research Center study found that, while 47 percent of conservatives
get their news from one broadcaster (Fox News), liberals spread 10
to 15 percent of their loyalty across each of four favorite sources.[20]
The result: there is no longer room for doubt about whether the
media marinates blocs of American voters with biased information
and disinformation. The public is, at times, made selectively ignorant
of important issues in a way that is little different from allowing the
prosecution in a court of law to sit on or skew information that might
damage its case.

Anti-intellectual neoconservatives aren't happy with science's
cautionary environmental messages, and they do what they can to

discredit or nullify them. When Arizona elected Fife Symington governor in the early 1990s, he initiated a biased agenda against environmental education that resulted in effectively closing the arm of the state's Department of Education tasked with environmental education.[21] According to the then director of environmental education, schools were ordered to pull in environmental materials that had been distributed by the Office of Environmental Education, and "green" teachers' efforts were reined in. That, and banning of certain environmental books, marked Symington's Arizona as the poster state for the anti-environmental arm of anti-intellectualism.

To gain that singular status, Arizona had to qualify on many fronts. First is distrust of the northeastern seaboard where prominent liberal movers and shakers were raised, many of them Ivy Leaguers born into a tradition of position and privilege that doesn't play well in blue-collar America—never mind that Symington was a Harvard-educated New Yorker. Others are seen as eggheads and nerds in the tradition of Adlai Stevenson and the Kennedys, many of them associated with legislation that holds social responsibility as important as personal responsibility. For even the dimmest of conservative propagandists, linking Northeast eggheads with the hated Democratic Party is a reflex. Conservativism's review of Democrat-sponsored legislation detected a deep-green streak that would sacrifice coal and oil to shave a degree or two from global warming. And tofu-eating easterners don't like cattle, and they attempt to rule public grazing lands with an iron hand. Enough said. Intellectuals aren't to be trusted.

That is why anti-intellectual candidates no longer address the public as voters, citizens, or even people. They say, "Folks, I am here to . . ." "Folks" sounds so, well, folksy. They pose as though from humble origins; as someone who can complete a twenty-minute speech without using a word of more than two syllables; and someone who, alongside us, might have earned a C in Mrs. Armbrust's third-period English class. The Powers That Be don't want a president who voters can look up to but one they could buddy up with from the neighboring stool at Jimmy's Sports Bar. Results from recent polls and 2016 campaign results spell a real danger that the conduct of the campaign pulled vision and accomplishment downward while trading inspiration and insight for crude expedients. Never underestimate the ignorance-driven naivety of the American voter.

ANTI-INTELLECTUALISM IN UNIVERSITIES

Paul Trout, a professor at Montana State University at Bozeman, offered an anecdote about a colleague in a special help session, asking, "Now, how would we do that?" A student at the back yelled out, "Who gives a shit!"[22] Though the student's outburst wasn't representative of Montana State's culture, it is emblematic of the lack of respect and motivation of a surprising number of students. For more than a decade, professors have been complaining about dealing with apathetic students' resistance to education. Apathetic students poison learning environments while advertising their anti-intellectual mind-set by refusing to contribute to discussions, griping about workloads, lobbying for lighter assignments, skipping class, and—this unkindest cut of all—giving low evaluations to courageous professors with the guts to maintain high standards.

It doesn't take many to poison a learning atmosphere. Neglecting to prepare for class, not consulting materials left on reserve at the library, not picking up handouts, ridiculing high achievers, and generally bad-mouthing intellectual endeavors and requirements as intrusions into personal time add to the degradation of the pedagogical experience. Depending on campus culture, students may shy away from discussing assignments or course content after class for fear of being cut off with, "Keep it in class." I even heard of one ostracized student who went to a counselor to ask if there was something wrong with her because she actually liked her classes. The problem is broad enough that college-bound high school students would be well advised to not only check out a college's offerings and ratings but also to try to gain a feel for its academic culture.

Of course, apathetic students have always bragged that they don't study. The difference today is that more first-year students are finding their educational goals compromised by campus cultures hostile to intellectual activity. At Virginia Polytechnic, a philosophy professor estimated that a majority of students are disaffected and that as many as 15 percent can't be reached. A chemistry professor at the same institution wrote that a majority of his students are generally uninterested and do the least work possible.[23] Although there is nothing new in this behavior, what is disheartening is the upward trend in the numbers, and that concerted lack of effort drags whole programs down to unacceptably low levels.

The problem is gaining momentum. With between 60 and 70 percent of high school graduates now entering higher education, colleges have reason to be concerned about what they are given to work with.[24] Temple University's Laurence Steinberg wrote that, whereas two decades ago a high school class would have three or four (profoundly) disaffected students, nearly half are uninterested today. He said, "It is potentially more harmful to the future of the wellbeing of American society than any of the other problems now grabbing the headlines."[25]

CAUSE AND EFFECT IN THE EDUCATION INDUSTRY

Pressure from anti-intellectualism has invaded campuses to lower standards by inflating grades. It keeps unmotivated students happy and enrollments up, and enrollees equal money. Because a university's financial stability requires full classrooms, regardless of whether students choose to learn or not, grade inflation becomes a bureaucratically acceptable tactic for supporting administrative needs and plans. Part of grade inflation can be written off to instructors' fear of receiving unfavorable evaluations for filing honest assessments of low-quality work.

Colleges adopt the bean counter's concept of students as consumers of education or, from the industrial standpoint, units of production, though that brings up the bothersome industrial issue of quality control. From the student's standpoint, the consumer model implies that the university should shape its services and approaches to satisfy the consumer's (student's) needs and desires. The downside is that, as consumers, students try to strike the best deals by going for the most product at the lowest cost, which means angling for high grades "earned" with minimal study.

As things stand, the quality of scholarly experience is slipping. The National Association of Scholars (NAS), a leading higher education reform organization, published a sixty-five-page report on courses offered at fifty top undergraduate universities listed in U.S. News & World Report's review of America's best colleges. The findings (paraphrased) are not encouraging:

Students are no longer required to enroll in common core knowledge courses that were once taken for granted as basic to a well-rounded education. In fact, many of the courses that imparted historical, cultural, political and scientific basics of society have been purged from required curricula.

The number of mandatory courses has been reduced from 9.9 in 1914, to 7.3 in 1939, to 6.9 in 1964, and to 2.5 in 1993.[26] The former universal requirement that students take survey courses that gave them broad understandings of the world and its systems have virtually vanished.

The college year has been shortened by nearly one-fourth while tuition continues to escalate. In 1914 classes were in session an average of 204 days per year; by 1939 the number had dropped to 195 and fell further to 156 days per academic year in 1993.[27]

The common complaint that students graduate without the ability to write may be a result of universities dropping courses in English composition. The number of universities requiring courses in writing has dropped from 70 percent in 1964 to 34 percent in 1996. (The survey found a similar drop in required mathematics, though there are signs in the new century that this unacceptable trend is being reversed.)

Whereas 90 percent of universities required courses in American History in 1914, that number dropped to 50 percent in 1939 and by 1996 only one of the 50 universities had a history requirement.[28] Literature, once required by 75 percent of universities, was not required in 1996 by any of the universities studied.[29]

From every standpoint, it appears that things may get worse before they get better. From upper-grade levels, educators look to younger grades to see what's coming up the pipeline, and what they see is not encouraging. Some critics write off youthful anti-intellectualism as the product of misguided educational policies, but that is hard to prove with family dysfunction and electronic distraction in play. Henry Bauer, author of *Students Who Don't Study*, reported this statement from a disillusioned college student: "Most kids nowadays just go through the motions of getting a college education . . . [and] colleges and universities go through the motions of teaching students."[30] The student was speaking only for himself and his peer group because educational excellence remains available to dedicated students even where anti-intellectualism poisons learning cultures. But the fact of a widespread negative trend, that cheating on tests is common even where honor codes are in force, that students hack into and change college records, that attendance and participation in classes are down all should serve as warnings to young men and women as they shop for quality educational experiences.

According to Peter Sacks, the effect on instructors is "frustration, indignities and moral danger."[31] He wrote that if a professor wasn't entertaining enough, stepped on students' sensibilities, or showed weakness, students would smell blood and, like sharks, move in for the kill. Evidence from across the map indicates that Sacks may be right. The situation between faculty and students in some schools amounts to undeclared cultural war. Considering today's cost of higher education, whoever is paying the bill would be well advised to do some investigating before writing the first check.

A SOCIETY-WIDE OVERVIEW

Society is faced with a conundrum: the very institutions entrusted with guarding and passing on intellectual vigor and traditions have become the target of anti-intellectual attacks. Placing the blame on higher education is as misguided as blaming public schools for unacceptable achievement without considering children's readiness for learning. Critics should look to cultural issues rooted in family life, entertainment, materialism, false goals, and failure of officials whose lives don't reflect the values they were elected to ensure. Just as parenting sets standards for children, leaders of every kind are obliged to lead by example. Critics of schools and colleges should look first at the anti-intellectual backgrounds against which they struggle. That includes voters harboring unhappy memories of school days that color their attitudes toward their children's schools' programs and needs. Homes where TV and social media take the place of reading and learning give scant support to intellectual ambitions, leaving promotion of excellence to idealists who, though they do come up with some impractical ideas, are generally principled enough to work for the general welfare. Their critics are more ready to settle for quick solutions that answer immediate needs but fall short of effecting real change. Example-setting leaders who work to clear their desks while focusing on only their side of issues lean toward substituting schemes based on what's permissible over what should be done. Whether from a president, teacher, banker, lawyer, or parent, a good example generally reflects knowledge of more than the personal side of an issue.

A telling correlation between density of newspaper distribution and achievement in local schools has long existed, though its significance may be fading with the dramatic drop in newspaper circulation. The simple truth remains that where parents take their news from print media, schools succeed. The reverse proves true where low-density newspaper deliveries correlate with low achievement. Yet when schools fail to meet state or national standards, critics are quick to blame administration, teachers, or curriculum, when a significant part of the fault lies with the non-supportive attitudes of an anti-intellectual subculture. Susan Jacoby, author of *The Age of American Unreason*, offers a different criticism, saying, "Spoon-feeding children with facts and figures designed merely to pass a standardized test will never prepare them to protect democracy."[32] Wise planners will recognize that these insights, along with all others, are needed to counter the effects of anti-intellectualism that will never leave us alone.

Certain interests gain from anti-intellectual attacks on liberal education, climate change, immigration policy, diplomacy, and reduction of carbon fuels. Anything having to do with taxes or government spending is a prime target. Interests that profit from use of carbon-based fuels deride advances in alternative energy. Conservative Christians may abandon reason to "Be fruitful and increase in number; fill the earth and subdue it. Rule over the fish of the sea and the birds of the air and over every living creature that moves on the ground." They allow themselves to believe that the biblical instruction from Genesis 1:28 (New International Version) justifies practices that contribute to extinction of species and degradation of the environment. Susan Jacoby adds, "This mindless tolerance, which places observable scientific facts subject to proof on the same level as un-provable supernatural fantasy,[33] has played a major role in the resurgence of both anti-intellectualism and anti-rationalism."[34] It is noteworthy that most attacks on intellectual activity are so rooted in history and tradition that those behind them fail to look ahead. If uncorrected, ignorant posturing has the capacity to diminish not only the nation's future as a center for creativity, discovery, and innovation but the odds that global ecosystems will survive.

History and tradition will always serve as stabilizing anchors for national cultures, but one who chooses the past for his or her intellectual dwelling place is like a passenger gone overboard from a moving ship to fall behind in the history of its wake. The reality of now disappears with the ship, leaving the history dweller lost in a sea of irrelevance.

CHAPTER 8

IGNORANCE IN EDUCATION

*Education's purpose is to replace an empty mind with an
open one.*

—Malcolm Forbes

Much was said about education in the previous chapter
because anti-intellectualism finds homes in certain niches
and practices within education. A broader view accepts that education happens all the time and everywhere: when a rock is thrown
through a window, when a car runs out of gas, or when a salesperson
exceeds a monthly quota. Whatever a person sees, hears, or experiences is in some way educational, which means that, for better or
worse, every moment is a teachable moment. Yet it has become easy
to think of education as the exclusive responsibility of schools and a
student's school years as the only proper time for education.

PUBLIC SCHOOL REALITIES

Poor public education. It is a rare year when it doesn't suffer an
excess of change and a shortage of money. Add to that, school administrators' normal knee-jerk response to lackluster achievement is the
invention of new paradigms. The things fixers get right are things
that can be seen: safety measures for school buses, better playground
equipment, chairs, desks, and test results. The things they get wrong
are the things they cannot see: methods that motivate, school hours

geared to children's best learning times, and physical exercise. Allocators of money fail to understand that motivated kids will learn nearly as effectively in drafty warehouses as in modern classrooms. It is what happens in classrooms and how children are treated and inspired that matter most, but those things don't compute as neatly as inventories of learning materials and equipment. Nuts and bolts have always been easier to deal with than concepts and vision.

Education endures constant criticism that keeps it on its toes. Being an inertia-burdened behemoth, it can't help but resist change. And resist it should, for society is overstaffed with reformers who would gleefully junk trusted curricula for trendy change, or scuttle modern education in favor of a return to the Three Rs. The touchy relationship between education and the society it serves generates a tension in which all parties manage to operate in a surprisingly moderate emotional climate. Considering the size of school budgets and the number of people involved, truly crippling issues are few, with mediocrity and limiting the cause and effect of Q and A instruction the enduring issues. Many of today's educational controversies center around a generational disagreement over how children of traditional parents should learn in the digital age. Another abiding issue arises from confusion over what the future can justifiably expect from children.

LOOKING FOR SOMETHING THAT WORKS BETTER

Howard Gardner's *Five Minds for the Future* lays out his vision of specific characteristics young minds must acquire if they are to cope with what is to come. Gardner wrote, "In the interrelated world where most of us live it is no longer possible to live the high life while others in distant or not-so distant places starve or succumb to curable disease."[1] That may not gain sympathy from people lacking Gardner's social conscience, but what is undeniable is that it has become more difficult to remain ignorant of the plight of the less fortunate.

Yet minds tied up in self-protective cocoons of social ignorance find it easy to ignore cruel conditions endured by others and deny obvious evidence that hope and opportunity are unfairly restricted from some to maximize the advantages of others. Gardner builds a case for five characteristics needed to qualify minds for coping with the future:

The disciplined mind that masters a number of ways of thinking.

The synthesizing mind that creatively blends information from different sources.

The creating mind that invents new ways of thinking to move boundaries of knowledge ever outward.

The respectful mind that welcomes and celebrates differences between cultures.

The ethical mind that analyzes every iota of change for its value, not to vested interests, but for the general welfare.

Gardner reasonably proposes that, to the degree that education fails to serve a population, its practices and goals should be altered, leaving the community to judge and propose change. He offers his *Five Minds* proposals as a working framework for change rather than another plan-in-a-can proposal that winds up hostage to flavor-of-the-times imperatives or changes in administration.

Public school teachers facing proposals for change will be eager to tell you, "We're buried in change. We haven't had time to adjust to last year's new approaches, and they're already redrafting curriculum—again. We simply don't have the energy or time to keep this up." They're right. Educational leadership, while operating with the best of intentions under pressure to do something, does *something*. They find themselves in the position of the trucker who pulled off onto the shoulder, climbed from his cab, and began beating the sides of his van with a two-by-four. A highway patrolman pulled in behind him with lights flashing and demanded to know what was going on. The trucker sheepishly explained that he had only a two-ton load permit but was carrying three tons of canaries so he had to keep a third of them on the wing to lighten the load. So it is with education, where well-meaning educational planners sustain a perpetuating state of flux that causes programs to be judged during rough settling-in periods before they have a chance to mature in practice.

JOHN GATTO, A VOICE FROM WITHIN

Rumblings within the system help to keep schools on their toes. John Gatto, New York State's Teacher of the Year in 1991, set off seismic rumblings in the nation's schools when he published bitter memories of his teaching experiences, writing,

> All of these lessons are prime training for permanent under-classes, people deprived forever of finding the center of their own special genius . . . that school is a twelve-year jail sentence where bad habits are the only curriculum truly learned. I teach school, and win awards doing it. I should know.[2]

Right or wrong, rants like Gatto's cannot help but generate hostility among school administrators. Though he was sincere in his criticisms, his harsh rhetoric heightened odds that decision makers would not give his arguments their due. The best that can be said of Gatto's approach is that his charges that schools are doing it wrong did command attention, and while his observations may be taken as accurate, broad-brush criticism seldom triggers reform. Better to start with some point that everyone involved can identify with. It is not difficult for staff at troubled schools to agree that identifiable things must be holding them from doing better while keeping the teaching/learning process from becoming more enjoyable. Teachers, like workers in any profession or trade, know that a job is easier when it's done right. But getting it right starts with admitting that you must be missing something.

Admission of ignorance opens doors and windows to possible

cures. Compare the forward-thinking openness of planners who expect to learn something new with backward-looking planners who interpret change as a mere reshuffling of what they already know. Imagine if Gatto's school's staff had united in admitting, "We don't know what we're doing wrong, but if we can figure that out, then we might be able to move on to figuring out the direction in which we should be moving." Gatto doesn't tell us why his personal experience went so wrong. Was he speaking to deficiencies in entire schools or the department in which he taught? Was he criticizing local deficiencies in leadership or a particularly bad time for his city's schools? He had more to say:

> Was it possible I had been hired, not to enlarge children's power, but to diminish it? That seemed crazy, on the face of it, but slowly, I began to realize that the bells and confinement, the crazy sequences, the age-segregation, the lack of privacy, the constant surveillance, and all the rest of the national curriculum of schooling were designed exactly as if someone had set out to prevent children from learning how to think, and act, to coach them into addiction and dependent behavior.[3]

Harsh as they are, it would be unwise to dismiss Gatto's observations. Gatto is a product of his times; his rhetoric was very possibly influenced by the tone of popular media messengers such as Glenn Beck, Rush Limbaugh, Ed Schultz, Charles Krauthammer, and even Rachel Maddow. Needless to say, excessive speech generates more heat than light, nudging diversity of opinion toward conflict. Gatto's book, *Dumbing us Down: The Hidden Curriculum of Compulsory Schooling*, is chock-full of accurate insider observations that deserve the attention of every career educator. That said, it must also be recognized that his elevated level of idealism cannot find a comfortable home in monolithic education. It could work if—and this is a very big if—so many of the parents of America's children were not superannuated children. Gatto's students' parents displayed ignorance of parental responsibility, a failing that stared them in the face each time their children failed to live up to expectations.

GROWING UP IN THE TWENTY-FIRST CENTURY

Any student of biology learns that the one overriding purpose of every living organism is to reproduce itself successfully. In the case of humans, "successfully" means dedicated nurturing until offspring gain an even chance at becoming successful parents to the next generation. Anything less breaks the chain. Ignorance of parental responsibility results in squandering children's time and attention by polluting home-learning atmospheres with trivial distractions and insufficient structured time for study. Of the 168 hours that make up a week, children sleep fifty-six, leaving 112 hours for conscious life. Studies show that kids surrender an average of fifty-five of those hours to television. School takes up thirty, and a Common Sense Media study revealed the impossible number of hours that children between the ages of eight to eighteen spend on cell phones and social media. The total exceeds a 168-hour week by twenty-three hours without figuring in showering, getting to school and back, eating, and going to the bathroom.[4] Days are made possible by attention-sharing laminations of mental activities that each deserve concerted attention. This is a major cause of low achievement, and it takes parents' rationalizing ignorance to believe otherwise.

Gatto studied the distractions that rob children of the hours needed for growing up properly and recognized them as the source of specific pathologies that make attempts at educational reform little more than fleeting façades. It is more than likely that some of the behaviors he observed in his classroom stayed with his students after graduation. Gatto's observations were the following:

Children are indifferent to the adult world, which is something new in human history.

Children demonstrate a lack of curiosity, and what little they have is transitory. Living in the moment puts crippling restraints on their consciousness.

Children have a poor sense of the future and how tomorrow is linked to today.

Children's thinking has become ahistorical, lacking any sense that history and yesterdays have any responsibility for what happens to today.

Children are cruel to each other, lacking compassion for misfortune, laughing at weakness, showing contempt for people who need help.

Children are uneasy with intimacy or candor. They are crippled by preserving a secret inner self and world inside an artificial persona made up of bits derived from entertainment.

Children are materialistic, having noticed that everything is for sale.

Children are dependent, passive, and timid in the presence of new challenges. This may be glossed over with bravado or aggressive demeanors, which, if tested, will prove hollow.[5]

The bulk of critical news coverage of public education comes from surveys indicating that high school and college students are uninformed. Questions such as "who is the chief justice of the US Supreme Court?" draw blanks. One-third couldn't identify the three branches of government, which survey sponsors took as proof that public education is not doing its job. Though the charge contains a large germ of truth, students' weak memory responses point to a different pair of related culprits: digitized information and a change in the way students process information.

DIGITIZED INFORMATION COMES TO SCHOOL

It is a rare student who doesn't carry a portable data device. Whether a tablet computer or smartphone, the effect is the same. When a question is raised, students don't fan through pages for information; they touch a few keys or just speak into their device. Even the simplest data devices can access more information than may be found in all the books of a public library, each brick-and-mortar building containing only a speck of the total of what the device can access. The new classroom routine consists of asking a question, consulting devices, and letting its answers gush forth—all in the space of seconds. Will school-age digital researchers remember what they find? Maybe. That noncommittal response won't produce as much concern as it once did because the new wave of education ranks skill in knowledge retrieval ahead of memorization, a change that does not serve students well when taking multiple-choice tests.

Once it was recognized that it has become as important for students to efficiently access information as to memorize it, there was no turning back. There are at least two justifications for this. First is the shaky nature of what was once taken as unshakable fact. Time spent memorizing information that will likely be revised or supplanted is a questionable use of classroom time. Second is the sheer weight of information. Google CEO Eric Schmidt announced at the 2015 Techonomy Conference that as much information is now created every two days as was created in the entire period preceding 2003, a staggering amount, too vast to be either taught or learned, suitable only to be accessed as needed.[6] The accessible body of knowledge contained in the Cloud and local data storage devices now serves as the student's outboard memory, or *extelligence*. With all that at their fingertips, young info navigators become accomplished connectors of dots and discerning discoverers of patterns. There is no turning back. Changing reality demands that minds be opened as never before.

Of course, that raises a problem. Without a solid core of practical background knowledge lodged in the mind, it is impossible to respond to the minute-by-minute challenges life throws at us. Daniel Kahneman explained in his book, *Thinking Fast and Slow*, that reflexive thinking is a pretty good director of immediate responses. He built a strong case for the general correctness of knee-jerk reactions that leap from preconditioned minds—preconditioned, preloaded, cocked and ready to fire without thought. It is memorized experience and learnings that feed this ability. Kahneman's thesis accepts a balance that honors both the digitally driven search paradigm and traditional acquisition of basic learnings. Achieving that balance won't happen fast, nor will it be easy, but honest attempts to get it right will certainly bring improvement to schools. As it is, educators are pressed to accept "future shock" levels of perpetual change in curriculum, an approach that leaves them feeling unanchored.[7] To expect otherwise is to expect that the accelerating pace of change will slow or stop, and that will not happen. Teachers who buck the trend by holding to outmoded traditions and practices of the past will feel pressure from administrators, dissatisfied students, and their parents.

ACCEPTANCE OF CHANGE IS A MUST

Of all the ignorance that hampers public education, the most common is the blind ignorance that denies change. Fortunately, recent crops of teachers and administrators are tuned to the times. Leaders balance their new mission with sensitivity to what aspects of traditional education must be honored. If the best administrators lack mastery over a range of subjects, it is only because no one can know it all. Every educational leader has zones of ignorance—insensitivity to music and the arts, an aversion to mathematics, disinterest in sports—but they are administrators, not rulers. Trained to properly respond to blind spots of personal ignorance, they delegate.

Trouble follows when administrators attempt to lead as though they do know it all while allowing ego to block acknowledgment of shortcomings. With regrettable exceptions, their time has faded from the scene. Most of today's school administrators necessarily act as agents of change, moving school cultures into new learning paradigms. The new way's routes are seeded in the past, directed toward the future, and couched in ways of learning that students relate to as being more natural than simply memorizing volumes of knowledge.

Schools haven't changed in that they still operate with mixed bags of teachers whose approaches to teaching, ranging from inspired to negligent, are applied to children who come to school reflecting as broad a range of parenting. Put that variety of teachers, children, and parenting together and anything can and usually does happen, which can be upsetting to parents who complain to principals who must then defend teachers' candid appraisals of children's performance. While a high school teacher can't know how 150 different home situations condition children's readiness to learn, parents are often ignorant of how their every word and gesture affects their children's confidence and security at school. They often forget that each second of every day contains teachable moments that play out in interesting ways in the classroom.

Parents too often fail to appreciate how time and effort spent on children's education pays off in the long run, for children brought up to be independent, creative, and socially useful are unlikely to become twenty-something couch potatoes living in their parents' homes. Parents would benefit from seeing their children's classes through teachers' eyes, where every day is another turn of the kaleidoscope that tumbles varicolored pieces into new patterns. Each day, youngsters walk into class changed from what they were the day before, ensuring that no two teaching days will be the same. Teachers plan their days as best they can, and then, because children are never the same as they were yesterday, the day happens to them. In the course of a high school teacher's day, 150 variables present unpredictable challenges across five or six periods, imposing a mental drain that often reduces teachers to staring at walls at the end of a day. Parents of one, two, or three children cannot appreciate the everyday challenge of having to inspire up to six batches of thirty kids who vary in readiness for learning.

UNIVERSITY-BRED IGNORANCE

While those excellent American universities that draw students from other states and abroad serve as training camps for creative thinkers, they also host peculiar forms of ignorance that hide behind distracting issues of soaring tuition costs, out-of-control Greek Row parties, and questions about whether an expensive university education is really worth a burden of student debt. In tradition-bound graduate schools, theses are written in academese, a language best suited to sleep study clinics. Turgid turns of phrase are peppered with obscure polysyllabic words salvaged from dustbins of scholarly history, rendering them unreadable to all but the initiated. When proofreading a nephew's doctoral thesis for the University of Edinburgh, I pointed out overuse of confusingly stiff constructions. He said, "That's the way my advisors write, that's how they talk, so that is how it has to be."

Some of academia's wordiness is necessary. As scholars discover new points of understanding, they may find that dictionaries lack words to describe them. Just as the words "ignoror" and "ignoree" were invented to meet the needs of this book, researchers in other fields invent new words and usages that may never find their way into barbershop conversation.[8] The result: English is split into social and academic dialects, leaving speakers of only social English on the anti-intellectual side of the language divide. That language gulf grows wider and deeper as public schools' increasing seriousness about education invites academic language into high school classrooms. Social language remains the language of bedtime stories, coffee shops, family gatherings, and cable television, while academic language rules communication in formal learning environments and science. For example, consider the common word "use." The University of Utah's list of spin-offs from "use" includes user, useful, usefulness, usefully, reusable, misuse, usability, unusable, disuse, and useless-ness. Not all of those "use" words are equally useful in street-corner conversations. Although academic language meets real needs, it also gives anti-intellectuals what they are looking for: an easy way to identify eggheads and fuel for widening the sociopolitical divide.

Depending on a college's academic traditions, the high priest advisors of academia who rule over the awarding of advanced degrees may find themselves bogged in hoary Hogwartsian reveries that hamper progress. They recall the days when a golden promise accompanied newly minted doctors of philosophy into the job market, confident that sheepskin symbols of achievement guaranteed secure futures. Today, a checkout clerk at Trader Joes is as likely to hold a PhD or master's degree as upper-level staffers in America's great institutions. A degree guarantees little today unless it is the right degree in the hands of the right person who found the right door that opened to opportunity.

Educated specialists who find their ability to address modern issues waning can look to narrowed education and interests as the cause. In a world where all things are connected, high-level decision makers need broad perspectives that result from exposures to breadths of intellectual experience. In the past, university students were required to bolster academic majors with ventures into other departments. But that faded as the number of general university requirement (GUR) credit hours dropped in response to society's demands for specialized, job-ready graduates. As universities assumed the role of high-level trade schools, they educated fewer well-rounded leaders.

Because an understanding of history is essential to good citizenship, much of what follows keys on the teaching and learning of history. The adage, "He who controls the past, controls the present," explains why inaccurate bits of popular history are responsible for shaping questionable decisions today. It takes an analytical approach to history to understand how scribes' omissions and distortions have masked America's checkered past by fashioning acceptable myths. The feel-good intention of constructing pride-inducing history leaves today's public prey to polarizing confusion about current tensions. Constitution worshippers collide with Constitution respecters, superpatriots collide with international negotiators, Greens collide with the-Lord-will-provide Christians, etc. In each of these conflicts, tension is fueled by ignorance of accurate history.

Though student researchers may find historical turf frustratingly overplowed and sifted, new understandings surface as the light of each new age illuminates events differently. The academic research mill grinds on even when not pulling new discoveries from the great unknown, as fresh interpretations elevate old details to new significance. Time morphs knowledge to ensure that a 1935 history of Central America won't agree with a 2015 history of the same territory, just as histories of our time will be fair game for future historians. Not so when historians attempt to edit knowledge of ancient Rome or Egypt, for history, like spandex, loses elasticity with age.

The viewpoints each generation casts on history are unique products of their times and support or ignore data according to contemporary views. Versions of truth and shadings of reality vary over time, as comparative readings of textbooks from the 1950s and 2010s demonstrate. Sometimes the difference will be a matter of emphasis—two paragraphs in the older book against one in the new edition. Other times, it's a difference in perception of the outcome of a battle, a trade agreement, invention, or a new view made visible by recent and supposedly deeper analysis. Much of the re-plowing and sifting of the past aims at unearthing flawed findings that must be amended. The goal, of course, is ultimately truth, but given that few written works are 100 percent free of the skewing effects of researchers' orthodoxies, preconceptions, and ideologies, analysts take conclusions with a grain of salt. Because we are flawed observers, the best of our understandings falls wide of the bull's-eye of truth, and because factual bases for knowledge do undergo adjustment, elements of what we take to be the truth have to be treated as moving targets. Because each age's perspective and research shine new lights on the past, there will always be more to be gleaned from the boneyard of history, where, thanks to digitization and the Internet, residents of disturbed graves of history, like B-movie zombies, keep popping up to re-explain themselves.

Like professionals in every field, teachers need to be nudged to update the materials and approaches of their profession. New textbooks, whether hardbound or downloaded, serve as nudges. And since curriculum planning is, on balance, corrective, change in education is generally positive. If the updated instructional content is invigoratingly different, students and teachers are stimulated and refreshed. But in most cases, demands for change don't sit comfortably against a foreground of classroom management challenges that include stacks of yet-to-be-marked papers and preparation for tomorrow's lessons. Unlike industry, public education cannot stop the factory to retool. And it is difficult for teachers to give up successful methods and materials they worked out over years to switch to mandated change. Many teachers aren't comfortable with relinquishing their positions at the front of the class to serve as roving guides and mentors in the "flipped classroom" model. Older teachers who grew in a tradition of bound textbooks will be less open to the twenty-first-century learning paradigm of using digital devices to navigate extelligence. Survival in the classroom will always require open-minded balance, and any teacher who is foolish enough to wholly embrace the wonders of extelligence to the exclusion of teaching to tradition will have earned the difficulties that ensue.

NEW DIRECTIONS

Departments of Education in state and private universities have a responsibility to expand programs that open minds. In November 2014, Secretary of Education Arne Duncan challenged schools by issuing preliminary rules requiring states to develop rating systems for teacher training that measure the quality of output, that is, teacher effectiveness. This action is well aimed, for if teachers lack competency, then the colleges that prepared them certainly bear a measure of responsibility, just as Wharton, Harvard, Stanford, Northwestern, and other leading business schools bear responsibility for tacitly endorsing business practices that cause sequential financial meltdowns. Are teachers who teach teachers partially responsible for promoting methods that turn out to be ineffective? I leave that question for the ethicists.

Learning begins by admitting that we don't know, and admitted ignorance has often been said to be the beginning of wisdom. By acknowledging ignorance, knowledge seekers demonstrate a respect for the unknown that helps purify the results of their probings. The results of their openness cause truth worshippers to flinch each time concept-altering twists on old truths are exposed. Facts are not forever, and life wouldn't be half so interesting if they were, for that would spell the end of much of the intellectual hunt. Michel Foucault wrote,

> [R]egimes of truth are the result of scientific discourse and institutions, and are reinforced [and redefined] constantly through the education system, the media, and the flux of political and economic ideologies. In this sense, the battle for truth is not for some absolute truth that can be discovered and accepted, but is a battle about the rules according to which the true and false are separated and specific effects of power are attached to.[9]

Knowledge is always subject to evolution, and the integrity of truth is obedient to whatever happens to knowledge. Admitted ignorance is the beginning of humble admission that our understanding is incomplete and it reflects the creative uncertainty of open minds.

A certain level of memorized content will always be essential, just as a certain level of programming is essential to a computer. Determining what that should be poses an ongoing challenge for curriculum designers. What it will *not* be is an encyclopedic body of ingested information because memory chips are far better than brains for that and they don't forget. Information technology and the need to maximize its potential have raced beyond the limits of the thinking and human memory that once formed the heart of education. The new partnership connects brains with extelligence by means of digital links. Though seeds for the transition have sprouted in schools, rigidity within the system continues to limit its growth. With one foot in the past and the other seeking footing in the new and changing way, insightful educators wisely keep asking, "What of the old must be preserved, and what of the new must be welcomed?"

Slavish adherence to traditional textbooks has moderated, but with the textbook market still dominated by three publishing giants—Pearson, McGraw-Hill, and Houghton-Mifflin Harcourt—the danger that a large share of educational content may be produced by a near monopoly on print textbooks remains. Texas textbooks are still vetted by a single board of censors, causing publishers to cater to the prejudices of Lone Star censors to win that market.[10] Add the fact that individual Texans are allowed to challenge adoptions that offend their sectarian beliefs and the result is a situation in which nationwide textbook selection is influenced by reactionary Texan sensibilities. For example, one Texas history text was edited to claim that slavery was only the third most important cause of the Civil War, a Confederate viewpoint.[11] A turning point came when the publishing giant Houghton-Mifflin Harcourt withdrew a text offering, announcing that their book had been written for national distribution, not to meet Texas standards. That marked the moment Texas began losing its grip on textbook content.

TRADITIONAL LEARNING MATERIALS LOSE DOMINANCE

Learning materials and teaching methods are constantly being reinvented to better align education with students' native learning skills and society's needs. Certain subjects still call for traditional textbooks, though their future usefulness is unpredictable in the face of open-source online substitutes that may be downloaded as easily as buying an e-book from Amazon. Digitized texts have matured from earliest offerings, shedding early errors in content and presentation. With costs as low as 20 percent of the price and an even smaller fraction of the weight, these substitutes for traditional texts cannot be ignored. Other advantages include rights of usage unavailable in traditional textbooks. Schools download master copies, then copy whole texts to students' devices. If lost, replacement is free or cheap. If editing is necessary, password holders can customize digital texts to meet local needs.

From the teacher's standpoint, easy mating of online texts with the universe of knowledge is liberating. The history of sectarian bias in text content and critics' power to dictate acceptable content for public school books have truly become just that—history. The content of four-pound textbooks can now be downloaded into devices students already carry, using only small corners of the devices' memories. Keyword searchability ends the frustration of fumbling through pages to locate bits of information, and that alone assures that e-texts are a game changer that is here to stay. An indication of the breadth of online textbook offerings may be found by looking into a web listing for "College Open Source Textbooks Community." The source lists universities' adoptions of online materials in chemistry, mathematics, and history, the three subjects that lead the online text movement.

Best of all, e-text technology leapfrogged sectarian frames that held generations of students in ignorance of indisputable scientific revelation. Misguided arguments against it melt against digital education's access to all that is known. With the barriers of flawed tradition thrown down, education is relieved of tensions that had eroded at everything from trust in teachers' credibility to the purpose of public schools. Ensuring the integrity of knowledge at the broad public school level is essential, since populations are as likely to be led to act on faulty knowledge as on verifiable fact. The job of sorting fact from fallacy falls, in part, to public education, where knowledge is reexamined every school term. The entire academic world jointly seeks out and discredits bad "facts," performing the same function as pulling spoiled apples from a box of fruit to preserve the whole. Bringing bad science and flawed history to light is satisfying ignorance-dispelling work, and in the digital age that work falls to every alert scholar, public school students included.

Until the advent of digitized texts, the textbook industry's history of profiteering kept textbook profits among the highest of all industries. Considering that the price of textbooks rose more than 800 percent over the past thirty years, a correction was long overdue. Education was not being well served. With the average college student spending over $900 for textbooks each year, something had to be done, and the Internet was where it was to take place.[12] Excessive profit taking by publishers provided the opening for tech-savvy independent publishers to gain a foothold in the market. But that was only one factor; time was another. The shorter time between conception of online text projects and their arrival in classrooms helped to tip the balance. Moreover, with new knowledge being more frequently in need of corrective change than oft-examined older material, ability to edit became increasingly important.

THE NEW ORDER

Control was wrested from the Big Three publishers in stages. They took their first blow when Internet marketers facilitated purchase and rental of used textbooks, undercutting publishers' sales reps' business and bookstore prices. Amazon and Chegg started it by offering college textbook rental through the web for periods of one to six months. The next step was breaking the hold that traditional textbook publishers had on the school market. The Big Three, seeing the writing on the wall, began phasing out the sales representatives who had maintained personal contact with schools until the opening of the century. When schools turned to buying directly from web marketers, the Big Three lost their absolute control over sales.

The fourth hit was the broadening of choice of open-source online materials. Early on, teachers in South Africa, teaming with over one hundred correspondents in other countries, spearheaded the development of a free online chemistry program. The quality of that program was so impressive that the world took notice and soon welcomed offerings from a mix of for-profit and non-profit publishers that addressed needs within most subject matter areas. The e-publishers Boundless, Flat World Knowledge, and Bookboon exemplify the growing range of plans and content, all of which offer keyword searchability, which no traditional book's index can match.

Today, Open Educational Resources (OERs) are offered to schools under licenses that allow editing by whoever might hold the password to a school's master copy. The advantages OERs hold for education caught the attention and support of the Gates and Hewlett Foundations, and once Congress endorsed the movement by allocating funds to support development of OERs for community colleges there was no turning back.[13] The sectarian hope that course content could be managed to serve ideological goals had died, and knowledge controllers who once infected schools with ideological bias were shut out of the process.

Students can now draw from over fifty thousand domestic and international OER offerings that allow easy synchronizing with Wi-Fi accessible content.[14] Once a course is downloaded, it doesn't have to be rebooted from the web for each use. Teachers love it because they can insert supplemental information and current events as needed. Taken together, the advantages amount to a frame-breaking, ignorance-eroding movement that holds the promise of uniting students of all tribes and beliefs in a unifying culture of shared knowledge. The OER movement may prove to be the world's best means of cross-cultural understanding. Among its less-desirable side effects is that the same advantages are available to terrorist propagandists for the radicalization and recruitment of naïve youngsters and development of webs of supporters and sympathizers.

TELLING IT LIKE IT IS

Learning how to tell good information from bad begins in early grades. A teacher might say, "When I was your age I was taught that . . ." and explain why that lesson was in error. When students are led to understand that every nation's history is imperfect, they can, without losing respect for their homelands, examine past misdeeds and misinterpretations of events in a corrective light that illuminates the path ahead. Truth matters, but if, according to one definition, truth is the most important opinions a person holds at any time, then information that forms the basis for truth needs careful study. Information is about as dependable as a fractious team of horses: useful, powerful, but not 100 percent trustworthy. Children deserve to be introduced to imperfect reality—with sensitive consideration of age and maturity—so that they are never left to suffer the ignorance of belief in inaccurate myths.

Good history teachers infuse classes with significant events of exploration, discovery, migration, invention, conflict, trade, and war. They confront puzzling myths and wring understanding from troubling issues. Because ignorance cannot be fought with boredom, the teaching of history must rise above semester-long routines of lectures, readings, films, homework, and tests. Few students could remain bored after discovering the following:

> What is written into history isn't always true.
> Things that really happened are sometimes omitted from the historical record.
> Events that did not take place may be woven into the record.
> History is sanitized to produce comfortable national myths.
> Written histories of actual events and their effects are too often distorted.
> Powerful interests work to suppress historians' efforts to produce a true record.
> Interested forces and pressure groups are accountable for distorted history.
> Unchallenged national myths self-perpetuate.
> The media is complicit in maintaining erroneous national myths.
> Cultural shadings impose bias onto otherwise factual accounts.

Imagine the involvement of classmates when a student launches a spirited discussion by holding up a sheet of notes and saying, "You'll never believe what I found out!" Emotional involvement in subject content should be happening in schools everywhere because, thanks to digitization and the Internet, the informational reach of young teens can tap them into what's happening anywhere at any time. Great lessons in every field are at their fingertips. Recent wars, being the nation's most controversial ventures, deserve special attention because of their embarrassing wrongness. The issues must be confronted with an openness that allows students of history to understand the pressures on media to stifle reports of the human, economic, material, diplomatic, and environmental costs of wars. The truth of history can't be abridged. Nor can powerful ignorors be allowed to drop curtains over essential questions, such as "is it possible for Western forces to win a land war in the Middle East or Asia?"

A BUREAUCRACY BUILT ON IGNORANCE

The larger problem is that public education is at war with itself. While most teachers and administrators work to do it right, a passion for accountability among education's bean counters hampers their best efforts. Teachers and students who struggle to bring subject matter to life must battle the mind-numbing tradition of packaging education in neat Question-Answer couplets that excel only at filling little blanks in classroom management software or grade books. Critics point to home-schooled kids who, when transferring to public schools without benefit of being tracked on the student-progress software of tax-supported schools, enter the system above grade level. Is it that homeschoolers do something better, or is it that public schools do it worse? Is it possible that factors peculiar to homeschool environments enhance achievement? Is it a matter of learning environments or of methods used? And, further, how might details such as flextime, interrupting bell schedules, and square footage per student affect the discussion? There is the issue of whether the advantages of charter schools make up for loss of the inspirational halo effect that talented kids cast over classmates in traditional classrooms. There are ideas to test, exemplary teaching to follow, and successful schools to study, but where passion for unfettered learning collides with institutional control issues, control usually wins.

Managerial excess within California's neediest schools caused 12.4 percent of their total instructional time to be taken over by analytical testing.[15] Surely, someone on the scene must have suspected that less learning equals more ignorance. According to a *Washington Post* report dated July 25, 2013, standardized testing became the central focus of the Bush era's No Child Left Behind policy and continued through Obama's Race to the Top.[16] The *Post* article determined that grade-level testing and test prepping accounted for nineteen full days per year in one California district and an amazing month and a half in the most heavily tested grades. One district reported that ending standardized testing would add between twenty to forty instructional minutes to each school day. Even the $700 to $1,000 per student spent on testing and evaluation is small compared with loss of educational opportunity due to reduced instructional time. It makes little sense. No industry, no matter how troubled, would shut down assembly lines 12.4 percent of the time to conduct mandated inspections.[17]

The more that well-reasoned schemes are tried, the better the chances of stumbling upon something that works no matter where they rise from: students in some of India's top schools share responsibilities for caring for facilities and grounds, a policy that bonds them to their schools while teaching responsibility. The Gates Foundation promoted small schools within a school for a time, then backed off.[18] Whatever the attempt, change should stress opening students' minds. While school catalogs list no courses dedicated to opening minds per se, creative teachers find that adopting tactics that move in that direction heightens students' sense of involvement. John Gatto was one of those. Teachers like him don't always enjoy popularity among their colleagues because their successes threaten traditionalists who can't or won't consider changing. He and other good teachers battle ignorance by awakening students' inner callings to *know*. Gaining habits of critical inquiry sets children on the path to responsible citizenship along with developing capacities for recognizing and defending against mind control tactics of the Powers That Be.

While teachers draw youngsters into habits of searching, evaluating, knowing, and understanding, too much of public schools' focus is aimed at issues of time allocation, sequencing, and testing. It isn't a matter of one priority upstaging others—all are necessary. It is when mechanistic demands of one erodes at others that learning suffers. It is when students' abilities to understand poetry, express themselves musically, question politicians' voting records, and speak other languages don't quantify well enough to satisfy bean counters that schools should earn low grades. Education serves up a diet heavy in little things—facts, dates and names, and numbers—while allowing ignorance of bigger things that are harder to evaluate. In reaching for the ultimate in accountability, a stubborn part of public education's support staff views students as products that schools process to a level of completion that can be measured in filled job openings and growth in GDP.

From the administrative point of view, it is essential that educational progress be measured numerically. Classroom management software that replaced yesterday's green grade books pipe numbers to analysts while allowing parents to log in to their children's accounts. Completed assignments, test results, pending projects, due dates, and what have you are ready for parents to examine, and that is good. What isn't so good is that to generate the numbers that result in grades, teachers must fall back on questions that generate quantifiable answers instead of projects that require qualitative appraisal. Critics should realize that by structuring education to generate easily quantifiable results, they cut into invention, discovery, adventure, and enthusiasm, countered only by thousands of gifted teachers who wage daily wars against ignorance.

COPING WITH CHANGE

It is strange that the Q and A system in which teachers pose questions and students respond with answers has lasted as long as it has. It is a perversion. It bears repeating that if questions generate curiosity while answers terminate it, it is the questions that students should value most, not answers. Compared with the shelf life of the average answer, questions live longer—some forever. Questions are the foundational substance from which answers are born—and die. As you read this, questions are driving new facts into data banks to displace old "facts" that are found to be obsolete or faulty. It happens in medicine, international relations, business, and the environment but not so much in educational practice.

Courses of study that aim at dealing with the future ought not to be based on uncritical belief in an oft-reinterpreted past. If educational practices were labeled similarly to versions of computer operating systems, today's educational practices might still be version 3.0 in a world that has moved on to version 4.3. Politics, too, is mired in an obsolete operating system where influential cadres of politicians steeped in selected myths of history struggle to build the nation's future from still photos of a past that can't be perpetuated. They remain infatuated with obsolete facts and myths that clash with contemporary issues. Lacking experience in seeking the right questions, they are left to sort from among the most readily available answers offered by history and experience. Being ignorant of the wealth of possibilities outside their walled-in personal universes, they are left to rely on what they know, and they defend that insufficient base against all reason. It is not because what they hold in memory is faulty but that their blindness to extelligence marks them as dangerously ignorant. It is up to education to see that this does not happen to another generation.

When change does manage to enter the system it sometimes fails to affect teaching, as illustrated by teachers' uneven acceptance of work done by curriculum reform committees. If curricular updates were implemented with the efficiency of Microsoft updates, the switch to updated content and practice would take place as soon as need is identified. Not so with curriculum revision. One reason is that individual teachers' frames don't always resonate with committee-generated plans. No matter how disciplined they may be, 100 percent of teachers will not welcome 100 percent of the change thrust upon them. Personal style and investment of self in creating their own lessons make it difficult to abandon tested ways, especially when trusted lessons are working well.

Think of course-by-course curriculum revision as an evolutionary process, similar to the way software progresses from version 1.4 to 1.5 or 3.0 to 3.1. Again using the Microsoft update example, major changes may be compared with a jump from version 2.6 to version 3.0 when content and goals change enough that new staff might have to be brought aboard and old books set aside. For instance, language study has been revolutionized to correct America's long-standing ignorance of foreign languages and the cultures that speak them. That correction was long overdue with global trade, foreign travel, and immigrants pointing out America's linguistic ignorance. Most of our newcomers arrived with enough languages to force schools to drop the designation *English as a second language* (ESL) and replace it with *English language learners* (ELL). For many newcomers, English is a fourth, fifth, or sixth language. Europeans enjoy needling Americans about their ignorance of languages by explaining that a person who speaks three languages is trilingual, a speaker of two languages is bilingual, and a person with one language is American. Just as every Norwegian student learns to speak English like a native and every Canadian student learns French, it is reasonable, given the number of Spanish speakers with whom we share the hemisphere, that we do the same with Spanish.

Colleges require second languages for admission, most accepting two years or more of study within one language. Dabbling in a number of languages doesn't impress college admittance officers, who prefer polished fluency in a language. Top-tier schools may require four to six semesters of study within a single language, but even that doesn't prepare students for the heavily accented English of foreign-born visiting professors. However, being multilingual is of some help even there because it provides a linguistic sensitivity that upgrades understanding of visiting professors' accents from impossible to simply difficult.

In spite of the obvious and growing need, foreign language and liberal arts courses are forced to yield to the higher priority of training job-ready graduates for twenty-first-century trades and professions. High school courses compete for a fixed number of slots in a school's time schedule, which means that selecting band or orchestra may rule out a student's preference for precalculus or Spanish 2, and opting for second-year German may rule out physics. Scheduling conflicts will happen. During registration, when students choose first, second, and third choices for each period, students who get half of their first choices are lucky indeed. Fortunately, public schools aren't the only places where learning takes place.

IDEOLOGY INVADES EDUCATION

Conservatives have been more active in censoring textbooks than liberals, while liberals have been more active in injecting controversial content. The Right tends to be more reactive since it holds to positions with greater certitude than the Left. The Right operates as though it has found its balance, while the Left is perpetually in search of a better balance. From a student's viewpoint, the Right enjoys an illusion of philosophical tidiness as though it is a party of pathological neat freaks, an organizational plus that, before Trump, benefitted party discipline more than society or the nation. Viewed from the same distance, liberals appear to be in bed with every disaffected group that society has to offer, including Bernie Sanders's Democratic socialism, which wrongly suggests that the Left has no identifiable philosophical center. When done right, education avoids the extremes of political zealots, allowing unbiased argument to guide students to consider all facts, circumstances, and offsetting influences of Right and Left. This level of classroom openness can and does upset partisan parents.

Political ideologues invaded higher education with the recent establishment of universities that boast conservative mission statements. Conservatives are quick to identify many universities as liberal, though rather than being founded to serve liberal political purposes, they evolved to host departments that foster social services, hence the leftist label. While university catalogs describe their programs in terms of curricular offerings, many schools are known by their political ideologies. It is when a school's benefactors are of one political persuasion and staff must pass ideological litmus tests to be hired that learning will not be objective and unbiased.

Diane Ravitch recounted an interesting fracas over public school ideology in her book, *The Language Police.* It picks up in Hawkins County Tennessee in the 1980s when the issue was, once again, textbooks. The case is listed as *Mozert v. Hawkins County Board of Education.*[19] In 1983, conservative parents went to war over the textbooks used in their children's schools, specifically those published by Harcourt Rinehart and Winston. Parents claimed the books promoted secular humanism, Satanism, witchcraft, fantasy, magic, the occult, disobedience, dishonesty, feminism, evolution, telepathy, one-world government, and New Age religion. They went on to charge that HR&W's books undermined government, the military, and Christianity, and they sued to force the publisher and school board to either prove without a doubt that none of that was true or remove the books. Once the wire services picked up scent of controversy, the case grew in notoriety, attracting support from the Concerned Women of America for the plaintiffs and People for the American Way for the school board. It would prove to be a five-year Left vs. Right donnybrook over censorship vs. freedom of religion. After the suit caught the public's eye, balanced national attention forced the plaintiffs to back off, and they settled for the parents' right to have their children read alternative books. Though the plaintiff parents lost, the case served as a warning to the publishing industry that potent forces stood ready to conduct prolonged challenges against words set on paper.

Any points that the activists might have scored from challenging passages or banning whole texts wouldn't have justified society's loss of accurate portrayals of reality. Liberals responded to the suit by challenging the teaching of flawed or incomplete content and questioning the plaintiffs' motives in sweeping content they disagreed with under anti-intellectual rugs. Conservatives countered by claiming that liberal science was amoral. The *Mozert v. Hawkins County* case is reminiscent of challenges to textbook content in Texas and California where state adoptions apply to every public school. When critics there challenged a book's portrayal of the United Nations as a peace-keeping forum, they proved their capability to stall the release of new textbooks for profit-diminishing months.[20] That power has since been taken from them.

Because every economic, social, or political issue attracts critics, schools may look forward to being challenged at every step as they move toward re-prioritizing curriculum. Educators will draw opposition whether doing something or doing nothing. They will be hit with questions about how improved access to the universe of knowledge might enrich life and complaints about how specific lacks of knowledge hamper opportunities and potential for success. If that question should gain traction, a new field of research might be born that would compare adults' achievements, purpose, and contentment with their formative educational experiences.

CHAPTER 9

IGNORANCE IN THE MEDIA

The task of the media in a democracy is not to ease the path of those who govern, but to make life difficult for them by constant vigilance as to how they exercise the power they only hold in trust from the people.

—Jimmy Reid

The best of American media does an admirable job of educating discriminating audiences, while the worst panders to audiences' eagerness for distraction, leaving them relatively ignorant of current issues. The media poses a trivial but annoying grammatical question: though it is a grammatical plural, it is commonly used as a collective singular. "The media are" or "the media is?" But grammatical accuracy is the least of the media's issues. It is a major battleground in a feud between enlightenment and ignorance. On the one hand, it bears responsibility for informing the public; on the other hand, it fails to properly discern critical issues it should cover, and it is guilty of faulty editorial analyses that upset markets, support hawkish proposals, and trigger fear-driven runs on guns and ammo. Throwing ill-considered information at emotionally charged issues is like tossing matches into gasoline, leaving editors to wrestle with the question of whether the right to know justifies the potential effects of disseminating knowledge. Or the question of how much knowing society can process before issues become incendiary. On balance, editors come down on the imperfect but better side of spreading rather than restraining knowledge.

The media maintains the informational trough at which American minds feed, but feeding can't be its top priority. First, it has to stay in business, which requires artful application of its two big Es: efficiency and entertainment. Cost-cutting serves efficiency; coverage of bizarre personalities and scandalous events takes care of entertainment. The industry's two Es harmonize with a culture of entertainment and electronic distraction that contrasts with the depth and quality of yesteryear's news coverage. In general, the news industry does a good job, just not good enough. The media alone is positioned to maintain the highest standards for informational integrity, but it fails to live up to that high calling because of the world in which it must operate. It bows to investors' demands, competes for sensational disclosures, panders to consumers' base tastes, and milks sensational stories after they've gone dry. Yet many media players try to do the right thing, just not hard enough. That dim appraisal is due in part to the media being lumped together with an infotainment industry that overshadows the inspirational work done by ethical reporters and publishers.

The media needs a conscience, and it has many. Because the sources that shape society's critical thinking about social, political, scientific, and cultural issues need inspection that can't come entirely from within the news industry, other concerned agencies have risen to the challenge. The national media watchdog group Fairness and Accuracy In Reporting (FAIR) has been serving up well-documented criticism of media bias and censorship since 1986. The Wisconsin Center for Journalism Ethics watches for accuracy in governmental integrity and quality-of-life issues. The staunchly nonpartisan Pew Research Center's Project for Excellence studies how journalists handle the information revolution. MediaChannel focuses on the media's political, social, and cultural impacts. PolitiFact.com and its partners wield their "truthometer" to rate published claims as True, Mostly True, Half True, Mostly False, False, and Pants-on-Fire False. Project Censored's mission is to tell the news that didn't make the news and why it was omitted. Partisan watchdog Media Research

Center "holds the liberal media accountable for shamelessly advancing a left-wing agenda, distorting the truth, and vilifying the conservative movement."[1] That voice is countered by Media Matters for America, which bills itself as a progressive information center dedicated to monitoring and correcting conservative misinformation. There are many more.

Experienced truth seekers understand that coverage billed as fair and balanced is neither fair nor balanced. That journalistic truth rises from the fact that it is unlikely that truth will ever be found in the center. One side will always be more correct than the other, which means the closest position to truth will be seated in one or another camp but not in some theoretical middle. Fair and balanced coverage has come to mean that both sides of arguments dominate microphones for equal minutes at equal decibel levels and spill equal amounts of ink. Objective journalism may be a goal, but it is never a fact. Every reporter has a slant, and every news agency has its editorial bias.

What the nation thinks and believes results largely from an informational diet that serves up more electrons than ink. If it were possible to examine our informational intake with the clarity of checking the contents of a shopper's grocery cart, we might be surprised—and disappointed. We should be disappointed at how much of the stuff we take in is not intended to better our situations. In fact, commercial and political propagandists' memes gull the population into uncritically accepting positions that lead society's rank and file deeper into twenty-first-century serfdom, a state of dependence on lords who progressively concentrate ownership of profit-generating facilities in fewer hands.

THE FIRST AMENDMENT AND THE POWER OF MEDIA

My German-born grandmother taught me about the power of print media when I was a child. She took it upon herself to settle dinner table discussions by declaring, "*Ich habe gelesen* (I have read it)!" Each time she threw out that conversation stopper, she confirmed that one shouldn't believe everything that finds its way into print, especially the pro-Nazi diatribes that came into her hands from who knows where. Yet like Grandma Graef, uncritical readers give undue credibility to print media's content. We accord this honor to print news as glum publishers watch readership shrink with the shift of audiences to electronic media. The timing is bad. Our need for good information grows more acute as shrinking budgets cause publishers to waver from their traditional responsibility to inform. Their sources for what passes as news and the Powers that control those sources steer public discourse according to ideologies that sway news sources for their role as the sharpest tool society has for determining election results that determine public policy.

Oscar Wilde observed, "In America, the President reigns for four years, and Journalism governs for ever and ever."[2] The twentieth-century journalist A. J. Liebling addressed another aspect of the news business, writing, "Freedom of the press is guaranteed only to those who own one."[3] An interesting balance is struck by the hand-in-glove relationship that connects media with government. With the press dependent on good relationships with government news sources and the success of government plans dependent on favorable media portrayals, their relationship is that of one hand washing the other. The periodic war footing society accepts could never have been developed without the media's complicity with government.

The community of interest linking government and media is strengthened when government-regulated media is controlled by a limited number of corporations. In the symbiotic world of media and media regulators, the government's need to control information is well served. Consider the unreasoning treatment the press lavished on the early years of the Iraq War, as documented in the Bill Moyers production, *Buying the War*:

> The story of how high officials misled the country has been told. But they couldn't have done it on their own; they needed a compliant press, to pass on their news and cheer them on. . . . As the

war rages into its fifth year, we look back at those months leading up to the invasion, when our press surrendered its independence and skepticism to join with our government in marching to war.[4]

Noam Chomsky added a perspective on the part the media plays in marking out the exclusive ideological territory of Left and Right, explaining that, while public opinion ranges widely, media analysts limit their view of politics to a two-humped distribution, chopped off at the ends.[5] The media assigns spans of ideological turf for Left and Right, ignoring voices outside the two humps. This serves the two-party agenda by consigning reformers' voices and ideas to the lopped-off outer fringes. So national debates carom between two defined party platforms, reweighing the merits of known ideologies while marginalizing creative candidates and proposals the public is seldom allowed to consider. That hindsight portrayal may have become history, given Bernie Sanders's Democratic Socialism; Donald Trump's platform of wild assertions; and the neoconservatives, having captured the Republicans' flag, carving a de facto third party from GOP ranks.

News media's responsibility for fair and responsible reporting has grown a bit ragged. Its once honored position was described in Edmund Burke's 1787 comment, "In the reporters' gallery yonder there sat a Fourth Estate more important that they all."[6] By "they all" he referred to the three bodies of Parliament: the Lords Spiritual, the Lords Temporal, and the Commons. By awarding reporters the title of Fourth Estate, Burke honored their courage to speak truth to power. Journalistic ethics in the colonies echoed the English tradition while leaving opinion considered too raw for Fourth Estate broadsheets to pamphleteers who printed the more controversial issues. The system worked well enough that in 1791 Congress drafted a First Amendment to the Constitution that forbade Congress from making any law "abridging the freedom of speech, or of freedom of the press." Such was the respect Congress held for the new nation's budding news industry.

By and large, print media acted responsibly and, with notable exceptions, earned readers' trust. Then came the 1898 *New York Journal* feature that blamed Spain for the explosion that sank the battleship *Maine* in Havana's harbor, a fiction that provided the excuse for launching the Spanish-American War. William Randolph Hearst's alleged statement, "You furnish the pictures and I'll furnish the war," served notice that his press would no longer be shy about testing ethical boundaries.[7] Ellen Goodman added a more subtle issue: "In journalism, there has always been a tension between getting it first and getting it right."[8]

The necessity for First Amendment protection of the media was highlighted by the Pentagon Papers scandal of 1971. Working from leaked materials, the *New York Times* published a series of classified Vietnam War documents that revealed how President Johnson had systematically lied to the nation and Congress and that the war had been secretly expanded as nations neighboring Vietnam were bombed. The leaker, Daniel Ellsberg, was initially charged with conspiracy, espionage, and theft of government property, but those charges were dropped after it was found that the Nixon White House had authorized so-called "plumbers" to break into the Watergate Apartments in an attempt to discredit Ellsberg.[9] The incident marked the beginning of the end of an age when controversial or embarrassing information could be hidden because it was thought possible and practical to do so. Once the WikiLeaks bombshell heralded the new age of transparency, the Powers That Be scurried to ramp up security while disciplining staffers to increased caution over what is written, said, heard, witnessed, archived, or transmitted. History will tell how that is working for them.

More attention is now paid to who gets to know what, leading to overuse of security quips, such as "that's above my pay grade," "it's a need-to-know issue," "for your eyes only," and the co-opted text of posters in security centers: "What you do here, what you see here, when you leave here, let it stay here." In the inane world of social media, teenagers post silly personal things on Facebook only to find that they go embarrassingly viral. Paparazzi, Facebook, Twitter, security cameras, and ubiquitous cell phone cameras ensure that nothing that catches the eye will go unrecorded. The new reality dictates that privacy in corporate and everyday life is, without safeguards, an illusion.

EFFECTS OF DECLINE IN PRINT MEDIA

News reporting has fallen on hard times. According to the *Huffington Post*, the number of working journalists in the United States dropped by seventeen thousand over the six years between 2006 and 2012, falling from fifty-five thousand to thirty-eight thousand.[10] It was strange for that to happen when the supply of newsworthy happenings was soaring. Of the remaining newspapers, the majority identify themselves as politically independent, though by conservatives' count, left-leaning journalists outnumber rightists four to one.[11] That split needs examination. Imagine a stake driven at the point of political neutrality in the political spectrum of 1970, splitting that year's newspapers by orientation to the left and right. Since then, hardening ideology caused neoconservatives to relocate the Right's HQ to the extreme right end of the scale. From the new rightist bastion, everyone positioned to the left was seen as liberal, including centrist Republicans who became labeled RINOs (Republican In Name Only). More recently, ultraconservatives moved even further to the right, creating even more leftists from what used to be their fellows.

From that extreme position, ultraconservatives can't help but view the bulk of objective reporting as biased. The picture is muddled by the fact that it is a rare reporter who is totally objective even when sticking to the facts of what, where, when, who, and why. Subtle inclusions and exclusions lend signature flavors to the excellent work of journalists, such as Will, Brooks, Robinson, Dowd, Kristof, Broder, Hersh, and others. Lesser scribblers allow their ideologies to take control, even to the point of proving that "a truth that's told with bad intent beats all the lies you can invent."[12]

That quote from William Blake remains a fair commentary on the pseudo-news emanating from think tanks where for-hire scholars with doctorates in economics, political science, foreign relations, and business mill out slanted pieces. A survey of editorial pages from all but America's most prestigious newspapers will turn up their writings, offered free of charge to an industry that, through layoffs of reporters, starved itself of professional-level journalism.

Walter Lippmann, dean of journalism throughout the mid-twentieth century, spoke for the imperfect newspaper culture, arguing that through it, the art of democracy is tasked with "manufacturing consent"—in other words, conditioning the public to support the Powers' agendas. Lippmann believed that was necessary because actual common interests are too often detached from public opinion and that it took a special corps of smarter responsible people to work things out. As Noam Chomsky observed, it was very much like the system Lenin envisioned, in which revolutionary intellectuals seize power so that they can "drive the stupid masses toward a future they're too dumb and incompetent to envision for themselves."[13] Like Lenin, Lippmann was contemptuous of the populace, saying, "We have to protect ourselves from the trampling and roar of the bewildered herd."[14] He did that by publishing what he thought the herd should know.

Lippmann showed little respect for an educated citizenry. He saw two factions operating in a democracy: one that thinks and plans and understands common interests and another composed of the bewildered herd that functions as spectators, not participants. Yet he allowed that it would still be a democracy in that voters could join to say "we want *you* as our leader," but not "we want to choose a leader." Lippmann's moral principle was that the public is too stupid to understand the great issues and would just mess things up, reasoning that responsible leadership cannot, in good conscience, let that happen. It follows that Lippmann would likely have viewed an entirely free press as too responsive to the "stupid" needs of the bewildered herd.

Lippmann believed that the herd must be tamed, its moods and desires controlled and directed through leadership's "art of democracy," which works to manufacture agreement and consent among the masses through liberal applications of benevolent propaganda.[15] Of course, this is hard for anyone outside the ruling elite to swallow. What is even harder to accept is that there appears to be more than a germ of truth to it, given that emotion-stirring theatrics of presidential candidates outpoll reasoned arguments. What Lippmann didn't address was that the Powers That Be, in order to promote self-serving agendas and keep the masses focused, bent ethical rules while championing a sterilized version of American history. Their ethic suffered from profit-motivated militaristic tunnel vision that foreign observers had no trouble recognizing while the American public was held in ignorance. Hermann Goering, Hitler's WWII air marshal, summarized the political practice of knowledge control at his Nuremberg trial in 1946:

> Naturally, the common people don't want war . . . but, after all, it is the leaders of the country who determine the policy and it is always a simple matter to drag the people along, whether it is a democracy or a fascist dictatorship or a Parliament or a Communist dictatorship. . . . Voice or no voice, the people can always be brought to the bidding of the leaders. That is easy. All you have to do is tell them they are being attacked and denounce the pacifists for lack of patriotism and exposing the country to danger. It works the same way in any country.[16]

Are Americans that malleable? Although the system will always be at risk from manipulators in high places, the American public's intellectual freedom still outshines that of most of the world. But can it stand? Challenges to independence of thought and reason that peaked in the first decades of this new century were articulated in President Theodore Roosevelt's prescient words a century ago:

> To announce that there must be no criticism of the President . . . or that we are to stand by the President right or wrong . . . is not only unpatriotic and servile, but is morally treasonable to the American public.[17]

MEDIA AND GOVERNMENT

People in high places enjoy quoting Founding Fathers—selectively, of course. Embracing inspirational quotes is basic to improving and polishing what has come to be known as one's "brand." However, the words of James Madison engraved outside the Library of Congress are religiously avoided by Beltway ignorors:

> A popular government without popular information, or means of acquiring it, is but a Prologue to a Farce or a Tragedy, or perhaps both. Knowledge will forever govern ignorance, and a people who mean to be their own governors must arm themselves with the power which knowledge gives.[18]

Howard Zinn said this of Madison's words:

> Madison's comment states a very important truth: Democracy is meaningless if the public cannot get accurate information. If information is withheld from the public by government secrecy, the public is misled by government lies if the media do not report these lies, and if the media do not investigate what the government is doing . . . then we do not have a democracy.[19]

Zinn once quoted a *New York Times* article that reported an instruction given by Fox network executives to limit information: "Well, you know, you shouldn't really play up Iraqi civilian casualties." Zinn's interviewer added, "I have a copy of that right here. It's dated July 20, 2004 and titled, 'The Communists had Pravda, Republicans have Fox.'"[20] Another Fox memo passed to a journalist said, "Let's refer to the U.S. Marines we see in the foreground as sharpshooters, not snipers, which carries a negative connotation."[21] Fox editors had to choose between informing the public and keeping their government sources happy. Hindsight judgments of right or wrong are matters of perspective that leave the question hanging: how might events have been different if the public knew the entire story of Iraq?

The public was not allowed to know. One disgruntled reporter said, "Our one raging controversy was over an interview with members of a departing National Guard unit."[22] The reporter, a vet himself, had quoted troops who expressed fear. That set off outrage among military brass that caused reporters to be banned from the armory in their own town. Overall, the quality of mass media coverage of the Gulf War was widely deemed horrible. Ted Koppel of ABC's *Nightline* said, "I'm not sure the public's interest is being served by seeing what seems to be such a painless war when 50,000 to 100,000 people [civilians] may have died on the other side."[23] Reporters' work was too often revised by management who said they felt it was too negative toward the US effort. Another reporter said news was "toned down because our sources in the military wouldn't be pleased with overly critical articles."[24] (See Greg Mitchell's book, *So Wrong for So Long*). Paul Reikoff, author of *Chasing Ghosts*, said, "American people don't know a lot about these issues. People abroad ask me, are Americans stupid? I say 'No, they just aren't told enough.'"[25]

When foreigners knew more about our war efforts in the Middle East than American consumers of domestic media news did, there was a problem. Blogger Richard Seymour, author of *Middle-East Bloggers Set Cat among Pigeons*, claimed that the blogosphere is more free to tell it like it is: "Bloggers are less afraid to go where mainstream media fears to tread. Frank images of war that never made it to television screens and newspapers in the West were distributed by bloggers and forwarded via e-mail to the world."[26] Seymour failed to comment on the negative effects of unbridled reporting, leaving historians to judge whether total transparency is always the best answer.

MANIPULATION OF MEDIA

The rich white males who manage the news maintain the myth that American prosperity and exceptionalism are products of the efforts and genius of rich white men who justly deserve the rewards. The ownership of television chains controls the choice of which policy wonks and public affairs analysts appear on panel shows. In a "git 'er done" climate in which the on-camera theatrics of extremists deliver high ratings, scholarly moderates appear wimpy, colorless, and not ones to git 'er done, whether the issue is immigration, ISIS, international hacking, or balancing the budget. Staged interviews and panel discussions provide, at best, biased insights into knotty issues and, at worst, a form of manipulative propaganda.

Consumers continue to trust media messengers whose credibility is openly tainted with bias and misuse of language. The commercialization of American culture reduced standards for media by mating truthiness and infotainment with pseudo-news to produce news-lite. Trust in media and government suffered from ignorors' use of the public voice to shape opinion, leaving audiences unsure that they could distinguish truth from fiction and knowledge from ignorance. The integrity of language was put at risk. The difference between accepted practice for published news and the gold standard for sharing information may be illustrated by comparing media's business-as-usual standards with the language of the Australian Aranda tribe, where to call something by name is also to trust and believe. While deceit in language is impossible for the Arandas, it is probable when ignorors have a job of convincing to do.

It was a short time ago that the FCC, the agency tasked with preserving the integrity of the press and broadcasting, underwent a housecleaning and restaffing. Out went regulators accustomed to carrying out the FCC's mission. In came deregulators who, under instructions from the Powers That Be, set about stripping away restrictions on media market monopoly, a change that concentrated a dangerous amount of the nation's information system in the hands of multinationals that enjoy symbiotic relationships with governments. Though there was opposition, the first significant whistle wasn't blown on home soil but at Paris's UNESCO headquarters, where the 1980 McBride Report, a UNESCO analysis of communications problems, called for democratization of communications at national and international levels. An excerpt of the report reads,

We can sum up by saying that in the communications industry there are a relatively small number of predominant corporations which integrate all aspects of production and distribution, which are based in the leading developed countries and which have become transnational in their operations. Concentration of resources and infrastructures is not only a growing trend but also a worrying phenomenon which may adversely affect the freedom and democratization of communications.[27]

The issue was personal to me. One of my pipelines into national and international issues had been commentary by author and radio personality Thom Hartmann. Hartmann is a gentleman who then honored his radio guests with a civil ear for whatever they might offer.[28] He guided measured discussions that, while seldom disparaging, reached to reveal others' beliefs and ideologies. A few years ago, I returned from some weeks out of the country and tuned in to AM 1090 for Hartmann's show. Alas, no Hartmann—just sports babble. I checked the frequency. Yes, it was 1090. Where had Hartmann gone? I checked the web. Not only was Hartmann missing from Seattle's KPTK 1090 but from Portland's radio KPOJ and also WTDY of Madison, Wisconsin. He had also disappeared from his time slots in San Francisco and Bangor, Maine. It seemed that progressive radio had been selectively shut down in areas where results in the last general election had tipped strongly toward liberal candidates. Were Hartmann's disappearances due to random broadcast economics, or might something else have been at work? For those who hadn't tuned in to his show, Hartmann is a psychotherapist, entrepreneur, author, and philanthropist with a global grasp on not just politics and economics but the pushes and pulls that move them. As an interviewer, he unfailingly showed courtesy to his guests no matter how strange their beliefs. After exposing his audience to contrasting viewpoints, he left it to them to form opinions.

I did some checking. The stations involved had come under the control of Clear Channel and its subsidiaries. The Clear Channel name refers to class-A ratings, which means they enjoy maximum freedom from interference from other stations and nighttime atmospheric issues. Clear Channel is also a subsidiary of Bain Capital, the corporate entity that founded Fox News.

This level of media monopoly appears so . . . Italian! In Italy, four-time prime minister Silvio Berlusconi owns half of the country's TV channels; most radio stations; the biggest advertising and publicity agency; the top publishing house; the nation's most popular news magazine; major newspapers; banks; insurance; cinema; video distribution; and Italy's premier soccer club, AC Milan.[29] With that kind of clout, it isn't surprising that Berlusconi was able to promote himself into high office. Such is the power of the press.

Clear Channel's assets are capable of affecting election results. Its radio empire and TV subsidiary, CBS, totaling 1,200 stations that dominate urban markets, is capable of influencing public dialogue and opinion.[30] Clear Channel owns four stations in the greater Seattle area, including KPTK 1090, where Hartmann once held the one o'clock to three o'clock afternoon slot. Unless things change, conservatives have won the battle of the airwaves. Liberals countered with MSNBC and other ventures but have not matched the conservatives' effective use of airtime. To the degree that each camp struggles to establish ideological turf, they veer from that mystical target of perfect compromise, neutrality, an ideal that leaves no one happy. The mind-set that politicians too often carry into bipartisan negotiations is "you are wrong and we are right," a position that betrays ignorance of the opposition and disdain for constituents' priorities. For use of broadcast frequencies, the federal government charges station owners with responsibility to serve the public interest, a responsibility politicized broadcasters cannot fulfill.

MEDIA UNDER THE LAW

Until the Reagan era rush to deregulate, the FCC enforced a policy that ownership of more than two major stations or newspapers in a single market was not in the public's interest.[31] The intent was to ensure that audiences would be protected from the effects of partisan domination of the airwaves. That limitation was relaxed in 1990, opening the door for Clear Channel to dominate AM radio in Seattle. Limits were expanded to hold single broadcast empires to less than 39 percent coverage of the nation's landscape, but shrewd distribution can make that 39 percent a telling influence on public opinion.[32] Everyone should make a point of listening to Clear Channel's conservative broadcasters and compare it with leftist radio to understand what politically charged content tries to do and how it appeals to emotions, not reason.

Democrats would love to match conservatives' coverage of the airwaves, but, given the laxness of control over mergers and acquisitions and their massive war chests, conservative broadcasters will keep building their media empire unless the tech-aware public's attention swings more toward social media, which it seems to be doing. Watch people on the street, on buses and trains, and even when dining together. Pocket-sized screens have so captivated the public that laws against distracted walking are becoming necessary. Knowledge controllers monitor hits on web traffic because new thinking has decided that that's where much of public opinion is now formed. Their challenge is how to gain control over diffuse webs of senders and receivers with a collective potential for triggering explosions of unpredictable opinion. Society may be approaching a time when established powers can no longer manage knowledge. One of two things may ensue: a more advanced democracy or chaos.

Meanwhile, partisan pundits trust that emotionalism will cloud thought. After Glenn Beck hosted a particularly harsh, emotionally charged session of Obama bashing, Color of Change, a progressive organization thrown together to rebut Beck's verbal excesses, challenged his charges with facts, which only added fuel to the fire. Hate mail spiced with F-bombs from Beck supporters filled Color of Change's inbox to demonstrate how misuse of the airwaves stimulates ignorant, visceral reactions.[33]

Inflammatory rhetoric had shunted reason aside to invite knee-jerk reactions. Beck used standard propagandists' tools for whipping up listeners who enjoy the rush of certain brain centers being stimulated. Thoughts of violence stir violent arousal as surely as autoeroticism causes sexual arousal. Pundits' stirring of violent fantasies in their audiences is akin to the mood-shifting effects of playing violent video games, which alters brain chemistry to produce cheaper highs than drugs. Giving oneself over to violent thoughts when joining with true-believing fans of radical media platforms of the Left or Right may become addictive. Rational thought gives way to ignorant mind-sets that are sometimes acted out to everyone's regret.

LIFE IN A CHANGING NEWS INDUSTRY

Reporters hanging onto jobs in a shrinking industry are understandably reluctant to oppose their publishers' policies. Few would dare to adopt the style of Hunter S. Thompson, whose "gonzo journalism" had his editors wondering if his captivating style justified his embellished stories. Thompson was the role model for the Doonesbury character Uncle Duke, whose disregard for journalistic convention was authentic Thompson.[34] Thompson's legacy of quips speaks of his disdain for media standards and practices:

> With the possible exception of things like box scores, race results and stock market tabulations there is no such thing as Objective Journalism. The phrase itself is a pompous contradiction in terms.
>
> As far as I'm concerned, it's a damned shame that a field as potentially dynamic and vital as journalism should be overrun with dullards, bums, and hacks, hag-ridden with myopia, apathy and complacence and generally stuck in a bog of stagnant mediocrity.[35]

Nobel-winning novelist and poet Toni Morrison added perspective to the situation facing modern reporters in her little book, *Burn This Book*. Morrison, a supremely gifted writer, had to battle her way up through the usual speed bumps and road closures that stand between African American writers and deserved professional success. Her views on pressures exerted on writers by the Powers That Be are uncompromisingly personal and honest, as is her life. If her words appear harsh, understand that Morrison writes to a world where the penalties for expressing truth are as she describes:

> Authoritarian regimes' dictators and despots are often, but not always, fools. But none is foolish enough to give perceptive dissident writers free range to publish their judgment or follow their creative instincts. They know they do so at their own peril. They are not stupid enough to abandon control (overt or insidious) over media. Their methods include surveillance, censorship, arrest, even slaughter of those writers informing and disturbing the public.[36]

Newspapers have taken a beating since the rise of television. The result has been closures, cutting back from broadsheet to tabloid format, two-newspaper cities cutting back to one, selling out whenever buyers appear, cutting staff, selling off labor-heavy presses, and farming out printing to regional print shops.[37] Just as it seemed that things could not get worse, a possible ray of hope appeared as the independent-minded superrich began buying troubled big-city newspapers. Jeff Bezos of Amazon forked out $250 million for the *Washington Post*.[38] Red Sox owner John Henry announced plans to buy the *Boston Globe*. Local movers and shakers bought the *San Diego Union Tribune* and the *Orange County Register*. Philadelphia's two papers, the *Inquirer* and the *Daily News*, sold for $55 million, quite a drop from their $515 million price in 2006.[39] The *New York Times*, which had bought the *Boston Globe* for $1.1 billion, sold it to Henry for $70 million.[40] With newspapers struggling, no one seems to know exactly how much they are worth, though their worth to society is immense. Newspapers are biased but openly so. The best of them, the *New York Times* and the *Wall Street Journal*, are oppositely slanted by some degrees but not enough to dim the quality of their opinionated content.

Time will tell whether well-heeled outsiders will promote more journalistic freedom than insiders or use their new acquisitions as personal platforms. Freedom and integrity were natural to the *Washington Post*'s erstwhile owner, the Graham family, who, unlike outsiders Bezos and Henry, were so steeped in newspaper culture that ink ran in their veins. Bezos has a reputation for preferring part-time and temporary workers at Amazon. On the other hand, his then estimated $25 billion personal fortune could allow him to exercise old-style journalistic integrity. Yet skeptics who compare print media's responsibility for informing the public with Amazon's business plan of eliminating competition are doubtful. In an open letter to the *Post* staff, Bezos sought to establish a personal commitment to good journalism, suggesting that, as owner, he hopes to channel the courage previous owners have shown. Bezos added, "That includes the courage to wait, be sure, slow down, get another source. Real people and their reputations, livelihoods and families are at stake."[41] In another market, observers fear that casino mogul Sheldon Adelson, who purchased the *Las Vegas Review-Journal* at an inflated price of $140 million, will turn his acquisition into a lapdog for his extremist views.[42] Adelson, whose billions came from casinos in Nevada and Macao, has been one of the Right's top contributors to super PACs. Time will tell whether knowledge or ignorance is served.

THE BLOGGERS

One benefit of shake-ups in the media community is the media's uninvited new arm, the blogosphere. Through it, an uncountable number of blog hosts, or bloggers, invite comment on pet topics. The can of worms opened by WikiLeaks was pure gold for bloggers who seized on the issue as a test of their ability to handle big issues from what seems an infinite number of angles. The blogger behind *Prairie Weather* comments,

Diplomacy can and does require deep secrecy, up to a point. But illegal wars sustained through ten years and counting—and through two administrations—are corrosive to democracy. Understanding and dismantling the secretive structure that makes illegal war possible is a responsible, not irresponsible, move. That's not to say they won't create huge problems for U.S. diplomacy for years to come.[43]

Bloggers are big on hyperbole, seemingly beholden to the attention-getter's logic that if something is worth stating it must be worth overstating. And since their self-appointed role is to provoke discussion, hyperbole works well for them and society in that unconstrained topical discussion is an enemy of ignorance. *Democracy Arsenal's* Michael Cohen weighed in from the Right: "Anyone who has worked in international affairs would understand (and this goes for Americans and non-Americans) that secrecy is an essential element of diplomatic relations. . . . To suggest otherwise demonstrates a shocking lack of understanding about how diplomats actually operate."[44]

The freedom of blogging continues to attract open-minded knowledge seekers who appeal to reason rather than ideological extremes. Andrew Sullivan, former editor of the *New Republic* and author of six books, is one of those. Sullivan wrote,

> For centuries, writers have experimented with forms that evoke the imperfection of thought, the inconstancy of human affairs, and the chastening passage of time. But as blogging evolves as a literary form, it is generating a new and quintessentially postmodern idiom that's enabling writers to express themselves in ways that have never been seen or understood before. Its truths are provisional, and its ethos collective and messy. Yet the interaction it enables between writer and reader is unprecedented, visceral, and sometimes brutal. And make no mistake: it heralds a golden era for journalism.[45]

Though Sullivan bills himself as a conservative, his independence is evidenced by his support for Obama and disdain for ultrarightist posturing. He operated the *Daily Dish* singlehandedly for six years before joining with *Time,* the *Atlantic,* and the *Daily Beast,* finally settling on an independent subscription format. Sullivan retired from blogging in 2015.

Blogging ensures that few opinions go unheard, which frustrates despotic demands for controlled media. Sullivan adds that "blogging is therefore to writing what extreme sports are to athletics: more free-form, more accident-prone, less formal, more alive."[46] Its immediacy and reach have turned the publishing industry on its head.

Glenn Reynolds, of the University of Tennessee Law School, launched his political blog *Instapundit* in 2001. Blogging was a new web phenomenon when *Instapundit* opened, and it managed to draw only a few hundred visits in its first days. But after 9/11, its numbers rose quickly until *Instapundit* was receiving more than ten million visitors per month at the end of its first decade.[47] Futurist David Brin calls the blogging movement the "Age of Amateurs," a time when the power of high authority and mega-media is challenged by what Brin calls the "Armies of David."[48] The Age of Amateurs and the Armies of David—imagery typical of the blogosphere's high-flying, free-wheeling voices that answer to no one but their own consciences or lack thereof, or, in the case of think tank bloggers, ideological masters.

CHAPTER 10

IGNORANCE IN POLITICS

The most important political office is that of the private citizen.

—Alexis de Tocqueville

The government's top offices are staffed by very smart people who, in exercising their lofty callings, focus. They focus so well that they develop issue-driven tunnel vision that obscures a wealth of pertinent information that lies outside the frames of their focus. Issue by issue, they impose limited vision analyses on a society that finds its values and opportunities affected Right and Left by political agendas. Limitations of time, energy, and money narrow the spectrum of federal and state projects to achingly visible needs and obscure political favorites. Focus on favored issues tends to sideline less dramatic proposals that address general welfare. Two sets of public information are readied to accompany the launch of projects: one massages citizens' social sensibilities to build support and endorsement, while the other paints the dismissal of alternative projects in acceptable colors. Throughout the process, information is selectively released, withheld, or altered as partisan "optics" require. The public is allowed to know in a process that might be aptly termed "trickle-down knowledge."

INFORMATION CONTROL IN PRESIDENTIAL DEBATES

Before the Trump and Sanders phenomena, one of the least visible examples of public information control was tucked away in the bipartisan process of fielding presidential debates. Elegant in its subtlety and blameless in the face it presented, the debate structure became a child of the nation's power elite. The past tense is used here in recognition of how reactions to the nation's 2016 campaign echoed fictitious TV anchor Howard Beale's famous rant from the movie *Network*: "I'm mad as hell and I'm not going to take this anymore!"[1] The Trump and Sanders campaigns leveraged Bealesque anger to derail the plans of partisan king makers, in part because campaigns had become too similar to the games in the Coliseum that kept Rome enchanted while the empire crumbled. Presidential debates had become political theater, which helps to account for an actor doing so well. And they earned reasonable ratings. Early on, the debates had managed to stay above beltway sleaze, but that only lasted until they were taken over by new organizers who infected them with limitations that clearly departed from the best interests of citizens and the nation.

Some history: Shortly before ratification of the Nineteenth Amendment to the Constitution in 1920, Carrie Chapman Catt spearheaded the organization of what was to become the League of Women Voters (LWV). The LWV's first order of business was to sponsor and organize debates between candidates for senatorial office, a function that had been absent from the political scene since 1860. It wasn't until 1976 that the LWV took on staging presidential debates. With a supermajority of homes then equipped with television sets and the public happily glued to the fascinating new medium, LWV strategists took advantage of the opportunity to educate America about its highest political choices. They aired presidential debates in 1980 and 1984, while Democratic and Republican higher-ups chafed at not being in on the planning and—horror of horrors—witnessing the LWV's willingness to consider third-party candidates. A power struggle between the LWV and the parties ensued, with the LWV wielding its unsullied principles against the parties' organizational and economic clout as centered in the parties' freshly minted Commission on Presidential Debates (CPD). A memo from one-time CPD chairman Frank Fahrenkopf illustrated the CPD's negotiating posture when dealing with the LWV:

> I'm just flat-assed telling you: We will not do a debate—we will not use the CPD to do a debate if the candidates come to us and they sit down and they negotiate and they say all right, we've agreed we're going to do three debates. We've agreed that so-and-so is going to be the moderator, we're going to do this thing. We'll say hey, we announced, we'll tell them, we announced a year ago what the criteria was going to be; we announced a year ago what the format was going to be and how we're going to do it. Your proposal does not meet our criteria. We will walk.[2]

The more idealistic LWV negotiated a compromise with the CPD that gave the latter certain venues to organize, with the LWV handling the rest. But the negotiations left a window open for LWV moderators to ask candidates uncomfortable questions that could cause the CPD's corporate sponsors to squirm. When the CPD jockeyed "forcefully" for more control, the LWV had had enough. LWV spokesperson Nancy Neuman said,

> The League of Women Voters is withdrawing sponsorship of the presidential debates . . . because the demands of two campaign organizations would perpetrate a fraud on the American voter. It has become clear to us that the candidates' organizations aim to add debates to their list of campaign-trail charades, devoid of substance, spontaneity and answers to tough questions. The League has no intention of becoming an accessory to the hoodwinking of the American public.[3]

The LWV had ample reason for reacting with such vehemence. The CPD had been hastily organized by the Republican and Democratic parties, funded by corporate sponsors and staffed by an eleven-person board with a near balance between Democrats and Republicans. The fact that it was a joint venture of Republicans and Democrats reflected the system's joint discomfort with the LWV's openness to fresh ideas. Foremost was their shared conviction that bipartisan US government should never slip toward a broader structure. In taking over, the parties rejected anything less than total control by cutting off challenges to the status quo. The chance that unwelcome change might sneak in through the LWV's lack of hostility toward third-party platforms was too much for the anti-Communist mind-set that ruled Washington. A *New York Times* editorial from 1996, titled "Fixing the Presidential Debates," summarized the media's opinion of CPD tactics and objectives:

> [B]y deciding . . . to exclude Ross Perot from this year's debates, the commission proved itself to be a tool of the two dominant parties rather than a guardian of the public interest. This commission has no legal standing to monopolize debates, and it is time for some more fair-minded group to get into the business of sponsoring these important events.[4]

After the CPD's takeover, the public was restricted to a limited informational diet. The questions, the format, and the venues were all chosen for political reasons. Seen in that light, there is a logic in why visionary plans for regulating industry and commerce were never broached and why proposals supporting renewable energy, environmental caution, and prosecution of white-collar crime weren't discussed. The debates became all but scripted, their content prescribed and the contestants limited to representatives of the two major parties, for to do otherwise would open presidential debates to corrective change. Beyond that, the CPD deemed it too dangerous to allow the LWV or any other objective voice of the people to engineer a forum that showcases presidential hopefuls. That may have ended when Sanders and Trump demonstrated that ignorors' plans to control knowledge may fail due to their ignorance of the force of current realities.

GROOMING THE PUBLIC'S POLITICAL MIND

Telephone traffic ramps up when elections draw near because the Do Not Call telephone registry offers free passes to three major botherers: political organizations, pollsters, and a mix of ethical and questionable charities. Ethical pollsters and truly responsible charities suffer from having to share phone lines with pollsters whose purposes are other than collecting fresh understandings of the public's will. Do you want more taxes? Are you in favor of killing unborn children? The intent behind such questions needs inspection.

It would be better for callers to ask, "What do you think stands in the way of real progress?" It's a question that might serve both liberal and conservative polls, for it zeroes in on what divides American politics. While liberals sort out results that identify barriers to social responsibility, conservatives cherry-pick responses that speak of barriers to personal responsibility. Put the leftist and rightist results together and the parties' issues are covered. But that is obviously too simplistic. The problem lies in which interests politicians are in league with and how they manage to divert debate away from the basic disagreement over which matters most: social responsibility or personal responsibility? A different analysis could point out the reasons that office holders choose to *know* and to *not know* certain information. That of course would map out a trail leading to the agendas of the interests that finance their elections.

Inflexible knowledge produces certitude. If liberals and conservatives were to join in figuring out how to effectively serve the nation, they would do well to begin by debating the upside and downside of certitude. The certitude that characterizes today's GOP is concentrated in the party's radical Right, a position that charges the more flexible Left as suffering a shortage of core beliefs. Both sides would agree on the appropriateness of dictionary definitions of certitude: "the state of being or feeling certain: freedom from doubt."[5] It is degree of certitude that separates how the parties think, and that influences what they think. Conservative certitude holds that it was unshakable moral posture that kept the population of the United States on the straight and narrow for two hundred years. Conservative keynote speaker Robert Ringer wrote,

> As one certitude after another has been shouted out of existence by "progressive thinkers" the national forum invites morally lethargic people to push the envelope of decadence ever further toward the edge and where it stops, nobody knows. One thing is certain: Violence is a natural offspring of an anything-goes society. After all, anything means anything—and anything includes violence. . . . Now all this may make a lot of anarchists cheer, but there's one problem they haven't considered. Once all certitudes have vanished and violence is totally out of control, a nation becomes a dictatorship waiting to happen.[6]

The full churches of the 1950s, along with literature and movies emptied of gratuitous sex, suggest that Ringer's GOP was on to something. On the other hand, liberals view certitude as a mind-set built from narrow frames that recognize only chosen parts of reality. A part of certitude's dictionary definition, freedom from doubt, pictures a mind that achieves the intellectual security of fixed beliefs by not doubting or questioning and, therefore, not sensing need for change. On the left side of the aisle, the strength and weakness of liberalism lies in its undisciplined mix of worldviews, united only by a fractious will to make things better. Liberals have no problem with change, while conservative critics can't stomach liberalism's openness to it. Nor can they trust liberals' assessments of how change should be managed or their predictions for its outcomes.

The freedom-from-doubt aspect of certitude appeals to closed minds, or if not closed, then lazy. When people lack zeal for questioning issues, learning slows to a crawl, especially when their leaders promote and model certitude. When peasants rise to challenge seats of power, they flex and adapt and study the trail ahead so they might anticipate their opposition's actions and reactions. They rise by flexing with conditions and events, but once they take up residence in palaces and their words become law, all that changes. The first order of business is defense of position, then defense of image. New rulers establish certainty of expectation. If you oppose, you will be jailed. If you steal, your hand will be cut off. No pleas, no variation of sentence. The once open-minded achiever adopts closed-minded certitude to remain in power. They must do whatever they see as necessary to ensure that their precious patch of turf atop the pyramid cannot be accessed by ambitious vassals. The view from the top of the pyramid becomes as narrow as its geography. That it didn't happen after the American Revolution is remarkable.

POLITICAL TENSION BETWEEN KNOWING AND NOT KNOWING

Tension between knowing and not knowing is natural and eternal. Some people know things that others don't know, which grates on the unknowing. Rather than a simple difference between what knowers and non-knowers know, what separates them is a difference in attitude between eager learners who welcome newness and those who don't hold new information in such high esteem because it is a precursor of change. People have always lived most comfortably with the security of knowing, imagining the realm beyond knowledge's horizon as terra incognita where fear of the unknown rules the landscape. For most, living on the firm ground of the Knowledge World works well enough to be preferred over uncertainty of the unknown. They find comfort there, believing, despite histories of suffering, that what you don't know can't hurt you. But what invariably happens is that inevitable change arrives to alter reality, which unsettles their relationships with the world and its inhabitants.

If active people with limited knowledge are left unaware of the negative effects inadequate knowledge casts on plans and ventures, they can't help but sow seeds of failure. The reality that people do resist corrections to faulty notions, often blundering ahead in the face of friendly corrective counsel, was once the subject of a discussion in which I proposed this rough relationship: "The knowledge people hold is often defended with ferocity that tends to be inversely proportional to personal supplies of knowledge." My friends dubbed it Graef's Law, a "law" so fraught with exceptions that it is best left as an inclination or tendency.

Envision a line dividing what we know from what we don't know. What we know has already been discovered, so it connects with the past. What we don't know is yet to be discovered, so it aligns with possible futures. The two realms flank the now, an exciting little slice of time so narrow that it is a confusing, roiled-up mix of past and future. More tidily, it might be thought of as the border separating what has been discovered from what is yet to be discovered. The book of the past yields up names, myth, knowledge, tradition, legacy, and so on. The realm of the future on the other side of the line is described with nonspecific, nonfactual descriptors: inquiry, speculation, theory, dreams, extrapolation, and imagination. While previous generations were more content to live within the knowing or past side of the divide, society's center is moving closer to the boundary where adventurous minds find fulfillment by venturing across it into the unknown. The two camps have come to be known as conservative and liberal.

Regardless of the ratio between stay-at-homes on the knowledge side and intellectual adventurers probing the unknown, it is each individual's unique relationship with knowledge and ignorance that determines consumer choices, faith preference, worldview, dreams, social tolerances, and political leanings. People firmly anchored in the knowing side tend to be more set in their ways, judgmental, and resistant to change. Inhabitants of border regions, rubbing up against differences as they do, are less certain. It is why college towns have a peculiar vibrancy and why the coastal trading cities of antiquity were awash with ideas. It accounts for Denver being more conservative than New York. In traditional societies, living, believing, doing, and thinking is centered comfortably within the what-we-know side of the line, but now and then great exchanges of ideas, technology, and unrestrainable mental activity upset tradition and order to redefine the relationship between traditionalists and explorers, the most notable example being the Renaissance.

We think of the two main sociopolitical groups as conservatives and liberals, with the more change-averse conservatives holding to time-tested intellectual ground. Liberals are on the move, believing that society is ready for and needful of knowledge that lies beyond their understanding but will soon be within reach. It is interesting how today's new knowledge, which will soon lie within the perimeters of tomorrow's past, reminds us that change is inevitable, a truism to people who accord greater value to what's unknown than others do. When seekers step out of tradition to probe the future, it is as though they leave home. When their minds take leave of the here and now, they leave others behind. When they come home again, they are changed.

Conservatives tend to be more anthropocentric, which focuses their values on human needs and wants, while liberals are more eco-centric, recognizing value and purpose in all forms of life, a difference that polarizes the two camps on environmental issues. The Left's advocacy for voiceless species collides with the Right's prioritization of economic growth. Rightists advocate for socioeconomics, while leftists include nature in their constituency. Both Left and Right claim they are correct, so, according to their separate perceptions, the other side must be ignorant of what counts. The difference between *how* liberals and conservatives think, together with other differentiating factors, determines the characteristics of what they think.

TOWARD OPEN MINDS AND AN ETHICAL POSTURE

Working with a mix of different types of thinkers is never easy, but it helps if open minds are positioned to steer the dialogue. Progress halts if those on one side become high centered on speed bumps of certitude that make it difficult for them to move from each moment's intellectual locus to better positions. But move they must. Those who refuse to move are wary of changes in their world. Radicals holding to old notions sometimes act out parochial fears by shooting up agencies of change. Refusal to recognize change after it has taken place leads to fear-induced rifts between threatened beliefs and reality. It takes unusual courage for the unknowing to challenge their own ignorance. It takes guts to grow and function outside bounds of crippling belief, to discern and to accept that the long-held core of one's personal code might be flawed or arbitrary. This requires a change from living in ignorance to living *with* ignorance so that ignorance, our link with the greater part of reality, can take its rightful but not dominating place at the table.

Now and then, a sitting president musters the courage to set aside masks of political expediency and tell it like it is. That is, to face up to not fully comprehending issues that government and society fail to properly address. In a special message to Congress on July 18, 1969, President Nixon said,

> For some time population growth has been seen as a problem for developing countries. Only recently has it come to be seen that pressing problems are also posed for advanced industrial countries when their populations increase at the rate the U.S., for example, must now anticipate. Food supplies may be ample in such, but social supplies—the capacity to educate youth, to provide privacy and living space, to maintain the process of open, democratic government—may be grievously strained. . . . How will we educate and employ such a large number of people? Will our transportation systems move them about as quickly and economically as necessary? How will we provide adequate health care when our population reaches 300 million? I believe . . . the Federal Government does have a special responsibility for defining these problems and for stimulating thoughtful responses. Perhaps the most dangerous element in the present situation is the fact that so few people are examining these questions from the viewpoint of the whole society.[7]

The upside of that outpouring was that Nixon, a Republican, gave top priority to the *general* welfare of America. The downside is that, in spite of his avowed concern about a growing population, what most concerned Nixon about the low birth rate of his era was that that it might stall economic growth. John D. Rockefeller III, chairman of the committee Nixon tasked with investigating the issue, reported, "We have looked for, and have not found, any convincing economic argument for continued population growth. The health of our country does not depend on it, nor does the vitality of business or the welfare of the average citizen."[8]

Though Nixon's hand-picked advisor contradicted his position, Rockefeller wasn't fired. A lively debate continued, but that was then, as opposed to the hard-edged acrimony of today's political gridlock. Nixon's position on population may have been wrongheaded, but it was clearly stated and openly debated. That collegial bit of history is offered to illustrate how much easier it once was for politicians to speak what they took to be truth and for opposing voices to be heard. With notable exceptions, Nixon had a fair record for opening issues to debate when holding people in ignorance might have been the more convenient path.

WHEN ANTI-INTELLECTUALS RULE THE DEBATE

From the beginning, America has suffered lapses in critical thinking, a problem perpetuated by entrenched anti-intellectualism. Given our background and Constitution, it seems crazy, but it is true. It doesn't make sense that the Founding Fathers, a body of truth-seeking, open-minded, would-be intellectuals should represent a society that reviled and ridiculed thinkers, but history is clear that such was and still is the case. The danger of anti-intellectualism was foreseen by Edward R. Murrow, who said, "A nation of sheep will beget a government of wolves."[9] He knew that the informed vote of every citizen is essential to keep majority rule from becoming a matter of too many wolves and not enough sheep.

The nation must be able to depend on truth-seeking media if it is to understand the facts behind issues. If the truth behind their sacrifice is kept from soldiers about to be deployed, they should not be put in harm's way. If Congress chooses to hold the public ignorant of the interests that push bills through Congress, those bills and their congressional and corporate sponsors should suffer. Corruption and the misuse of truth have diminished trust in government, and the people don't seem to know what to do about it. Here's a bit of a paradox: in 2014, when the approval rating for Congress stood at 11 percent and the nation was clamoring for change, polls showed that 96 percent of incumbents standing for reelection would win.[10] Bipartisan voters' ignorance perpetuated an unrepentant, change-resistant system that Ambrose Bierce, in *The Devil's Dictionary*, defined as a nonchoice:

> Conservative, n: A statesman who is enamored of existing evils, as distinguished from the Liberal who wishes to replace them with others.[11]

Negative campaigning, a favorite of both liberals and conservatives, has proved effective in controlling information through distraction. Mudslinging diverts attention from candidates' many qualifications and instead focuses on real or hyped-up misdeeds. In the case of John Kerry, there was no truth to the charges against him, but enough mud stuck to cost him the election. Misinformation more than satisfied the media-assisted suspicions of those who chose to believe the worst and still believe the anti-Kerry lies. As history tells us, voters take stands with equal vehemence, whether informed, misinformed, or uninformed.

Former Speaker of the House Newt Gingrich, a master of issue-skewing power words, distributed a body of advice to neophyte conservatives that has served as a guide for his party's speechwriters for decades. He composed it after admirers pumped him for the techniques he used to win the day for the GOP time after time. He offered the lists below to help strengthen the campaigns of Republican hopefuls by use of words that lend positive or negative power to messages. Gingrich said that his power words will help to develop the positive side of the contrast with liberal opponents, giving the community something to vote *for*.[12] A good tactic that was nothing more than what advertisers do every day.

Gingrich also advised against any hesitation to use contrast in defining opponents. He explained that word choice should create a difference and that power words can create a clear and easily understood contrast when oppositely loaded words are applied to the opponents' record, proposals, and party. It was a powerful strategy, but Gingrich's lists were largely neutralized as Democrats copied his tactics. Gingrich's positive power words included the following:

> Actively, activist, building, candid(ly), care(ing), challenge, change, children, choice/choose, citizen, commitment, common sense, compete, confident, conflict, control, courage, crusade, debate, dream, duty . . . [and so on through to near the end of the alphabet.][13]

When describing the opposition, Gingrich offered, "These are powerful words that can create a clear and easily understood contrast [when applied] to the opponent, their record, proposals and their party":[14]

> Abuse of power, anti-flag-family-child-jobs, betray, bizarre, bosses, bureaucracy, cheat, coercion, "compassion" is not enough, collapse(ing), consequences, corrupt, corruption, criminal, crisis, cynicism . . . [and so on to near the end of the alphabet.]

The degree to which blatantly manipulative language has become stock-in-trade for communicators of both parties testifies to the climate of cynicism that rules Congress. The words shade truth with distracting emotional baggage, the goal being to obscure issues in thickets of rank verbal growth. The intent is not to inform but to pump up emotions until they displace knowledge as the basis for making decisions. It is a manipulative process that leaves the public influenced but ignorant. Knowledge and language suffer along with the integrity of candidates, office holders, and the institution of government.

THE RIGHT KNOWLEDGE GROWS FROM THE RIGHT QUESTIONS

When committees convene, discussion often begins with, "Well, what do we know?" This signals committee members to rummage about in past experience for bits and pieces drawn from past projects that may or may not address the needs of the current problem. These offerings provide footholds in tasks, but, like first pitons set in cracks, they won't help the ascent if their position is wrong. Method is flawed when projects are begun without proper respect for all that might be off course or not known.

What follows are naïve questions about military planning from a person who, aside from a hitch in Korea during the last years of that conflict, knows the art of war only through studying historical accounts.[15] One has to wonder what Pentagon planners actually knew as the costly Middle East wars struggled on. With so much at stake, they were certainly pondering to the best of their ability, but their descent into aimless mission creep frustrates historians' attempts to find purpose in those adventures. The wars' initial justifications and lack of exit plans left everyone wondering, especially its planners.

If the planners had no credible answer to the question of why the nation went to war, they stand answerable to the harsh judgment of history. Perhaps they should first have asked themselves, "What don't we know?" When contemplating involvement in a foreign scene where the history, culture, and traditions of native peoples can't be understood unless one is born and raised in their reality, committee members might have been wise to put off deployments until they had a better grip on all they did *not know*. If they had held back, more attention might have been focused on the many poorly understood factors that might upset their best laid plans. Having lived among the natives of another culture for some years, I have no doubt that Iraq posed mysteries that Western minds could not fully understand.

Did they know if all enemy factions answered to one central command? Did they know if hostilities were coordinated or if hostile factions flexibly seized opportunities? Did they know exactly how arms and supplies were routed to insurgents or who was supplying them? Did they have a plan for a stable Iraq if they won? Did they know how much of the population was truly in sympathy with the United States? Did they understand the ambitions of potential postwar Iraqi leaders? They could not know how much hostile factions were willing to suffer or if they had a breaking point. They weren't clear on how the enemy was financed, nor were they clear on inter- and intra-tribal animosities. They still haven't come to grips with the hater-hated relationship to fully understand why they hate us. They aren't sure whether the help they received from neighboring states was popular, tribal, governmental, or a blend. They have yet to fully understand radical Islam's chains of command or how fluid the answers to any of these questions are.

It is only after planners take the breakthrough step of acknowledging their ignorance of important issues that they become better prepared to convert ignorance into questions. If analysts had recognized their ignorance before going in, they might have asked what depth of knowledge of tribal animosities, affiliations, what attitudes toward the United States, what desires for separatism or nationalism, what desire for peace, and what other motivating attitudes needed to be understood before considering military engagement. Where were the other side's technical people schooled? How good were they within each specialty, and did they still draw support from the schools they attended? For nations or tribes involved, how strong was the popular support from their areas of origin? What supplies and armament were they most likely to run short of, and how might resupply have been interrupted? How might movements of money have been interpreted as preludes to hostile actions? Of what significance were sectarian differences within the movement, and how might they have been used to destabilize central command?

There is every reason to believe that a ramped-up questioning approach might have served better than an unbending intent to invade. Because reality is a harsh but effective teacher, it is certain that points like those above guide planners toward more measured responses today. But that might be wishful thinking for a culture that begins deliberations by tossing declamatory statements into the mix and treating desires, beliefs, and facts as though they carry equal weight. The run-up to the Iraq War was built on an impressive stream of unfounded commentary, as though war planners were contesting for prizes for unfounded opinion:[16]

Vice President Dick Cheney: "In Iraq, a ruthless dictator cultivated weapons of mass destruction and the capacity to deliver them."

President George W. Bush: "The weapons of mass destruction have got to be somewhere."

Deputy Secretary of Defense Paul Wolfowitz: "We have no idea what kind of ethnic strife might occur in the future although, as I have noted, it has not been the history of Iraq's past."

President George W. Bush: "Mission accomplished."

Winston Churchill cautioned war planners with a statement that is read by every militarist of conscience. It had to be known to the Pentagon's chiefs of staff as momentum built to invade the Middle East, and yet predictions made about the duration of hostilities, the outcome, and casualties indicate willful ignorance of Churchill's words. It is inconceivable that a modern commander in chief could be so ignorant as to not study it, or, if he did study it, to be so blind as to ignore this warning:

> Never, never, never believe any war will be smooth and easy, or that anyone who embarks on that strange voyage can measure the tides and hurricanes that he will encounter. The Statesman who yields to war fever must realize that once the signal is given, he is no longer the master but the slave of unforeseeable and uncontrollable events. Antiquated War Offices, weak, incompetent or arrogant commanders, untrustworthy allies, hostile neutrals, malignant Fortune, ugly surprises, awful miscalculations—all take their seats at the Council Board on the morrow of a declaration of war.[17]

AMERICAN EXCEPTIONALISM IS BASED ON IGNORANCE

The cause for the disconnect between what the nation should do in international affairs and what it does was spelled out in *Strategy and Force Planning*, a textbook prepared for the US Naval War College. It reflects a background of policy seeded during the Cold War that, according to recent proposals for dealing with Middle East issues, still guides the United States' interventions in world affairs. A sample:

> Our first objective is to prevent the reemergence of a new rival, either on the territory of the former Soviet Union or elsewhere, that poses a threat on the order of that posed formerly by the Soviet Union. This is a dominant consideration . . . and requires that we endeavor to prevent any hostile power from dominating a region whose resources would, under consolidated control, be sufficient to generate global power. . . . Our strategy must now refocus on precluding the emergence of any potential future global competitor.
>
> Peace is the result of an imbalance of power in which U.S. capabilities are sufficient, operating on their own, to cow all potential challengers and to comfort all coalition partners. It is not enough to be primus inter pares [first among equals].[18]

Because those statements might not have carried sufficient weight of threat, the authors, Barry Posen, analyst for the Department of Defense and the Center for Strategic and International Studies and director of Security Studies at MIT, and Andrew L. Ross, Naval War College professor of strategy research, now professor of International Affairs at the Bush School, explained the direction of US foreign policy as follows:

> The U.S. must show the leadership necessary to establish and protect a new order that holds the promise of convincing potential competitors that they need not aspire to a greater role or pursue a more aggressive posture to protect their legitimate interests. In the nondefense areas, we must account sufficiently for the interests of the advanced industrial nations to discourage them from challenging

our leadership or seeking to overturn the established political and economic order. . . . We will retain the pre-eminent responsibility for addressing selectively those wrongs which threaten not only our interests, but those of our allies or friends, or which could seriously unsettle international relations.[19]

Those teachings explain American exceptionalism, a concept that makes news without explaining its roots. Perhaps the biggest flaw of American exceptionalism is its one-way view of other peoples and their situations without sufficient consideration for how it affects their image of the United States. It is at once imperialistic, arrogant, intrusive, and uncompromisingly self-serving. It is definitely not reflective of the mind of the American people, though foreigners don't always understand that distinction. It is a projection of a governmental uber-culture in which elements of the military, industry, finance, media, and federal government conspire to pursue initiatives that don't make the news until stuff hits the fan.

Walter Wink identifies integrated power structures as the Powers That Be, and when the Powers are knitted seamlessly into all-powerful organizations, he views them as Domination Systems.[20] Domination Systems derive their ethics from their goals, and their goals justify their means. The bigger that controlling organizations get— and Domination Systems are the largest—the greater their need for control of knowledge. America's Domination System, operating within and beyond the United States' borders and regulations, links powerful corporate, organizational, financial, and governmental actors to perpetuate American supremacy. It trusts that well-financed American exceptionalists will keep the rest of the world in line, as prescribed in the Navy War College Manual. The Powers function as a shadow government, pulling strings that commit the nation's assets to action or inaction, depending on projections of profitability and protection of national interests. Because they are most profitable when public ignorance removes obstacles, they do what they must to maximize profits.

WHEN IDEOLOGIES DRAW HARD LINES

It is the government's responsibility that citizens should enjoy peaceful relationships with the world, but that becomes difficult when ambitious power elites harbor global ambitions. That danger is further complicated when ideological certitude disdains observers' competing beliefs and sympathies. A corollary to ideological certitude says that the standards one's own culture holds are elevated to where it looks down on those held by other cultures. Consider how less materialistic peoples and cultures are ranked down by insensitive charges of poverty and squalor when the yardsticks for comparison are designed to reflect what we are and do. While conservatism has trouble valuing societies with lower levels of consumption and productivity, liberals are more likely to suspect that contrasting cultures offer opportunities for learning.

Members of Nigeria's brutal Boko Haram are ignorant, not stupid. Had they grown up in Amsterdam; Austin, Texas; or Buenos Aires, their outlook on the world would be radically different and they might have earned high marks in the Western education they abhor. Their futures would be as various as their imaginations, some even considering service with the Peace Corps. Or if they had reason to disrespect the systems that did or did not educate them, they might have become radicalized. One effective way to keep young men and women from accepting terrorist ideologies and to eliminate reasons for terrorism is by opening their minds to all that is possible and by setting positive examples and meaningful challenges before them. That happens when governments encourage free and open access to information. That judgment, correct in general, was painted with too broad a brush here, for the imperfect democracy of Boko Haram's Nigeria is not despotic.

The paternal condescension of developed nations toward the so-called Third World has not been particularly benevolent and has demonstrated an embarrassing history of cultural ignorance. With materialism the West's cultural standard, thatched clay-walled homes containing few materialistic trappings are seen as indicators of poverty when, in fact, the infectious value of African and Amazonian village life at its best engages European and American expatriates so deeply that they suffer stressful periods of readjustment upon returning home.[21] I personally struggled for more than a year to find peace in America's Pacific Northwest after two and a half years in Africa, a normal period of adjustment for returnees from extended stays in stable parts of the continent. Wherever one is from, whatever the culture from which one springs, cultural contrasts trigger judgments among the ignorant that block understanding. While the average Western traveler might do well with quiz show questions about far places, that person rarely has what it takes to be trusted and accepted by the people of those places. Western education can be part of the problem, though not of a scale to warrant a Boko Haram–type reaction. The evangelist Billy Graham put it this way:

> Partial education throughout the world is far worse than none at all if we educate the mind without the soul. . . . Turn that man loose upon the world [who has] no power higher than his own, he is a monstrosity, he is but half educated, and is more dangerous than though he were not educated at all.[22]

It isn't necessary to approve Graham's entire criticism to agree that the legacy of Western interventions leaves something to be desired. Nonbelievers might express Graham's comment about soul in more worldly terms while still agreeing that where intercultural education falls short of building understanding, ignorance speaks through condescension or cruelty. Understanding and mutual respect are built on painstaking intercultural study and contact. Achieving it is never easy or cheap, but it cannot be allowed to be expedited or done wrongly. Attempts to establish working relationships with other peoples must fit their pace of acceptance, understanding that both parties must be willing to change, which unfortunately may take decades or a generation. At worst, intrusions that create power vacuums backfire to leave occupied peoples worse off.

It takes time and dedication to learn how to laugh at local jokes, share village meals with ease, and—this may be the toughest one of all—to honor their traditions by being humble in their presence, for feelings of cultural superiority will be sensed and resented. Anything less will leave the visitor gaining, other than tourist sights, little more than a burden of estranging ignorance.

Travel guru Rick Steves emphasizes the ambassadorial role of travelers. When young, he learned that when Americans visit foreign villages they become the face of our nation. When they depart, their hosts fashion images of the United States and its government and people from impressions travelers leave behind, a responsibility that most travelers willingly accept. Visitors from across a congressional aisle; across Christianity's denominational schisms; across racial, ethnic, or tribal differences might practice being ambassadors in the best sense of the word. It is in acknowledgment of ignorance of folkways unlike one's own that the thwarting power of not knowing is defeated. If American society opened its heart and mind to the ways of strangers with the same zeal it gives to hardline *isms*, video games, social media, or putting balls through hoops, good things could happen.

CHAPTER 11

INSTITUTIONAL IGNORANCE

Organizational inertia makes large institutions insensitive to knowing when it is time to change.

—Reid Duerchi

In his book *American Vulgar*, Robert Grudin describes social and institutional ignorance as vulgarity, a characteristic that is at once ignorant, harmful, and popular—i.e. vulgar.[1] Grudin identifies vulgarity with oligarchs' unapologetic grasping for power and profit, their great institutions qualifying as vulgar through purposeful ignorance of people's situations and their effects on the world at large. Grudin's concept of vulgarity focuses on the dominant commercial culture that operates as the law of the land. He explains how society is misled by professional controllers of information—politicians, advertisers, media manipulators, and others. The overall result is a dumbing down of public information's content that leaves the electorate mired in ignorance.

THE GROWTH TRAJECTORY OF INSTITUTIONAL IGNORANCE

Corporations, churches, school districts, universities, unions, NGOs, cities, counties, states, and the United States government have been and are afflicted with institutional ignorance. A tipping point toward institutional ignorance is passed when individual perception and expression is overwhelmed by groupthink. It takes hold when mantras such as the domino effect, a Communist presence on our doorstep, too big to fail, or trickle-down economics are implanted in national consciousness and editorial policies. Public trust that the media will responsibly inform diminishes. When the news industry fails to blow whistles on wrongdoing, it announces that the nation has lost informational protection.

America was formed near the end of the eighteenth century by visionaries whose mental processes were quickened by the recent Enlightenment and the Enlightenment that was a natural follow-up to the Renaissance and Reformation. Surrounded by overwhelming space for vision, the colonists were hampered only by personal limitation. The new nation had not yet accumulated enough history of failure to dim optimism, nor had it yet suffered crippling institutional ignorance. Rather, its main challenge was a surplus of inspiration, drawing as it did from leading voices of the Enlightenment. Two cores contested for dominance over society's thoughts: divine law, as interpreted from the Holy Bible, and the Enlightenment's concept of universal reason, which held that there is but one rationality based on truth that accounts for our humanity.[2] The two were blended in three principles that the signatories of the Declaration of Independence and Constitution agreed upon. Note the emphasis on reason:

Government should be dedicated to the rational interests of all citizens, and must be structured so that no authority can overwhelm them.

Reason conflicts with unquestioning faith, and so government should stand separate from and independent of religion but with faith its counselor.

Science is based on reason, and so government should recognize, honor, and develop scientific knowledge.[3]

The focus on reason was fallout from the Enlightenment. Two centuries of French intellectuals' criticism of the excesses of monarchy and church inspired the themes for the colonies' founding documents: freedom, liberty, and equality. While the thoughts of the Enlightenment's Rousseau and others might not have captivated Daniel Boone and friends, it directed the thoughts of Thomas Jefferson and other nation builders. A great pendulum had swung. Released from its far position of controlling ties with church and monarchy, it swung toward an opposite extreme that shunned church dogma and regal control. The Founding Fathers, being fans of the French rebels, were caught up in the change. They rejected authoritarian rule and belief as dictated by King George and church hierarchy. The best testament to the new colonial mind-set is the Jefferson Bible, or, as Jefferson titled it, *The Life and Morals of Jesus of Nazareth*.[4] In the irreverent spirit of French Revolutionaries, he cut out passages from the King James Version and pasted them together to produce an abridged New Testament that omitted miracles and other passages that spoke of spiritual mysteries. They would be omissions that could never dim the founders' awareness of spirit and mystery. The spirit of Jesus's social gospel was left intact: love your neighbor—enemies too—visit the sick and prisoners and feed the hungry, do unto others as you would have them do unto you. Fast-forward to today's Congress, and though Jesus's social ministry is firmly imbedded in the Declaration of Independence and Constitution, the votes of Congress's most rabid document worshipers show the least respect for Jeffersonian social gospel. Since their oaths of office contradict any chance of their being unfamiliar with the documents they so loudly worship, their actions indicate willful ignorance of the spirit of the Constitution.

Vote by vote, the government's priorities have changed to allow profit-motivated entities to overwhelm the interests of lower income strata, demonstrating that Congress no longer operates in accordance with the way the Constitution's signatories intended: in the rational interests of all citizens. This means that either ignorance of the founders' intentions or deliberate misinterpretation works to cause loss of homes, unavailability of healthcare (especially for veterans), and multiple overseas deployments of home guard troops. Monsanto's patented gene lawsuits against neighboring farmers plus countless other offenses confirm a need for the constitutionally instructed courts to revisit the three priorities cited above.[5]

THE WAGES OF INSTITUTIONAL IGNORANCE

In spite of its impressive brainpower, the Pentagon suffers the same institutional ignorance that has afflicted General Motors, the US Department of the Interior, the US Senate, and public schools. In her book *Willful Blindness,* Margaret Heffernan gave an example of what happens when highly placed officials limit their view of reality: years after the Vietnam War, Robert McNamara met with former Vietnamese foreign minister Nguyen Co Thatch, who said to him, "Mr. McNamara, you must never have read a history book. If you had, you would have known that we weren't pawns of the Chinese or Russians. Don't you understand that we have been fighting the Chinese for a thousand years? We were fighting for our independence. And we would fight to the last man."[6] The limiting frames of Cold War ideology had blinded McNamara and his colleagues to the primary motivation of the North Vietnamese. His unbending adherence to the domino theory testified to his ignorance.

When planners proceed on the basis of models, they may not appreciate that everything of relevance is never incorporated into a model. Plans are limited by frames, and even the sum of the frames surrounding a planning table cannot help but leave much of reality outside the door.[7] Or plans may suffer from willful blindness. In law, willful blindness is the state of mind of a person who intentionally fails to be informed for any number of reasons, none of them good. The law doesn't care why one chooses to remain blind, only that they do. That being the case, it is easy to see why the definition of willful blindness is raised in cases of money laundering or drug trafficking. Should prosecutors pursue cases when acts are committed under veils of ignorance or willful blindness? It does little lasting good to bring actions against individual offenders unless offended parties address the institutions that support those acts, what keeps society from recognizing wrongdoing, and why warnings of institutional ignorance routinely go unheeded and uncorrected.

Alan Greenspan is an imperfect example of what happens

when the willfully ignorant hold high office. There was much about finance that Greenspan chose not to understand because his fixed and narrow frame was closed to evidence that he might be wrong. Greenspan, a friend and disciple of Ayn Rand,[8] once told network interviewer Mike Wallace, "I am opposed to all forms of control. I am for complete laissez-faire free and unregulated economy. I am for the separation of state and economics."[9] Greenspan's lasting affection for Rand was no secret. His attachment to her philosophy was so transparent that having Greenspan steer the economy was like having Boko Haram run the Peace Corps.

Warnings were served by respected critics Muriel Siebert and Brooksley Born, but few took heed.[10] In fact, Greenspan's cronies blasted Born's warnings out of the debate. After the financial meltdown, Greenspan answered Senator Henry Waxman's charge during a congressional hearing, saying that his model had not worked. "Precisely. That's precisely the reason I was shocked, because it had been going for forty years or more with very considerable evidence that it was working exceptionally well."[11] He had trusted his experience, not the greater reality that surrounded it. Excuses such as Greenspan's have been termed "ostrich behavior," and they normally carry heavy costs. Whether one's head is buried in the sand or just laid prone along the ground as ostriches actually do, it is a poor posture for defense because one certainly cannot deal with a problem without first acknowledging it. Dodging acknowledgment of responsibility is a favorite tactic for avoiding liability. If you deny that you are connected with an error, there is a chance that you won't be held responsible for it, which summarizes the obfuscating efforts taken to insulate higher-ups from prosecution. Nothing gets fixed, as demonstrated by the way the finance industry repositioned itself after the meltdown to resume some of the same behaviors that brought about the crash.

THE BASICS OF GROUP IGNORANCE

Sheer force of personality often allows charlatans to keep hapless victims in the dark. Examples include tragic incidents in religious sects and the social fallout of extreme politics. It allowed the mass murder-suicide of 913 followers of Jim Jones's Peoples' Temple in 1978, the tactics of L. Ron Hubbard's Scientology, and Uganda's Movement of the Ten Commandments that killed 900 in March of 2000.[12] At least a dozen more incidents made the news in recent years, and now, in what has become the mother of all extremist outbreaks, the world has ISIS's selectively violent attachment to the Koran to deal with. These movements are related in that they all demand that followers limit their thoughts to a movement's dogma. Their shared characteristics include the following:

> Reinforcing or excusing unethical and violent behaviors.
> Suppression of dissent, doubt, critical thinking, or independent judgment.
> Irrational magical thinking and bizarre claims or statements.
> Anti-scientific thinking.
> Isolation from other worldviews and control of what is read.
> Ganging up on or brainwashing vulnerable members to coerce them into compliance.
> Preventing contact with outsiders or ex-members.
> Blind obedience to directives from leaders.
> Hoarding of money and power by leadership.
> Double standards of behavior for leaders and followers.
> Orwellian doublespeak, in which language is manipulated to suggest opposite meanings.
> Enforcement of conformity in dress and behavior.

Branches of Christian conservatism limit their outlook to closed interpretations of biblical teachings. When they compare the Bible's instructions with what the world offers, they find reason to reject worldly knowledge as corrupt, so they wrap their lives in defense of the Bible, though Jesus said, "I came that they may have and enjoy life, and may have it in abundance."[13] That verse offers support to liberal theologians who see God in science, music, nature, and each other. Pope Francis's courageous corrections of certain Roman Catholic traditions are in keeping with his admission that the Catholic faithful have been held in ignorance. In their ignorance, unquestioning followers could not know that they had become complicit in supporting faulty policies. Worshipful adherence to the letter of the Constitution of the United States is no different. Certain political activists have not noticed that the United States is not the same nation that was founded in 1776. It has a past to learn from, pressing current issues to respond to, and a future descending upon it that will find the nation unprepared—because of what its leaders choose not to know.

When political conservatives courted the Christian Coalition by agreeing to deny the undeniable science of accredited scientific organizations, they endorsed the lie that a significant number of scientists disagreed with majority warnings about environmental issues.[14] Corporate backers' interest in the issue made the deniers' intent smell of purposeful ignorance. George Lakoff wrote that it was no accident that Al Gore's blistering critique of the George W. Bush administration's denial of environmental threats was titled *The Assault on Reason*, largely because the administration's anti-reason activists had promoted fossil fuels over alternative energy as the key component of a yet-to-be-determined national energy policy. Anti-reason policies that favor corporate agriculture over smaller producers remain in force in spite of the negative effects of Big Agri's increased per-acre chemical applications; anti-ecological monocultures; increased soil depletion; and concentration of agricultural ownership in the hands of MBAs and investors, not farmers.

STAGE 1 OF CORPORATE IGNORANCE

Corporate agriculture's understanding of farming is rooted in profit, not principles of responsible farming that ensures the health of the land. Ignorance positioned itself to work its way up to where it could treat soil as a consumable commodity. Bad ideas became institutionalized when people were hired to fit those ideas. Seeds of ignorance germinated in Human Relations departments where hiring managers lacked training to recognize sociopathy. Paul Babiak and Robert Hare documented this issue in *Snakes in Suits*, citing the frequent error of HR managers mistaking charm and aggressiveness for executive-level problem-solving skill when interviewees were, in fact, demonstrating sociopathic behaviors.[15] Hiring sociopaths ensures a higher level of corporate ignorance.

Up to the time when sociopathic executives' excesses come to light, their behaviors are easily mistaken as indicators of administrative talent.[16] Sociopaths are drawn by nature to climb ladders of organizational success, aggressively stepping on and over peers. M. E. Thomas gave us a list of profile-defining questions in his book *Confessions of a Sociopath: A life Spent Hiding in Plain Sight.*[17] Though employment law prohibits asking certain questions like the ones below, interviewers must bear them all in mind:

Are you superficially charming and intelligent? Although not happy with "superficially," a sociopath would say, yes.

Do you have delusions or other signs of irrational thinking? Sociopaths would say no. They are coldly rational.

Are you overly nervous or have other neuroses? Sociopaths will answer no. They are rarely anxious or afraid of risk.

Are you reliable? Sociopaths will answer yes, though their group is notoriously unreliable.

Do you tell lies or say insincere things? Sociopaths have no trouble lying when the truth doesn't suit their purposes.

Do you feel remorse or shame? Sociopaths rarely feel guilt or shame.

Might your behavior be antisocial for no good reason? Socio-paths display inappropriate and unwarranted behaviors to situations.

Do you have poor judgment and fail to learn from experience? Sociopaths think they are smarter than others. Failure from bad judgment seldom slows them down.

Are you pathologically egocentric and incapable of love? They are.

Do you generally lack the ability to react emotionally? Sociopaths cannot experience the emotions of the general population.

Do you lack insight? Sociopaths are not reflective or meditative.

Are you socially responsive to others? Interestingly, sociopaths have to fake emotional responses to appear to be functioning normally.

Are you a party animal? Sociopaths will display wild behaviors, with drinking or without. Sex may be frequent but meaningless.

Do you make suicide threats? Yes, sociopaths have a flair for the dramatic.

Have you failed to follow a life plan? Sociopaths find it difficult to hold down jobs or maintain relationships requiring obligation to others.

STAGE 2 OF CORPORATE IGNORANCE

Thanks to rampant deregulation during the 1970s and 1980s, a flood of acquisitions, mergers, and breakups triggered industry-wide shake-ups, opening corporate doors to ambitious sociopaths. In the chaos of deregulation, a trend developed across the business world to become more sleek, lean, and efficient. Corporations redefined their organizational style, opting for simpler systems that granted executives more room to make snap judgments in fast-paced envi-ronments. The change caught the attention of Nobel laureate econ-omist Daniel Kahneman who inspected the new way in his book *Thinking Fast and Slow*. The profile for the sought-after executive had changed from the organization engineer to the mover and shaker who could get things done faster. Executive headhunters easily found work for candidates who projected images of charm, confidence, and strength, traits that often coupled with egocentricity and insensitivity in what seemed to be an acceptable trade-off in the new accelerated and dispassionate climate of business. Once the trend caught on, it washed through Harvard, Wharton, and other prestigious business schools to find acceptance across corporate culture without correction. Sociopathy, and sometimes its evil big brother, psychopathy, had found a home. Cutting corners and shady manipulation became business as usual, setting the stage for the savings and loan crisis of 1989, the popping of the dot-com bubble in 2001, and the global financial crisis of 2007–08.

Stage 2 of corporate ignorance took hold when ignorors gained the power to manage information. The trend progressed to where a significantly higher percentage of corporate executives exhibited sociopathic behaviors than could be found in cross sections of the population, imprinting a new style of abrasive-oppressive management on corporate America.[18] In *What Would Machiavelli Do?* Stanley Bing wrote that sociopaths bring insensitivity and hardheartedness in place of decency to the job; are recognized as difficult to deal with; hold opposition at bay; are self-centered by nature; and are unpredictable in the good-cop, bad-cop mode by switching between violent rages and wild euphoria.[19] To sociopaths, competitors deserve no mercy. They were aptly personified in Michael Douglas's portrayal of Gordon Gekko in the movie *Wall Street* and their worldview summarized by Gekko's monologue:

> The point is, ladies and gentlemen, that greed, for lack of a better word, is good. Greed is right. Greed works. Greed clarifies, cuts through and captures the essence of the evolutionary spirit. Greed, in all its forms—greed for life, for money, for love, knowledge— has marked the upward surge of mankind. And greed—you mark my words—will not only save Teldar Paper, but that other malfunctioning corporation called the USA.[20]

Stage 2 of institutional ignorance is characterized by narrowed operating concepts and procedures. Its compulsive demand for precision couples well with viewing the world through fixed frames. Though never fully comfortable in any situation, leaders with sociopathic tendencies are discomforted by change, which causes them to react against much of what transpires outside their frames. Whatever they do not personally understand they mistrust. It follows that sociopaths adhere strictly to chosen procedures or schools of thought to the exclusion of all else, as Alan Greenspan did with his handling of the US economy. George Lakoff zeroed in on this flaw in *Don't Think of an Elephant.*[21] He described frames as defining portals of thought. Once a narrow thinker develops an ideology, incoming arguments that don't fit that ideology bounce off it, leaving little impression. Frames act as specialized basketball hoops with rims that allow only certain sizes and shapes of balls to pass through. Whereas a home team (institution) might shoot nearly 100 percent on its home court, their ideological precision may be a total mismatch for a rival's home court. Executives whose minds are structured to love precision derive comfort from drawing sharp lines between their personal orthodoxies and all that lies outside them, a practice that removes the greater part of reality from consideration.

GOVERNMENT: A NATURAL HOST FOR INSTITUTIONAL IGNORANCE

Institutional ignorance thrives when officers of organizations promote versions of truth that support personal commitments and ambitions. The flaw exposes itself when one accepts a leadership position while lacking the openness and trust that allows delegation of responsibility to cover blind spots. Ignorance of one's incapacities may be benign or willful. Assuming that shortcomings are normal products of limited education and life experience, members of administrative teams will have scatterings of blind spots that they cover for each other. But when executives demand personal control over untended issues, their willful ignorance ensures that there will be problems for their organizations.

It should be no surprise that institutional ignorance thrives in federal government, for any bureaucracy of size is a natural host for ignorance. The effects on the government's branches vary. If government ignorance might be ranked by misconduct of mission, Congress would draw the worst ratings and the military the best. Congress has, by most measures, become an increasingly ineffective Byzantine maze that is seemingly designed to prevent progress. Inefficiencies are so embedded in the system that it defies correction as though status quo is the way things ought to operate. As James Wilson wrote in his 1989 book, *Bureaucracy*, "Government has to be slower, has to safeguard process. . . . It is not hyperbole to say that constitutional order is animated by a desire to make government inefficient."[22]

George Will adds to Wilson's point in the introduction to his book *The Leveling Wind*: "On the other hand, there is frank bewilderment about what is to be done. That is not necessarily bad. In politics, bewilderment is preferable to misguided certitude."[23]

The fact that the US government has never been overthrown in spite of all its faults testifies to its staying power, but, given the challenges of the digital age and the issues of a fractious world, it cannot, without adjusting, serve the nation as it did when originally conceived. Nations that adapt more quickly to opportunities presented by digital technology, changing alliances, and availability of resources pass us by, in part because we do not aggressively educate our young to lead us through challenges and partly because too many of America's leaders are simply too old to be sensitive to all that technology offers. The median age in the United States is 37.1 years while Tanzania, typical of African nations, posts a median age of 17.4 years.[24] Young digital natives could contribute more if the old didn't drag their feet.

I was working on a project in Malinyi, a Tanzanian village of ten thousand with no electricity and no roads, just paths. The nearest town with power lay a day's drive to the east over sixty-five kilometers of rutted track. When in discussion with village leaders, I heard a familiar ringtone, at which point one of the group pulled a modern cell phone from his robe. Not burdened by hardwired phone infrastructure, Tanzania's developers leapfrogged into cell service that connects the land's remotest areas. The system's designers had been tasked with connecting the nation under one plan, unlike US cell service, which capitalized on lucrative urban markets first. Although Western powers still have the advantage of working from bases of established industries and research facilities, web access to technological data has allowed less developed nations to catch up with lightning speed. They have traveled and seen, and now they want. Unlike America's congressional ideologues, Tanzanians look to the future, not the past. They want more for their nation than NGO demonstration projects provide.

Dysfunction within government has been linked to Congress's supermajority of lawyers' enjoyment of debate. TED lecturer Stewart Brand described the issue as a conflict between Congress's mission of solving problems and congressional lawyers who insist on debating them to death.[25] The conflict has been attributed in part to the training and experience that they bring to their jobs. The *New York Times* reported in 2012 that the 435-member House of Representatives had one physicist, one chemist, one micro biologist, six engineers, two dozen with medical training, and most of the rest were lawyers who set the tone.[26] When problems arise, they are debated, not solved. Imagine the reduction in debate time if problem-solving engineers replaced the lawyers as committee heads. Their problem-solving tactics would displace the lawyerly gridlocking debate in the style of *Jarndyce v. Jarndyce*, the interminable case described in Charles Dickens's *Bleak House*.[27] Lawyers certainly know their stuff, but when it comes to efficiently moving issues from need to action, they find themselves bound by nature and professional tradition. Given their numbers in Congress and being representatives of a legal industry characterized by maximizing billable hours, they may be expected to perpetuate the inefficient MO that rules the system.

That doesn't have to be. A new approach to combating governmental ignorance is gaining traction in smaller venues, thanks to the efforts of people like Jennifer Pahlka, whose thick résumé lists years of creative work with the web. Pahlka's chance meeting with a techie working for Teach for America started her thinking that programmers with a passion for public service might jump at a chance to put their expertise to good use by fixing the government's notoriously troublesome systems.[28] She asked herself, if Teach for America could gather qualified volunteers to teach where needed, why not enlist programmers to fix underperforming public systems? So Pahlka started Code for America (CfA), enlisting teams of programmers who, in 2014 alone, served Atlanta, Charlotte, Chattanooga, Denver, Lexington, Long Beach, Mesa, Puerto Rico, Rhode Island, and San Antonio. Thanks to Pahlka's leadership, CfA technicians are proving that it is possible to overcome institutionalized ignorance of digital technology. The difference between Pahlka and institutional obstructionists is that she throws her frames as wide open as they need to be. Ignorance is her starting point, not her burden. Ignorance wrongly worn is why obstructionists' contributions stumble.

Gavin Newsom, lieutenant governor of California and former mayor of San Francisco, holds up technology as a tool for engaging citizens as collaborators, not spectators. Though his focus on technology may overshadow credit due to other forms of creative input, he makes the point that it is engagement through technology that will pull society together to get things done. Newsom's vision has engaged the Internet in helping to foster a level of citizenship that enables a more effective level of governing. In his book, *Citizenville*, Newsom offered a new road map for restoring effectiveness to the government and reinventing citizenship. Newsom wrote, "It's not about elites taking charge, controlling the system, and telling us what's good for us. . . . We have to accept the fact that top-down hierarchy is no longer working and it won't ever work again."[29]

Top-down hierarchies may not have read the signs, and if so they become vulnerable. The old guard's decision-making power suffers as leakers' revelations and demands for transparency weaken the hierarchies' best efforts. And the informational chaos of the blogosphere further diminishes their power by affecting debate more rationally than structured TV panels and partisan editorials. Yet there can be no clear victor in the war between ethical bloggers dedicated to shedding light and propagandizing bloggers with axes to grind. The voices of greed and power won't go away. For obvious reasons, their tools of obfuscation and purposeful misinformation will remain formidable foes.

Should officialdom choose to turn a blind eye to the expertise and insight of the Pahlkas and Newsoms of our country, it would be supporting governmental ignorance, for genius springs from free spirits more readily than from organizational committee action. The broadest knowledge about how to use technology to fix things rests with an informal army of independent programmers, not in the hands of inertia-crippled institutions where frame-narrowed vision cripples progress.

IGNORANCE IN THE VOTING BOOTH

The ability of the Powers That Be to lengthen and strengthen their control depends on their ability to manipulate public information. A review of broadcast networks' coverage of the run-up to the 2014 federal elections revealed a theme of demonizing Obama's policies and then tying Democratic candidates to those policies. The thought behind the propagandist scheme was that, if stirred up, the Democratic Party might harbor enough closet racists, right-to-lifers, small government advocates, and birthers to yield up a few points to the Right. On the eve of the election, broadcast TV featured unflattering photos of President Obama along with claims of 52 percent unfavorable against 47 percent favorable ratings.[30] What they failed to quote that night were poll results concluding that the nation approved of the vast majority of President Obama's accomplishments. Something remarkable was happening. On the brink of an election, the nation was being coached into detesting a president who gave the people the very programs that earned their approval.

A *Washington Post* poll unearthed an undercurrent it published under the banner, "Polls Show Record Obamacare Support, but That Doesn't Mean Much."[31] That bit of faint praise reflected University of Texas pollster Sheril Kirschenbaum's grudging finding that "America disagrees on many things about energy . . . but they seem to agree on wanting to promote renewable energy. The President's plan seems to speak to that."[32] About gays serving openly in the military, a 2006 poll of 545 troops who served in Afghanistan and Iraq found that 72 percent were personally comfortable about interacting with gays and lesbians.[33] In April 2007, Admiral William Crowe, chairman of the Joint Chiefs of Staff under Ronald Reagan and George H. W. Bush, said that he had long believed that the policy against gays was based more on "emotionalism than fact" and that he thought it was time for the policy to end.[34] On foreign policy, the *New York Times* wrote that "the results with Syria, Russia and Iran remind us that when American foreign policy is led by painstaking diplomacy, it seeks multilateral consensus and acts with an understanding of its own limitations, it can produce positive results. More often than not, boring is better."[35]

Question by question, polls measuring support for President Obama and his programs showed, with few exceptions, substantial levels of approval that contrasted with lackluster popularity ratings. History was left to sort out how an unpopular president was able to pass successful legislation. Once the leavening effects of passing years dampen anti-Obama rancor, it will be found that entrenched interests had worked to overwhelm voices of quiet reason to make the popular unpopular with landslides of misinformation.

The greater issue for the nation is not whether President Obama's policies are popular or not but how opinion makers poison national dialogue in order to achieve their sponsors' aims. People who form personal opinions solely from what popular media offers seldom realize how far their opinions are led from truth. As the famous Fairleigh Dickinson University study determined, watchers of Fox News had a poorer grasp on US affairs at home and abroad than respondents who watched no news at all.[36] Comparisons of the facts about issues with votes on those issues show clearly that a great number of voters are propagandized into voting against the best interests of themselves, their families, and the nation. What election observers see is cultivated ignorance in action.

IGNORANCE IN THE PEWS

Faith-based organizations are especially prone to institutional ignorance. When believers' faith is burdened with over-reverence for scriptural detail that hampers larger understandings, they might get it wrong. Or if they hold early-acquired understandings that aren't allowed to mature through change, limit God's reality and dynamics to that listed in the Bible, or in any other way lock down their understanding of the deity that is beyond human understanding, they embrace ignorance. Certain conservatives believe that to be true to their faith they must stand separate from the world, which cuts them off from important learnings. Believing that they must yield their will to a greater power seen only through the spiritual lens of selected parts of the Bible, all else becomes suspect. In fact, there is little in holy books that prescribes standing separate or denying learning—unless it is pulled out of context and misinterpreted, as in Romans: "Do not be conformed to this world."[37] If the God of Christianity, Judaism, and Islam created the world and all that's in it, it seems reasonable that studying that creation and its processes should be acceptable to him or her.

Hal Marcovitz, author of *Religious Fundamentalism*, contrasts the spiritual posture of sects with inspirational acts of faithful individuals. He describes how sects define their spiritual and cultural turf in terms of a type of tribal separatism that uses sharp-edged litmus tests to authenticate membership.[38] Anyone who fails a sect's tests is not only excluded but lumped with outsiders as unworthy. It is why the world's religious sects and *isms* account for more lasting hatreds and conflicts than any other cause. Yet central passages in the holy literature of all major religions paint each of them as peacemakers, the Christian Bible calling for pounding spears into plowshares and loving one's enemy. And sects not only choose to make war with other sects but do violence to their own, as demonstrated by the Great Inquisition of 1245–1246, questionable applications of Sharia law, and compulsory female circumcision.

Thanks to globalized communications, religious ignorance takes a hit now and then as seekers learn to sort truth from fiction. Learning opportunities abound, one being films shown at international film festivals that show a mix of pro- and anti-faith films of varying quality, some finding their way to arthouse theaters and Netflix. Ayaan Hirsi Ali, a Somali activist, partnered with Theo van Gogh to produce the film *Submission*, which documented abuses against Islamic women.[39] Hirsi Ali works on, though van Gogh was murdered for his efforts.[40] Malkie Schwartz, who was raised as a Hasidic Jew and rebelled against oppressive practices of fundamentalist Hasidic Judaism, formed an organization that helps fugitives from Hasidism adjust to contemporary society.[41] More often than not, it is individual women who lead the charge against ignorance that holds faiths from fulfilling their promises, and it is men more than women who close their minds to all but the ways of their *isms* and act out against liberalizing factions.

Conservative Christians tend to restrict understanding of their faith to teachings set down soon after the Christ story was documented for the New Testament. That discipline is good and necessary to keep denominational belief pure. But with the great faiths of the planet all founded on the existence of one powerful creator god who lives on beyond the time of those writings, denying the ongoing works of such a deity is to refuse to learn from his actions this side of the time when his or her will was revealed to the people of Israel. As Islam's enduring Sunni-Shiite conflict between fixed and less fixed factions indicates, their squabbles have little to do with under-standing what the will of Allah has in store for a body of believing individuals.

Though these things must be discussed, core issues of faith are not openly discussable everywhere. Depending on the campus, cor-poration, agency, club, administration, or sect, conformity police erect barriers that forbid discussion of different understandings of the Great Mysteries of Faith and even forbid descriptors that identify origins or orientations of people. In churches and on campuses where inquiry should not be inhibited and thought should be encouraged, overblown policing of political correctness and thin-skinned cultural sensitivities have chilling effects on dialogue and narrowing effects on formative frames of young minds.

FAITH, SCIENCE, AND IGNORANCE

You are right in speaking of the moral foundations of science, but you cannot turn around and speak of the scientific foundations for morality.

—Albert Einstein

The Great Body of the Church finds itself in a quandary here: its timeless messages can't flex in every breeze like the wise bamboo, but even theological reality must change with growth of understanding. Because change threatens inflexibility, conservatives take up the role of defenders of the faith in spite of their conviction that an omnipotent God has no need for downfield blockers. To keep the faithful from wavering, they promote tradition, even as timeworn interpretations, liturgies, trappings, and behaviors fail to draw new members, and old members chafe at being discouraged from voicing important questions for the Church in their time. As Pope Francis so clearly recognizes, social practices within the Church must change. A great awakening and reformation is sweeping through the Church, while an old guard—and some not so old—refuse to release followers from the ignorance of tradition.

Conservatives within Christianity, Judaism, and Islam hold to the ignorance of certitude as an expression of faith, which is not hard to do when the definition of faith is "belief without proof." Adherents to the great faiths don't anchor their faith on knowledge; they *believe* and would be proud of their belief if pride weren't considered a sin. Faith doesn't require tangible evidence to prove God's existence. In fact, believers are happy to not know, accepting the not-knowing aspect of belief as a blessed state that supports their call to humility. Though it may seem strange, faith and science share variations of that attitude, with both fields accepting that when ignorance is acknowledged, it becomes a portal to knowledge of things beyond present understanding.

CERTAINTY AND HUMILITY CANNOT COEXIST

It is not uncommon for Christians to believe that knowledge isn't necessary for growth toward spiritual maturity, for profound spiritual experiences have even visited convicts locked in solitary confinement. Religious fervor and not knowing seem to go hand in hand when the new in faith, having only scratched the surface of Christianity's foundations, express rock-solid belief while giants of Christianity, after lifetimes of study, find themselves caught up in doubt—not doubt about the foundations of their faith but about accepted interpretations of their church's treasured myths and traditions. Over time, both newbies and seasoned clerics experience the "believer's enlightenment" as last year's great revelations become this year's naiveties. For the young in faith, it takes time and maturity to moderate youthfully exuberant certitude. Christians grow in faith, and when they grow they change, and as they change, their understanding progressively morphs into something greater. At no time during growth can they say with certainty that they have all the answers. The growth never ends.

This was beautifully illustrated when Bill Moyers assembled four dozen prominent theologians, thinkers, artists, and writers representing Christianity, Judaism, and Islam to ponder the book of Genesis together.[1] They met in teams of seven for a monumental ten-part PBS television study, and transcripts of their meetings were published by Doubleday as *Genesis: A Living Conversation.* One remarkable and refreshing outcome of the project was the consistent willingness of everyone involved to admit that *they did not know*. They openly questioned God's purpose and were unsure of which actions of his chosen people served holy purpose. Their lack of certainty is refreshing to simple believers because, if leading theologians are uncertain about God, then it should be permissible for the rank and file to doubt and question. It follows that, in matters of faith, admission of ignorance and doubt are not bad things. If faithful Christians are called to be humble, then certainty that one *knows* all that underlies their faith cannot help but torpedo humility. Certainty and humility cannot coexist.

Admission of ignorance is an honest tactic that serves well under most conditions. When a personal computer goes haywire and the Geek Squad is called in to set things right, any feigning of knowledge by the device's owner will only set the IT geek to talking over the owner's head, leaving the owner with instructions he or she won't understand. It takes no more than a few self-aggrandizing errors to get a person to understand that pride should not be allowed to paint a knowledge-base for more than it is. Admitted ignorance works better.

Admission of ignorance may come harder to pastors and priests than to lay persons because one of the hazards of the profession is that congregations hold them up as ultimate local spiritual authorities. They are stuck with the role, which some handle with grace and humility. Others will sometimes reject questions that range outside the frames of their life experience or religious studies. This is played out when educated parishioners with lifetimes of study of their faith seek to engage pastors in discussion about a theological point, only to run into pastoral certitude. Older pastors may claim the excuse of being brought up in a tradition of unquestioned clerical authority. Even younger pastors find themselves trapped by congregations' expectation that ordination is proof of superior spiritual authority. It doesn't help that pastors are expected to live the metaphorical role of shepherds to flocks rather than as examples of how to live and think. The pastoral image has been handed down from ages past, when the priest was the only literate person in many villages and exclusively tasked with the responsibility of reading Scripture. Martin Luther sought to undo that concentration of priestly monopoly with his call for "the priesthood of all believers," yet it lingers on five hundred years later.[2]

Christian spiritual authority was long seated in the Church of Rome, where a self-perpetuating cadre of functionaries maintained an all-powerful spiritual fiefdom. Disciplined adherence to tradition held the Church unassailable, even to the point of protecting pedophile clergy from justice. Unquestioning obedience to the Church was defined by Ignatius of Loyola, sixteenth-century founder of the Jesuit Order, who wrote, "What seems to me white, I will believe to be black if the hierarchical Church so defines."[3] Half a millennium later, and as a demonstration of change, it was one of the Jesuits' own, an Argentine priest by the name of Jorge Mario Bergoglio, who endorsed change in his 2011 book, *On Heaven and Earth*:

> Dialogue is born from an attitude of respect for the other person, from a conviction that the other person has something good to say. It assumes that there is room in the heart for [another] person's point of view, opinion and proposal. To dialogue requires a cordial reception, not a prior condemnation. In order to dialogue it is necessary to know how to lower the defenses, open the doors of the house, and offer human warmth.[4]

THE QUESTIONING CHRISTIAN

Bergoglio, now Pope Francis, the pontiff who has formerly disaffected young Catholics flocking back to the Church, saying, "It's cool to be Catholic now," is no friend of certitude. He clearly respects holy mysteries as much as Church doctrine and, at the age of seventy-nine, is a young-at-heart, open-minded seeker of knowledge. His rejection of institutional ignorance finds parallels among new theologians in Judaism and Protestantism. Much of Pope Francis's background works against religious certitude, allowing him to focus on another Jesuit thrust: finding God in all things. As a practical chemist, trained at Buenos Aires's Escuela Tecnica Industrial, he has a feel for science's contributions to faith.

I keep company with retired pastors. We meet for coffee and swap books by twenty-first-century theologians who, like scientists, use not-knowingness as springboards for exploring mysteries of faith. It is in their retirement that they feel spiritually liberated, not from, but toward their faith. Their newfound freedom allows them to soar off like spiritual Magellans into the terra incognita of spirit, where they sense new depths and dimensions. It also causes regret that they had not matured into their new spiritualities when serving congregations.

Now and then, a theologian carves out a church career without slavishly bowing to the constraints of orthodoxy, even within a liturgical church. One such was Donald Cupitt, an Anglican whose radical pondering of great questions was taken as heretical or inspirational, depending on where his critics stood. Cupitt may not be a giant of the Church, but he does stand out for being an open-minded thinker while remaining rooted in faith. While at Cambridge, he switched his major from physics to theology, was ordained an Anglican priest, defied orthodoxy by denying the existence of the devil, studied the then out-of-favor Kierkegaard, and argued that religion cannot be based on *knowledge* of the divine but must involve a complex way of living. He turned to scolding his Church for insincere, ironic references to their deity. For example, when misfortune hit a colleague, they would joke that God must have been annoyed. To Cupitt, that jocularity spoke of a distance separating traditional church language from the conscious belief of the speaker.[5] He tested the archbishop of Canterbury's tolerance by suggesting that the kind of religious imaginings we engage in dictate the sort of God we end up with. Even Cupitt's book titles were provocative: *Who was Jesus?*; *Is Nothing Sacred?*; *The Old Creed and the New*; *Jesus and Philosophy*; *The New Religion of Life in Everyday Speech*; and *The Dethronement of Christianity*. Cupitt is an example of theologians whose faith is on the move, growing stronger and deeper with each turn. He was radical enough that, while he may not be the ideal poster boy for freedom in faith, he would have fit with Moyers's panelists in setting orthodoxy aside to share doubts and questions.

INSTITUTIONAL FAITH MAY FOSTER IGNORANCE

Church history is punctuated by challengers to orthodoxy who were crushed or marginalized. Their questions provoked such strong reactions because they had less to do with the essence of Christianity than how it was practiced. To be fair, when comparing offenses against God carried out by orthodoxy and reformers, it is difficult to determine which body is furthest off base and does the most damage. If some attempt to sort that out, chances are that they will be pulled toward their own comfort zone, whether reform or orthodoxy. It is a pursuit that faintly resembles avoidance of personal ignorance. Discomforting calls to acknowledge ignorance may not lead to perfect objectivity, but they do set seekers on the unending path toward freedom from bias and prejudice.

Because no one, no matter how deep in faith, has the entire picture, we must be cautious with criticism. We don't *know*. I once taught a class with members split between orthodoxy and New Age liberalism in a typically split church that had a traditional service with organ and piano followed by a contemporary service with guitars and drums. Let's just say the group wasn't wholeheartedly accepting of each other's approaches to faith and didn't mix much socially. One Sunday, it became clear that open discussions of issues were further dividing the class, so the next Sunday I hung a patchwork quilt the ladies had been assembling over a portable whiteboard and said, "We're going to take a look at God." I passed out half lengths of Starbucks drinking straws and asked them to punch the straws through their discussion outlines so as to limit their scope when viewing patches of quilt through the straws. They were asked to sketch the parts of the quilt they saw through their straws and compare their drawings with their neighbors'. The point was that each person saw a small portion of the whole, that what they saw was a real part of the same quilt, and that it would take a lot of viewers to perceive the whole of it. Discussion led to recognition that it is natural but wrong to assume that my view of God is more valid than yours, or that what another sees can't have anything to do with the God I know. If the viewers were screened off from each other, they would believe that what was on their own field of vision could not have been of the same thing others saw, which is pretty much the situation believers face when comparing their separate knowledges of God, except for the unifying influence of the Bible. One of the class members said, "You made your point, but it's not going to change human nature."

We are, and always will be, ignorant of the big picture, which is reason enough that no one is justified in letting the uniqueness of what one experiences cast clouds of negativity or doubt over what others experience. An individual's imperfect receptors feed imperfect thought processors that operate in a tiny corner of space and time. We cannot know it all. Clearly, admission of incompleteness and ignorance form the best intellectual posture in that it throws all the doors and windows open. Claiming that one's view through a personal metaphorical straw reveals the wholeness of God would be the ultimate statement of ignorant piety. As Soren Kierkegaard put it, "Deepest down in the heart of piety lurks the mad caprice which knows that it has itself produced its God."[6]

FAITH COLLIDES WITH SCIENCE

Whereas religions introduce holy mysteries, people want cut-and-dried answers, or, if open-minded, they may settle for progress toward answers. Science is better at nailing down findings or making progress toward findings than religion, so when twenty-first-century sociologists study where people put their faith and hope, they find a movement toward science. Could this mean that scientists are assuming the mantles of the future's priests? Shamans and priests of antiquity, who monopolized knowledge of calendars, "determined" the day when crops should be planted and when short days would start to get longer. By wielding passed-down knowledge, they posed as controllers of natural events. But since the science of meteorology has put shamans, priests, and cultish mystery out of the weather forecasting business, perhaps there is reason to consider that God may be speaking through scientists who work to understand his creation.[7]

In fact, it's science's open admission that it is driven by informed ignorance that places it on more solid intellectual ground than the knowledge base of religious sects that believe in a creation date of six thousand years ago. The notion that informed ignorance could possibly represent a more solid intellectual base than inflexible faith isn't a new one. The situation was beautifully drawn in E. B. White's classic *Charlotte's Web*, in which the spider, Charlotte, weaves love notes to Wilbur, the pig, into her web.[8] When the farmer's daughter, Fern, discovers the words, "Some pig," woven into a web, her uncle Homer took it as a miracle, while her mother, Mrs. Arable, became so upset that she took Fern to a doctor. She asked the doctor, "Do you understand how there could be any writing in a spider's web?"

Dr. Dorian said, "Oh, no. I don't understand it. But for that matter I don't understand how a spider learned to weave a web in the first place. When the words appeared, everyone said they were a miracle. But nobody pointed out that the web itself is a miracle."

When Mrs. Arable countered, saying that a web is just a web, Dr. Dorian said, "Ever try to spin one?"

"No, but I can crochet a doily and I can knit a sock." Dr. Dorian stopped her by pointing out that while someone had taught her to do both, no one taught the spider to weave, which made it a miracle. Mrs. Arable conceded the point, adding that she certainly didn't understand the business of words in webs and that she definitely did not like what she did not understand.

Dr. Dorian said, "I'm a doctor. Doctors are supposed to understand everything. But I don't understand everything, and I don't intend to let it worry me."

Well said. If there is a God, and that God is as they say—omniscient, omnipotent, unfathomable, and so on—then the great mysteries may be meant to be just that: great mysteries, intended to be pondered but not laid out on pathologist's tables for dissection and analysis. A case may be made for understanding more about the mysteries of faith by knowing less about them, whereas in science the need to know and do is a mover that propels the curious from one level of understanding to the next. The possibility that science's strides may have assumed the momentum to, according to some observers, become uncontrollable has awakened a measure of caution. Anti-science forces within the world of faith use the label "scientism" to identify their concept of what they take to be a new fact-based religion with ungodly high priests, believers, supporters, and a not-always-high calling. Avowed skeptic of science Bryan Appleyard wrote in *Understand the Past: An Alternative History of Science,*

> Science is not a unique, omnipotent force that will, by itself, make a better world. It is not a truth about the world that renders all other truths obsolete. It is not on the verge of explaining what Douglas Adams called life, the universe and everything, nor will it ever be. And finally, its past achievements have not proved unambiguously good for the human species or the planet.[9]

About doubtful achievements of science, Appleyard cites cloning, weapon research and development, bovine spongiform encephalopathy (mad cow disease), environmental degradation, designer babies, bioengineering's issues, and technologically adept terrorism. He should check his facts on the cause of mad cow disease.

SCIENCE AND FAITH'S CONTEST FOR ALLEGIANCE

Traditionalists complain that scientific and religious education compete for the minds of students on an uneven playing field. Their best e-Bibles lack science's space-age technological theatrics that lead youngsters into believing that everyday reality is not enough. When Appleyard asks if science is delivering what it takes to care for people and the planet, it gives him little comfort that the best answer is *maybe*. But that unsure response isn't entirely different from unsure expectations for answers to prayer. In matters of faith, one cannot expect to nail every spiritual hope in place when the basis for prayer is, at least in part, personal. The closest one can come to owning evidence of the greatest of mysteries is that there is something undeniable about life being more a matter of becoming than arriving, that simply *being* means little and answers nothing, that the Taoists' core concept of constant transformation echoes a biblical call to grow that Christians should reassess. And if those thoughts are in any way acceptable, then science's generating of more questions than answers—which it constantly does—may be another contribution toward deeper understanding of God's creation and purpose for us. Science is not the enemy of faith; its search into the nature and dynamics of all that is shouldn't be thought of as altogether separate from faith's inquiries into the nature of God.

Because humanity wants and needs some measure of intellectual comfort, we split our allegiance, according a measure of credit to science for its capacity for tinkering with mysteries of the great unknown. The other part is rooted in hope for something better, an intangible something in which we can have faith if knowledge fails. We can't bench science because it is our knowledge factory, because new products of industry were once science's spin-offs, and because science wrings information from the unknown to dispel ignorance. Beyond being fascinating to follow, every scientific discovery opens windows to more new mystery than it solves, adding to the scope and depth of what we don't know.

Science believes that no experiment fails. If the equipment blows up or refuses to function, something is learned: don't bother to do it that way again. If test results scatter wildly across graphs, meaning might be found even in the randomness. Well-planned research often hits walls that leave teams scratching their heads and wondering, "What do we do now?" I once put the question of what happens at those times to a managing director of Seattle's Battelle Northwest research facility. His answer was to the effect that they then look to God. This happened many years ago, so there is now no way to determine whether that gentleman was speaking from a personal platform of faith or as spokesperson for Battelle. Faith serves as a sea anchor that provides a measure of security and stability during revolutions in thought when competing interpretations of what matters most lead to tension and conflict.

Alien onlookers gazing down on us would believe that we are most certainly crazy. They would see oppressors ruling from strength while choosing not to understand or care about the oppressed who feed them, for caring leads to vulnerability. As long as top dogs can stay ignorant of the plight of those they torment, they will continue to do so. It explains why hawkish Americans prefer to operate through strength, not diplomacy, which allows intellectually lazy militarists to rest on confidence in military superiority without troubling themselves to earn understanding of the nations and peoples they would invade. Parallels can be found in the histories of industry, politics, and religion.

Brutish action comes more naturally to limited thinkers. The less they know of other people, the less they feel responsible for them, which amounts to sociopathic indifference to others' problems. Open minds are more generous. A friend with a natural gift for knowing everyone he met had a way of giving companions his entire attention by steering conversations onto what made them tick. His remembrances of past meetings with others were so keen that when he and I shared a ski area hot tub with eight others near Oregon's Mt. Bachelor, he recalled having met three of them over past years and even pulled up bits of what they had talked about. He was incapable of handling people roughly because it was his habit to know them. He *knew* the three in the hot tub. While the Christian Bible says little about gaining knowledge about strangers, it is consistent in advocating kindness to the point of holding up a Samaritan, a traditional enemy of Judaism, as an example of setting aside tribal animosity to care for a wounded Jew.

THE SEARCH FOR MEANING

In the confusion over the relative moral standings of religion and science, religion enjoys certain advantages. For one, while science satisfies specific material needs, desires, and protections, it thus far has failed to meet humankind's desperate need to understand why we are here and what humanity's purpose might be, other than as the out-of-control species that messes up the balances of nature. The depth of curiosity about our purpose is indicated by the number of listings under an Amazon search string for "a life of meaning." Amazon's first page of titles offers the following: *The Meaning of life*, by Bradley Greive; *On the Meaning of Life*, by Will Durant; *Finding Meaning in the Second Half of Life*, by James Hollis; *Meaning in Life and Why it Matters*, by Susan Wolf; *Meaning of Life*, by David Friend; *Man's Search for Meaning*, by Viktor Frankl; *Jeremy Fink and the Meaning of Life*, by Wendy Mass; *Meanings of Life*, by Roy Baumeister; *The Meaning of Life*, by E. D. Klemke; *Meaning in Life*, by Thaddeus Metz; and *The Meaning of Life*, by Terry Eagleton.

A scan through four more pages of titles reveals that the difference between page one's content and that of following pages is not a dimming of focus on the meaning of life but a gradation into more cryptic titles. Clearly, the search for meaning is a big deal, spurring cartoonists to picture Ziggy and others ascending peaks for audiences with gurus. Monty Python had a go at it with their outrageously tasteless 1983 production, *The Meaning of Life*. The theme generally places wise ones in remote places far from influences of Western civilization where they may be approached only at great personal sacrifice. In this symbolism they get it right.

Why are we here? What is our purpose? What messages to us are written into this creation? These questions were being asked before humankind's inept reach was eloquently painted on the Sistine Chapel ceiling, showing Adam's maximum reach failing to bridge the enigmatic gap between his and God's hands. Yet the human need to reach is all important, for failing to reach has dire consequences.

Not bothering to reach and dream beyond the here and now leaves one empty of purpose, as portrayed by Peggy Lee's somber rendition of Leiber and Stoller's 1960 song "If That's All There Is."[10] In the song, a woman narrates three scenarios from her life, ending each vignette with a despondent complaint that says if that's all there is to it, why not have a drink and get the party started? In the first scenario, she and her father escape their burning home, and, as they watch it destroyed, she accepts the loss without feeling, asking herself if that's all there is to a home. Next, she tells of being taken to a circus, and, after seeing the acts and pageantry and animals, she's not impressed. And when a man comes into her life only to leave after some years, she reflects back over their time together with the same hollowness. As before, nothing has meaning to her so she asks if that was all there was of the relationship. Her understanding of people, things, events, and relationships was shallow and unformed. Somehow, her developmental processes and experiences had left her ignorant of what makes life meaningful.

Emptiness of purpose and meaning leaves people without peace. We must aspire. To or toward what is the question. Like Michelangelo's Adam, we reach toward the Great Mystery, while enlightened churches provide sympathetic centers for reachers. Reaching toward what? Perhaps we are not meant to know exactly, only to be drawn toward the mysterious *It*.

Great minds have explored this. Stephen Hawking, author of *A Brief History of Time*, envisions a time when science will discover how to unify all creation in one mathematical expression. His search centers on discovering the mythical universal constant that connects all states of matter and energy. If this does come to be, Hawking predicts that it will be in a form that will be understandable to everyone. It is an audacious proposal, for, in a way, Hawking proposes a recipe for ending much of the reason to search, but if history is in any way our guide, humankind *needs* ignorance to spur us on. Hawking failed to hold that in mind when he wrote,

Then we shall all, philosophers, scientists, and just ordinary people, be able to take part in the discussion of why it is that we and the universe exist. If we find the answer to that, it would be the ultimate triumph of reason—for then we would know the mind of God.[11]

SCIENCE, FAITH, AND CERTITUDE

Hawking's view was countered by Bryan Appleyard in *The Brain Is Wider Than the Sky*. In his mission of calling fouls on science for what he takes to be its excesses, Appleyard says that science is not only a neutral commodity that equips people with the West's material power, but a corrosive power that burns away ancient authorities and traditions. He pictures scientists taking up the mantles of witchdoctors and wizards with experiments as their rituals. He asks, "[W]hat kind of life is it that science offers to people? And what does science tell us about ourselves and how we must live?"[12] Appleyard charges that science "does not tell us why we should do things or how we should live; it offers, instead, solutions." He moderates his criticism by calling for a "relativizing" and humbling of science from the structured form of mysticism that presents problems that only it can solve, a view that betrays his ignorance of science's acceptance that most lab results prove little or nothing. Appleyard wrote that science's effectiveness becomes "almost inevitable because it narrows the possibility of refutation and failure." He expresses a hope that science will learn to achieve a balance with faith:

And that should mean that science can become itself again rather than the quasi-religious repository of all our faith as defined by the popularizers. We would have forced science to co-exist by turning it into something else, something more human.[13]

Despite his inaccurate appraisal of science, Appleyard's following testifies to the breadth of the battle between religious sects and the measurable world. He argues that if science were merely a methodology, the problem would be minor. But science has become the dominant way of understanding the world and how we relate to it, shaping, analyzing, and defining everything from economics to medicine, even sociological processes. Appleyard claims that science has, to a large degree, defeated religion and that the power of science has overwhelmed other outlooks to the point where religion represents no more than another "interesting" viewpoint. He worries that since religion's answers cannot be proved, science has come to be the more believed contestant.

Appleyard wrongfully claims that religion and science are as contradictory as Islam and Judaism—absolutely and irreconcilably conflicted. First, Islam and Judaism have much in common; it is their adherents who emphasize differences. Next, a more flexible mind might find that science, along with everything else, may be of God. Though Appleyard would be loath to admit it, it is through certitude of his platform that he expresses ignorance of the very situation he seeks to understand. Though much of what he writes deserves attention and his calls for change are often on the mark, his charges against science carry the taint of ignorant dogmatism, and his defenses of religion are reminiscent of history's self-appointed defenders of the faith. If God is anything close to what Appleyard envisions him to be, then God needs no such defense.

Of course, Appleyard is right that science errs. He is right that religion's impact has waned somewhat against science's ascendency. His warning that it is dangerous to put a level of faith in science that elevates its deep thinkers to priestly status is probably good advice. Where he errs is in not remembering that his God, as envisioned by centuries of Christian believers, is greater than his beliefs, greater than his church, greater even than Christianity, and greater than the reach of science. Appleyard puts himself dangerously within the grasp of certitude, that self-defined confidence of correctness that negates whatever might conflict with one's argument. A more balanced understanding would say that there is much that makes one a bit fearful of science, but maybe that is because it is difficult to know what it's all about. The universe is filled with mysteries, but, as Dr. Dorian said, that should not keep us awake at night. It is all right to not know.

For the faithful, certitude should be seen as a greater threat than science. As Sir Thomas More put it, "God help me to always seek the truth, and protect me from those who have found it."[14] That quotation is an excellent introduction to the connection between knowledge and power, an inseparable pair in this modern world. The French thinker Michel Foucault spent much of his career exploring that partnership, titling one of his books *Power/Knowledge*. His thesis was that those with knowledge use it to strengthen their own positions and to impose their will on others through colonialism, imperialism, multinationals, and cartels.[15]

Walter Brueggemann, an Old Testament scholar, is one of many across history who have pointed out that whatever comfort certitude might deliver is overrated. It is at the root of fundamentalism of every brand, whether in government, religion, education, military, or anywhere else. Note that there would be no fundamentalism of any kind without narrowed frames and restricted fields of thought and learning. Brueggemann provides this view:

> We all have a hunger for certitude, and the problem is that the Gospel is not about certitude, it's about fidelity. So what we all want to do if we can is immediately transpose fidelity into certitude, because fidelity is a relational category and certitude is a flat, mechanical category. So we have to acknowledge our thirst for certitude and then recognize that if you had all the certitudes in the world it would not make the quality of your life any better because what we must have is fidelity.[16]

CERTITUDE TERMINATES THE SEARCH FOR KNOWLEDGE.

Imagine a Christian about to face death wrestling with his concept of final judgment. The books are about to be closed on a life. Whatever he had done or thought across the course of years is almost wrapped up. This person wonders, "Is the God I followed more likely to ask, 'Did you always do the right thing?' or 'Did you live the way set before you to the best of your ability?'" If he had been victim to certitude he would have presumed to know precisely what the right thing was and would have done that. But if he had acknowledged his ignorance, then doing his best meant moving out of ignorance to do better. That path is not always smooth, but, on the other hand, acknowledgement of not knowing gives better footing than pretending to know.

Knowledge can't be unchanging in a time of rapid change. A marketing expert recently reported that new tech products commonly spend more time in research and design than on store shelves before being displaced by something newer. It is this apparent instability of a world in which facts, small truths, and reality refuse to hold still that makes certitude so attractive. Fixed codes provide comfort even when wrong. We vote for candidates who promise resurrection of the past and reject office holders who adjust with the times, calling them wafflers. The craving for certainty is natural. When a ten-year-old map can't guide one properly, when last month's budget won't cover this month's costs, when it is only a matter of days before an Adobe Reader pop-up announces still another update, we look for solid ground.

Planets and stars and classics of literature can be trusted. Definitions give a comforting sense of what is. Creeds provide the comfort of familiar words in familiar settings that reflect beliefs that sustained the Church over time. These things can be held to, while dreams and visions and imagined things come and go. Yet imagination is the mind's most enjoyably creative process. It is the root of "what if?" questioning. Via the Theater of the Mind, Bible readers travel into the midst of long-ago actions to ask one of Jesus's disciples, "Hey, why in God's name did he do that?" Imaginative Christians don't fixate on the here and now as though it is as good as it gets. They understand that mystery is at least as fascinating as knowledge because there is more of it, and it is certainly more powerful. They come to honor questions even over answers, having learned that living is a journey from what's known to unknown destinations. On a good day, they might convert a bit of unknown into known. Ignorance is the starting point. Stages of ignorance are waypoints and springboards without end and should be accepted as just that. To enlightened believers, they come to be welcomed as blessings.

Certainty lends an illusion of control, and when things seem to be getting out of hand a bit of control is comforting. But control can become addictive. Control over a machine, control over a family, control over a corporation—that type of control produces expectations that things will work out according to one's plan, come hell or high water. But hell and high water are in the natural order of things, so chances are high that a person's confidence that things will or won't work won't match up with reality. According to the Hungarian thinker Karl Polanyi, knowledge of how the world works will always exceed what's understood.[17] Shallow knowledge shapes plans without the benefit of deeper understanding: I trust that the bridge will support me without understanding its engineering. One might become an expert racecar driver without understanding the mechanical mysteries of a high-tech car. The car and the driver may operate well on the track without the driver knowing all that's happening inside the engine because the driver has faith, not knowledge, that the machine will work.

Successful church programs are headed by leaders who, if asked, will say that they don't know exactly what, other than faith, makes their programs work. Of course, organization, preparation, and money also figure highly, but that's not the whole picture. On the other hand, many of the Church's thorniest problems are caused by the certitude of leaders who can recite, chapter and verse, what their plans are and how they are to be carried out. They *know*, and if things don't work according to plan, then there is no shortage of externals to blame. Fallible human leaders have been known to seize not upon discomforting truths to explain failure but upon more comforting excuses, spiced with sufficient truthiness to create illusions of blamelessness. Well-intentioned plans are never wrong; they just run into problems. Whatever specks their proponents mistake for whole truths are installed as unifying principles for congregations, industries, and governments while competing thoughts are set aside as unworthy. This is ignorant certitude on steroids.

Insecure but highly placed leaders *need* followers to adopt certainty that their personal beliefs reflect a holy light that labels all other variants on belief as misguided. They are overly alert to dissatisfactions, variations in interpretation, different styles of music, ecumenicalism, variant worldviews, and criticism of management style. Schisms pop up to turn mainline congregations into battlegrounds, splitting them into dissidents who righteously justify reasons for leaving versus stalwarts who have ridden out storms before. These tawdry divorces discourage onlookers from giving churches a try. Religionists should also recognize that politics is more likely to change one's denomination than religion is to change one's politics.

Once there was the protestant church of Luther in Germany that splintered off from the Church of Rome to form a body of worshippers distinguished by inspired protest that awakened churches in Switzerland, England, and elsewhere. It would be enlightening to know what transpired over the years to fragment Lutheranism into three main branches and smaller splinters. Baptists hold the title for most prolific splintering, as the number of every city's First and Second Baptist churches of various persuasions indicate. An online search for the churches of Florida's Apalachicola, a strip town bordering US Highway 98, displays about twenty-eight Christian churches with various labels. Apalachicola (pop. 2,334) is served by twenty-eight churches that, by simple division, average eighty-three men, women, and children per congregation.[18] Considering the usual number of backsliders, fishermen, weekend golfers, travelers, shut-ins, confirmed atheists, and Sunday workers, attendance at the average church will be reduced to where it would be more practical to hold services around tables in Apalachicola's city park. Clearly, more are caught up in what separates them than what they hold in common, indicating that some might still have more to learn about God Is Love.

CHAPTER 13

PROPAGANDA

To swallow and follow, whether new doctrine or old propa-
ganda, is a weakness still dominating the human mind.
— Charlotte Perkins Gilman

History paints propaganda as an instrument that power seekers wield to manipulate minds with lies and half-truths. It is so unrelentingly prevalent in one form or another that populations fail to notice its presence even while still reeling from the effects of its past attacks. It will always be with us because leadership will apply whatever it takes to maintain control and ensure profitability. Governments of every type—democratic, despotic, Communist, Fascist, and Socialist—use propagandist tactics of population control to bind people into supportive bodies. When leadership's thought-control messages prioritize power and profit over what should be done, they distance their news releases from public information and marry them to propaganda.

Propaganda works best on homogenous populations. In Germany, Japan, and Italy of 1940, propagandists had only to appeal to Germans, Japanese, or Italians. Compare that with the challenge Nigeria's propagandists face nowadays trying to pull that nation's more than 250 ethnic groups together. While the Nigerian government generally supports education, many Nigerians hold a dim view of Western-style education due to a history of favoring the well connected of certain tribes that have enjoyed more benefits than others.[1] Nigeria is a somewhat oil-rich nation that has used part of its oil money to educate well-connected young men and women in the world's universities. In past years, graduates with newfound world-liness returned home to be slotted into high-paying positions of advantage, not responsibility. From street level, recipients of Western education appear corrupt. The favored ones' rise was also enhanced by "long legs," the colloquial term for the ability to step over others on the way up, aided by tribal or family connections. Attempts to pro-pagandize Nigerian radicals into docile citizenship remain slim in a nation with a history of awarding unequal advantage to members of its many tribal minorities.

THE UNBROKEN HISTORY OF PROPAGANDA

The fact that populations fall for manipulative messages while the ravages of previous propaganda campaigns have yet to be forgotten doesn't square with the old maxim "Fool me once, shame on you. Fool me twice, shame on me." People allow minor truth bending to slip by, passing it off as business-as-usual politics or salesmanship. Hardcore propaganda is recognized only in hindsight, for it is only in hindsight that artful propaganda can be judged for what it did. Propaganda would be the equal of public information if its bene-ficiaries were other than its sponsors. Public information supports movements, such as acceptance of vaccines, eradication of commu-nicable diseases, use of seat belts, and minimizing smoking as accept-able change. Think of propaganda as public information's evil twin.

Propaganda is a reliable tool for amassing power and profit. It takes possession of thought with the stealth of magicians relieving volunteers of wrist watches and billfolds, achieving its goals through distraction, misinformation, and fearmongering. When distracted, its targets lose sight of what they were thinking before becoming dis-tracted, and that in itself may be enough to satisfy propagandists' aims. Subtle misinformation works because "a truth that's told with bad intent beats all the lies you can invent."[2] Or they may whip up jingoistic fears of threats to life, liberty, and the pursuit of happiness plus, of course, threats to "national interests." Antiwar activists counter with claims that conflicts are promoted to keep a population's attention on the horror and drama of combat and off home front issues that would otherwise suffer under scrutiny.

Propaganda is as old as despots' efforts to control underlings' thoughts. Its applications have been as various as propagandists' ambitions, though its indelible image is tied to Germany's misinformation campaigns before and during WWII. Without it, Hitler could not have pumped up support for ethnic cleansing and forceful domination of neighboring states. While Hitler's demonizing of Germany's "undesirables" serves as the textbook example of propaganda's potential for poisoning thought, we are accustomed to a diet of it based on the same principles but called "advertising." Its aim is to convince us that Fords are better than Chevys and that Cialis is better than Viagra, or vice versa. One of the earliest writings that sought to define programs of mind control was written by Edward Bernays, a nephew of Sigmund Freud. Bernays wrote,

> The conscious and intelligent manipulation of the organized habits and opinions of the masses is an important element in democratic society. Those who manipulate this unseen mechanism of society constitute an invisible government which is the true ruling power of our country. We are governed, our minds are molded, our tastes are formed, our ideas suggested largely by men we have never heard of. This is a logical result of the way our democratic society is organized. Vast numbers of human beings must cooperate in this manner if they are to live together as a smoothly functioning society.[3]

Can this be true? That our minds are molded, our tastes formed, our ideas suggested so easily? If the amount spent on advertising is a measure of the effectiveness of commercial propaganda, then much of the direction of our thoughts is truly not of our choosing but implanted and groomed. Internet advertisers spent $42.8 billion in 2013, for the first time topping the $40.1 billion spent on ad sales for broadcast TV for one year.[4] The effectiveness of Internet pop-ups and TV spots has been tried, tested, and is backed by studies proving that sales and profits more than justify the seemingly exorbitant cost of electronic media exposure. A thirty-second spot during the 2011 Super Bowl cost $3.5 million.[5] It cost $425,000, more or less, for a spot on *American Idol*.[6] Automobile manufacturers shell out just under a billion dollars per quarter to convince us to buy their products. They aren't dummies. They know beyond whatever we suspect that artfully composed propaganda can and does control thoughts and actions. Robert Shiller and George Akerlof's enlightening book, *Phishing for Phools*, offers an abundance of examples.

PROPAGANDISTS' CONTROL OVER BALLOT ISSUES

Propagandists for hire were tasked with defeating a Washington State ballot initiative calling for mandatory labeling of foods containing genetically modified organisms (GMOs). The bill, designated I-522, exempted restaurants, which raised the question, "What is a restaurant?"[7] A line was drawn to exclude vendors of precooked foods, such as Domino's Pizza, not a perfect solution, but solutions are never perfect when drawing lines across complex issues. Another line was drawn that limited the labeling requirement to first-generation foods with GMO content, not second- or third-generation GMO content, such as chili made with beef that may have grazed on GMO-tainted hay.

The anti-GMO movement is driven by three concerns. First, many GMO crops are bred to survive overloads of poisonous pesticides and herbicides that contaminate human food in measurable amounts. Second, when food plants are reengineered in GMO labs, their natural nutritive value is lessened. Third, when non-GMO farmers' crops are accidentally tainted by GMO pollen drifting over property lines, Big Food's lawyers sue the invaded farms for unauthorized use of patented pollen, sometimes driving them out of business.

Since genetic engineering generally decreases nutritive value, Big Food's motive for meddling with nature wasn't improvement of nutrition. Rather, GMO advocates aimed to boost profits by reducing certain challenges native to farming, like bugs and weeds. To defeat I-522, Big Food needed Washington voters to believe that (a) agricultural chemicals wouldn't harm them, (b) that the levels of residual poisons in foods are not harmful to human health, and (c) that farming without toxic chemicals would cause the price of foods to soar. Lab tests and marketing results had proved all of those points untrue, so Big Food mustered a war chest from out-of-state donors and hired a tested engineer of public opinion, campaign consultant firm Winner & Mandabach, the public relations machine that had successfully torpedoed California's anti-GMO issue.[8]

It would have been nice had both sides debated their cases in an inform-the-public forum, but since most of the true facts accrued to the anti-GMO side, while the false facts burdened GMO supporters, the anti-GMO forces had to come up with something else. It wouldn't be a ground-breaking tactic: Hitler had already written the book on how to handle such things, writing, "Tell a big lie and tell it often and you will be believed."[9]

Winner & Mandabach's operatives opened by warning that Washington would become the only state to require GMO content labeling. In truth, Connecticut, Maine, and Alaska already had GMO-labeling laws in force and dozens of other states had similar laws pending.[10] But W&M repeated their statement often enough that voters came to believe it. Then there was the bothersome fact that sixty-four nations requiring GMO content labels discriminate against importation of genetically altered American foodstuffs. W&M warned that labeling genetically modified (GM) foods would cost taxpayers millions every year, but Trader Joe's and PCC Natural Markets had already made the change at no cost to consumers. Nor had there been a measurable uptick in prices when lists of nutrients were first required on labels. Then the propagandists said that GM foods pose no safety risks. If Big Food's scientists had tweaked genetics to make apples more colorful or sweet corn sweeter, that might have been more accurate. But when the GM foods carry poisons so toxic that responsible farm owners clothe workers in hazmat suits when applying them, the public had reason for concern.

HOW TO SELL "ALTERNATIVE FACTS"

Winner & Mandabach reported that the world's recognized health study organizations had concluded that GM foods are safe. In truth, the World Health Organization, United Nations, and American Medical Association had called for premarketing safety testing, a call that US food producers have yet to respond to.[11] W&M's claim was bold in the face of published opposition to untested GM foods by the National Academy of Science, American Public Health Association, Washington State Nurses, Breast Cancer Action, and other reputable organizations. W&M claimed that GM crops reduce the need for herbicides and pesticides, when the record shows that the quantities of toxins GM crops are bred to tolerate lead to the survival of superbugs and super weeds that require even heavier applications to control.

Backers of GM foods were relying on their agents' ability to distract the public from nutrition issues and health hazards, causing observers to wonder if questionably sharp business practices had crossed into the realm of evil.[12] The I-522 issue was symbolic of more than a battle between consumers and producers.

If voters' educations had better prepared them to defend against misinformation, Initiative 522 would have passed by a large margin. Instead it was rejected.[13]

THE IGNORANCE OF RADICAL PROPAGANDISTS

Every printed or broadcasted attempt to sway thinking deserves close inspection. The style and excess of Alex Epstein's article from *Capitalism Magazine*, "Why You Shouldn't Keep an Open Mind," typifies that of pundits who manage to develop followings in spite of their illogic.[14] Their socially destructive work needs close scrutiny. First, it is necessary to understand where they are coming from. Epstein's columns are printed in *Capitalism Magazine*, a Bahama-based online daily that describes itself as having a "pro-capitalist, laissez-faire, pro-individual rights perspective."[15] It echoes the philosophy of the Ayn Rand Institute in rejecting the position of mainstream conservatives who don't demand a completely unregulated capitalist economy. To broaden his audience, he should suggest, insinuate, and imply. While the most effective propagandists are at once forceful and subtle, Epstein is short on subtle and long on force, suggesting that he preaches to a limited choir. Follow him as he tries to disguise his attempt to manipulate readers' thoughts as an appeal to reason:

> An open mind is one that is open to all ideas, values, and behaviors. It is often accepted as the unbiased, non-dogmatic alternative to the closed mind—the deliberately stunted intellect that clings, dogmatically to a set of beliefs, despite the many facts that contradict them. An example of this latter type is the Christian fundamentalist who rejects the theory of evolution, instead claiming that "Creationism" as described in the Bible is true. He holds this belief despite the massive amount of fossil evidence, carbon dating and laboratory tests confirming the theory of evolution, while providing no real evidence supporting "Creationism."[16]

If Epstein had managed to hook a few readers, some among that number might be curious enough to see what he had to say next. His next step is to question open-mindedness, proposing that it becomes a receptacle for both good and bad:

> The first question to ask the person who tells you to keep an "open mind" is, "Open to what?" Nazism? Creationism? Female genital mutilation? Binge-drinking? . . . The answer is generally that one should be open to all philosophies, religions, cultures, and behaviors. . . . After all, rejecting any of these ideas or behaviors would be closed-minded.[17]

Epstein suggests that the open-minded have abandoned values. Should any of his readers still be hanging on, he puts their discernment to the test by asserting that anyone with an open mind has given up all moral and ethical grounding, assuming that some among his audience will accept everything they hold themselves open to hear. Epstein goes on to claim that the open-minded yield up all inclination to make independent judgments:

> The fallacy of the "open" mind is that it treats all ideas, values and behaviors, no matter how disconnected from reality or destructive of human life, as worthy of consideration. It gives no means for deciding between contradictory ideas, only the order to be open to all of them. Since one should be open to philosophies, religions, and cultures that preach reason or unreason, adherence to the facts or a denial that facts exist . . . one literally has no means of coming to any definite conclusions.[18]

Epstein's call to question others' beliefs but not your own supports ideologues' efforts to polarize politics. Committing to hold firm to one's beliefs when they, like everyone else's, are flawed robs society of its best opportunities for correction because the person anyone has the best chance of changing is one's self. If the open mind is a cover for mental laziness, then Epstein's call to never question your personal beliefs is an endorsement of the blind followership of mental laziness. The radical position of Epstein's camp cannot be ignored because it demonstrates a power to draw followers.

When conservative economists' certainty that economic regulation is wrong brought about the Garn–St. Germaine Act of 1982 regulatory controls were relaxed and ushered in decades of deregulation.[19] The fiscal irresponsibility that followed nearly sank the economy while open-minded critics of deregulation were marginalized or discredited. Subsequent congressional hearings determined that the authors of deregulation's reports reflected a tunnel vision belief that was impervious to criticism while ascendant predatory practices abruptly concentrated wealth in the top one percent,

proving that an entire government and population can be held ignorant when media is bamboozled into turning a blind eye to practices
that wouldn't pass a real investigative reporter's smell test. Ignorors
succeeded in carrying out a game plan of pure, unprincipled genius.
They are still at work. Watch for their identifying fingerprints on
political news and be alert to appearances of these tell-tale propagandists' weapons:

Loaded or hot-button words: peace, war, terrorism, freedom,
liberty, weapons of mass destruction, abortion, gay marriage, neocon,
theocon, welfare state, firestorm, hardball, etc.

Testimonials: raising up partisan "experts" whose quotes and
studies are used to add authority.

Name-calling: tax-and-spend liberals, warmongering neocons.

Plain folk and comforting tales: rolled-up sleeves, no tie or jacket,
sharing a beer, folksy phraseology.

Glittering generalities: "Wherever I go in this great country I
see . . ."

Undercutting: "Their claims are empty and their accomplishments few."

IT DOESN'T HAVE TO BE TRUE TO BE BELIEVED

Propaganda's purpose is to redirect large numbers of people's sense
of reality. Given the US Army's propagandized versions of what happened to Pat Tillman and Jessica Lynch, the reality of their situations might never have become known had it not been for the persis-
tence of Tillman's family and Lynch's humility.[20] Though an autopsy
proved that Tillman was killed by friendly fire and Lynch testified
that she was injured when her truck crashed and then cared for by
Iraqi doctors, Pentagon propagandists had chosen to cast both in
heroic roles that, aside from willingness to serve, had little basis in
truth. The Pentagon had adjusted the accounts to help put the best
face on a questionable war effort.

Propagandists are a major presence in the blogosphere, where they spread the informational equivalent of smog: dangerous to health and restrictive to visibility. The growing popularity of blogs offers a cheap and effective way for special interests to clutter bandwidth with input from special interest think tanks and trade associations. Success is somewhat automatic when all it takes is igniting audience feedback to provocative arguments, which then generate provocative responses. It is a lot like lighting fires that have a capacity for fueling themselves. The authors of the American Enterprise Institute's climate and energy studies are especially effective at enflaming like-thinkers while agitating newbies into their fold. Few blogs are neutral. An indication of partisan bloggers' success is seen when catchy phrases gain enough traction to go caroming around the blogosphere. Echoes of these were found to be rebounding about in like-thinking blog sites: "to expose the **flawed jobs reasoning** of President Obama's new carbon plan";[21] **"you just can't out-gloom an environmentalist"**;[22] **"wealth distribution from red to blue states"**;[23] "new scare for **eco-apocalyptics**";[24] "Green jobs, like **shovel-ready jobs, proved a myth**;"[25] "the **fight against climate change has fizzled**."[26] Two "fizzles" found in a single search session suggested imitative responses.

The method was simple: interesting phrases were picked from partisan blogs and launched back into the blogosphere. The bolded phrases above triggered avalanches of bloggers' responses, indicating that like-thinking responders borrow expressions from each other in an in-group choral exercise that proves its popularity through growth. The next unsurprising determination was that faithful conservative responders cluster around sponsored conservative blogs, just as Centrist to Left responders cluster around liberal blogs to sharpen their differences. Though nothing less than control of the nation's economy, social fabric, resources, and profit-taking policies are at stake, polarizing blogs erode at the public's ability to vote from clear and unbiased understanding.

HOW TO RECOGNIZE FASCISM

Four men sat a short distance from me in a Pacific Northwest coffee shop. They were big men with big voices, so there was no trouble catching their drift. The two Lefties vs. two Righties took each other's political teasing in stride until the topic swung to affordable healthcare, at which point one of the Righties became emotional. He stabbed a finger toward one of the Lefties, said something about waiting months for appointments like Canadian Socialists have to do, and slapped a hand on the table, which turned some heads. He growled that the Fascist-liberal government was out to strangle business and f— up jobs. The Lefties laughed. He muttered something I missed, shoved away from the table, and headed off with his friend in tow.

A proper education would have taught him that the Fascism label doesn't fit liberals. That the Right and Left reflexively throw it at each other so carelessly reveals a worrisome ignorance of history. Given the terrible cost of WWII, concerned citizens should study up on what Fascism really means if they are to avoid the penalty in George Santayana's warning that those who don't learn from history are doomed to repeat it.

The big fellow at the coffee shop showed ignorance by linking liberals with Fascism. Real Fascists are with us, though they hide in plain sight under other labels. You can spot them by their signature mean-spirited warping of truth; contempt for anyone who looks, speaks, or thinks differently; and love of violence. Though the destructive practices of WWII's Nazi alliance should have warned the world against Fascism, it still lives, and there are signs that it is rearing its ugly head again in America and elsewhere. Its resurgence under other names is made possible largely because people are so blinded by ignorance of what Fascism truly means that they are unable to defend against it.

Nazi-type propaganda's roots are buried so deep in history that it would be futile to attempt to assign it a time of origin. Nero employed it when he cast blame on Christians for the burning of Rome. Fascist-type propaganda figured heavily in Niccolo Machiavelli's classic treatise on government, *The Prince*. But the most famous Fascist propagandist of all time was Adolf Hitler's minister of propaganda, Dr. Joseph Goebbels, who wrote,

> It would not be impossible to prove with sufficient repetition and a psychological understanding of the people concerned that a square is in fact a circle. They are mere words, and words can be molded until they clothe ideas and disguise.[27]

HITLER AND MUSSOLINI

Hitler adopted Goebbels's understanding that words are tools to be shaped to satisfy lust for power. Of course, open-minded respect for knowledge was counterproductive to Nazi purpose, hence the book burnings in Germany's town squares. Yet seventy-five years after Adolf Hitler and Benito Mussolini tried to impose Fascism on the Western world, the coffee shop debater was clueless about what Fascism is or that true Fascism is the wedding of a strong dictator with a nation's corporate structure. Hitler reflected cynical confidence in his ability to control his people's thoughts in writing, "I use emotion for the many and reserve reason for the few," and "If you tell a big enough lie and tell it frequently enough, it will be believed."[28]

Snippets from Hitler's playbook for manipulating the consciousness of his nation give a picture of the man. Believing in his heart that he would, in the manner of Alexander the Great and Napoleon, rule the entire Western world, he wasn't shy about setting down thoughts about how he would make that happen. Hitler studied Machiavelli's works, from which he read, "Politics have no relations to morals" and "Men are so simple and so much inclined to obey immediate needs that a deceiver will never lack victims for his deceptions."[29] Hitler understood that whoever controls language controls the nation, and by means of his dynamic speeches and dominance over media, he narrowed Nazi Germany's dialogue. His words took on a steely sense of aggressive purpose when he went to war, writing, "It is not truth that matters, but victory," and "The very first essential for success is a perpetually constant and regular employment of violence."[30]

While Hitler's words reflect a pathological coherence, the illogic and excess of Mussolini's propaganda makes it difficult for twenty-first-century historians to understand how he managed to drag Italy, an idealistic young nation cobbled together from city-states, into war. Italians, with a shortage of experience in dealing with dictatorial excess, simply fell victim to a megalomaniacal despot. By force of personality and ruthlessness, Mussolini amassed a concentration of personal power his young nation had not experienced before, a power so absolute that he was able to force national support for a senseless attack on Ethiopia so that his war machine might acquire a taste for blood. More than Hitler, Mussolini was fond of sounding off about what he took to be the virtues of Fascism: "Fascism should rightly be called Corporatism as it is the merger of corporate and government power," and "The truth is that men are tired of liberty."[31]

Fascist dictators were convinced that unfettered access to knowledge was dangerous. Knowledge had to be suppressed, censored, selectively ducted and denied—even created. The Fascists' use of language, though grossly perverted, is instructive in its belief that politics has everything to do with ambition but little to do with responsibility. Nazi purpose was furthered by a social tunnel vision that dismissed the worth of every genetic variation outside the pale of "Aryan superiority."[32]

THE WEST ADOPTS PROPAGANDA

Before Hitler's rise to power, Charles Masterman, chief of Britain's War Propaganda Bureau, or WPB, established the tone for Allied military propaganda during WWI. Masterman wrote that his department's policies were intended to "direct the thought of most of the world."[33] Since official voices avoided speaking of propaganda so forthrightly, it was a bold move indeed and one that would soon be copied in the United States. President Wilson, who swept into office on a platform of "Peace without Victory," had actually been angling for a way to join the war. He commissioned a propaganda office known as the Creel Commission to copy what the British had done—that is, direct the thoughts of people—and before long, images of Nazi atrocities had pacifist Americans demanding German blood.[34] This is not to say that the United States should have stayed out of it but that the tool for uniting the nation behind the war effort was sharpened by publicizing not only war facts but exaggerated facts, which was deemed necessary at the time.

Wartime propaganda played a role in the development of Walter Lippmann's Progressive Theory of Liberal Democratic Thought, a scheme for manufacturing public consent to support the government's priorities.[35] Lippmann, the most influential journalist of the mid-twentieth century, saw weaknesses in uncontrolled public opinion and set out to correct that. Between the two World Wars, American propaganda was strategized to manufacture public consent for whatever topped leadership's agenda. When leadership chose a direction, the public mind was shaped to support it, and the deal was done. Genetic markers of the techniques showed them to be indistinguishable from those used by Stalin, Hitler, apartheid regimes, imperial Japan, Mussolini, and every tyrant who bothered to study power politics. The underlying thought shared by Lippmann and the Powers was that it was necessary that a select few who shared higher-level understanding steer the masses toward a future they were too dense and uneducated to comprehend. To bring that about, the Powers had only to keep the people ignorant of other options.

The Select Few believed they were joined in a moral purpose that justified whatever they chose to do. If the masses were left to make decisions for themselves, the wheels would soon fall off the socioeconomic cart, causing widespread distress. Better to save them from themselves and save the nation from profit-diminishing recessions, strikes, and social strife. On the public side of the Great Oz's curtain, feel-good buzzwords and phrases woven into propaganda's fabric held the masses together. Behind the curtain, planners plotted the best ways to protect their interests from what Lippmann called "the trampling and the roar of a bewildered herd."[36]

The Select Few believed they were a people set apart. Insiders came to know them as the "Specialized Class," or the "Caste," a super-class that tended the duties of planning, prioritizing, and executing projects that favored the Powers That Be. To become a member of the Specialized Class, one had to be socially connected or demon-strate zeal for the Powers' agenda. The Specialized Class developed a special mentality that stood above constraints of oaths of office and general welfare. As codes for economics and governance took shape within the Caste, so did their functional bodies of knowledge and ignorance. The Caste's knowledge base centered on the dark art of political expediency. Their non-knowledge, born of willful igno-rance of the needs of the bewildered herd, put self-interest above general welfare. Should that description seem a bit hazy, a reading of Dennis Thompson's book *Ethics in Congress: From Individual to Insti-tutional Corruption* explains how truth was distorted to keep citizens from marching on the capitol.[37]

CAN WAR'S IMAGE BE SANITIZED?

The nation's record of involvements beyond its borders—Nicaragua, Panama, Iraq, Grenada, Chile, Guatemala, Vietnam, and the list goes on—involved unpublicized incidents that would have left stains on the nation's image had they not been swept under carpets of national security classification. A neutral onlooker might have asked what, aside from protecting identities of operatives and delicate negoti-ating points, needed to be hidden. In fact, much of the dirt involved embarrassing accounts that could have ended careers if brought to light. But secrecy is necessary. In defense of the practice of classifying documents that would otherwise be open to the public, it is easier to keep the ship of state on course when free of distracting revelations and damning accounts of misdeeds that question office holders' fitness for public service. It was, in part, that type of revelation that had officials' knickers in a bind over WikiLeaks's revelations. More hacking attempts will take place, if only to earn the reward of embarrassing the high and mighty, which is enough reward to keep copycat hackers chipping away at walls of secrecy. They despise not knowing. Citizens, likewise, should despise not knowing, for it is impossible to correct improper practices that are held secret.

The will to penetrate government security is fueled in part by idealistic contempt for federal shenanigans and the somewhat subjective definition of terrorism. According to US Army manuals, terrorism is "the calculated use of violence or the threat of violence to attain goals that are political, religious or ideological in nature . . . through intimidation, coercion or fear."[38] When comparing the offenses of al-Qaeda, Boko Haram, the Taliban, and the Red Brigade with great nations' uses of violence, it becomes clear that both sides' hands are unclean. The comparison teeters on whether the overt savagery of Islamic beheadings and coldhearted Sharia Law exceed the awful total of noncombatant deaths and injuries during Middle East and Asian wars.

When it comes to generating wartime deaths, the United States is near the top. The count of 100,000 to 120,000 Iraqis killed during the initial conflicts continues to climb due to the dusting of Iraq's countryside with powdered residue of US projectile tips made from depleted uranium (DU). Radiological effects from depleted uranium are the cause of skyrocketing rates of childhood cancers and birth defects according to Iraqi and World Health Organization surveys. Iraq's 1991 incidence of cancer stood at a stable 40 per 100,000. By 1995 it rose to 800 per 100,000 and climbed to 1,600 per 100,000 in the year 2000. The rate of neurological defects in newborns has risen to thirty-three times that of Western Europe.[39] The incidence of birth defects near Fallujah is at a level where women fear becoming pregnant because the local rate of birth defects due to radiation stands at fourteen times that of Hiroshima and Nagasaki following the explosion of nuclear bombs there.[40]

Depressing reports of the effects of DU are brushed aside by news of brutal beheadings and assassinations. If there is to be any progress toward making the planet a peaceful home for children, people must be informed of what Paul Harvey called "The rest of the story," and that includes the raw cost of war to both sides. But since the goal of propaganda is to control the thoughts of a population, one of its most effective tools is suppression or omission of uncomfortable information, such as the Iraqi cancer statistics cited above. Balanced understanding becomes impossible when news is purposefully filtered to craft a history more capable of generating respect and support for the government's initiatives. But with the conduct of wars necessarily secretive, their sponsors and agents are the only ones privy to tactics, deployments, and uncensored results, while home folks are privy to a different package, one aimed at building support for the war effort. The lasting effects of wartime propaganda confound peaceful intentions, since the invaders and the invaded write contrary histories, the losers' histories being significantly more accurate in ways that help explain ISIS's hatred of the West. Contrary histories, both of them flawed, ensure mutual ignorance that holds peace at bay.

FEDERAL AND CORPORATE PROPAGANDA

Noam Chomsky, a plain-spoken Jewish intellectual, wouldn't have survived Hitler's Germany, where racially pure groupthink left no room for his kind. Chomsky has become a modern-day prophet who speaks truth to power, which fails to endear him to the Powers That Be but earns him accolades from thinkers who admire his courage. In his book *Media Control*, Chomsky sets down reasons why politics' questionable adventures into dis- and misinformation tarnish the nation's standing with citizens and trading partners. The following paraphrased excerpts from it form the core of his observations on the government's use of propaganda to misinform and disinform:

Lavish applications of verbal cover-up cosmetics laid on to disguise behavioral or policy blemishes.

Discrediting unrelated opposing opinions well fortified with facts.

Fabricating horror stories and inciting fears to gain support for taking the nation to war.

Injecting hot-button revelations when the public needs to be distracted from focusing on domestic needs that aren't on the official agenda.

Directing blame for failures or excesses toward the opposition.

Making silk purses from sows' ears by dressing up images of unpopular initiatives or stretching the qualifications of unqualified appointees and candidates.

Justifying plans, outcomes, appointments, purchases, voting records, treaties, finances, and political bedfellows that can't stand on their own merit.[41]

While Chomsky addresses the government's manipulation of knowledge, corporate America's adventures in propaganda deserve equal attention. Corporate propaganda may be as innocent as arranging to showcase a brand of muscle car during a TV car chase. Or it may involve sifting consumer reviews to publish only the positive. But it also crosses into the darker zone of masking information that could cast a pall over a brand's reputation. The R. J. Reynolds Tobacco Company (RJR) case was a textbook example of how commercial propagandists handle such issues.

The nationwide antismoking campaign had RJR on the ropes. Sales of Winstons and Camels were down, and the future for cigarette sales was looking dim. Ads that coupled smoking with success, glamour, and adventure were no longer working, signaling a need to change the theme and the message. The new face for smokers became Heartland Man, a healthy middle-aged Minnesotan with a baseball cap and a pickup. He was a man's man whose scripted message said, "I'm one of America's 45 million smokers. I'm not a moaner or a whiner. But I'm getting fed up. I'd like to get the government off my back."[42] He went on to explain that banning cigarettes was just a first step. Next, the government will "go for liquor and fast food and buttermilk and who knows what else. There's a line of dominoes a mile long," said Heartland Man.

Small-government advocates were delighted. RJR's Heartland Man ads, while falling short of rescuing cigarettes' reputation, were more effective at implanting suspicion of governmental intrusion into private lives than anything the Powers had tried. Shortly after the first Heartland Man ad aired, the firm of Mongoven, Biscoe and Duchen, RJR's propaganda specialists, recommended that Heartland Man become the centerpiece of RJR's advertising campaign.[43] The new campaign deemphasized smoking and nicotine, focusing instead on the wrongness of an invasive, intrusive, and too-powerful government. The next step was to enlist hundreds of organizations from across corporate America to join the movement, which was by then known as GGOOB, for Get Government Off Our Backs.

The US Chamber of Commerce embraced GGOOB, as did the NRA; the Traditional Values Coalition; Small Business of America; the Seniors Coalition; and Americans for Tax Reform, headed by none other than Grover Norquist.[44] In the stampede to join Heartland Man's opposition to Big Government, it was all but forgotten that RJR had initiated GGOOB. RJR had planted a seed in fertile conservative ground where it thrived and grew. While GGOOB provided only a modest success for RJR, it was a huge success for neoconservatives, whose followers happily chanted, "Get government off our backs!"

By the end of 1995, there was evidence that the GGOOB campaign had moderated the downturn in cigarettes sales, but that was only the tip of the iceberg. Norquist and others managed to leverage GGOOB's considerable antigovernment influence to put a freeze on new health and environmental regulations.[45] Three men, Thomas Synhorst (former aide to Senators Charles Grassley and Bob Dole and an RJR smokers' rights advocate), Douglas Goodyear (an RJR staffer on the GGOOB project), and Timothy Hyde (who served as RJR's public affairs chief), joined to formulate bigger plans for GGOOB. It had grown to become a propagandist's dream come true.

In 1997, the three formed a Washington, DC, lobbying firm, calling it the DCI Group, a generic name that carried no negative baggage.[46] DCI offered a special service for politics and business that builds movements by pulling strings in the shadows. It is staffed with expert propagandists who engender "desired outcomes" by creating illusions of public support. From a single-issue beginning at RJR to GGOOB to Grover Norquist to the DCI Group, one disingenuous movement within a stressed tobacco company grew to become a for-hire service specializing in manipulating the mind of America for clients able to pay their fees. Thanks to RJR and Big Tobacco's trials, DCI rose to royal status among ignorors.

PROPAGANDA: THE BIG PICTURE

Propaganda is useful and necessary when bonding a nation against belligerent enemies, and it is certainly a treasured part of Americana for whipping up support for favorite sports teams. When commercial propaganda touts fire sales or rock concerts, it is simply hawking opportunities for consumers, but when misuse of language, censorship, suppression of knowledge, or distortion of truth are willfully used to control public thought, some agency should be positioned to call foul. This is not a new idea; versions of it keep witnesses from lying to juries and restrain applicants from cheating on job applications.

When public information's evil twin, propaganda, moves to pollute public dialogue, media is its messenger and should be liable for a share of the penalties when journalistic due diligence is not employed to identify the actors behind wrongdoing. It is a matter of ethics, not law. US culture is begging for an effective ethic that promotes halting, censuring, and penalizing propagandists who cross the line, no matter how high their position. Since laws are invented when society fails and society has dropped this ball, a case exists for criminalizing willful public lying. The importance of this cannot be overstated, for the practice of publicizing expedient lies (i.e., propaganda) to secure profit or power has become embedded in corporate and governmental culture, weakening society and the nation. Ignorors cannot be permitted to continue their everyday practice of polluting public dialog and vandalizing language.

CHAPTER 14
COSTS AND CONSEQUENCES OF IGNORANCE

*No one knows the cost of a defective product—don't tell me
you do. You know the cost of replacing it but not the cost of
a dissatisfied customer.*

—W. E. Demming

Except for acts of God, forces of nature, wear and tear, and the erosive passage of time, the cost of things gone wrong may be charged to ignorance. When things go badly, the culprit is seldom bad luck, that "stuff happens," or abject stupidity. If one corporation were tasked with cleaning up the messes caused by ignorance, it would be the biggest business in the land, but costly effects of ignorance don't have to be so extreme. They are minimized when people admit their ignorance and open their minds.

In a perfect world, ignorance wouldn't be as great a concern as it is in the confusion of our here and now. In a utopian dream world, news, political campaigns, sales pitches, sermons, watercooler gossip—every word would reflect pure natural reality. Que será, será. No manipulation, no exploitation, no disinformation in a world free of ignorant meddling. No ego trips or inflated ambitions allowed. People would accept whatever befell them with equal resignation and without being misguided by the faulty notion that it is solely the faults of other people that bring about negative effects that should result in punishment. In our vanity, we believe that someone should bear the blame for every bad outcome and someone deserves the reward for every good one, as though the effects of nature's interventions would halt should humans cease their activities.

PAYING THE COST

The cost of ignorance-tainted outcomes may be measured in different currencies. For example, the costs of conducting an ill-conceived war without knowing the consequences are complex: civilian casualties, destruction of infrastructure, life-long incapacity of those wounded, a furthering of regional instability, provocation of international terrorism, and diverting national treasuries from meeting internal needs. None of those can be measured solely in dollars. The budgetary problem is further complicated by untraceable losses of currency, diplomatic setbacks, and the gray area of funds spent on private armies of civilian contractors.

Not knowing causes missed opportunities when market fluctuations say buy or sell, or when a medical exam would have discovered a small, operable tumor. Not knowing burdens college graduates studying for degrees in fields already overpopulated by applicants. It is the villain when debt incurred from casual spending transfers control of one's future to financiers. Not knowing turns an experimental recipe into a culinary disaster. Whenever not knowing is involved, actions reliably diminish in value and cause personal injury, pain, regret, loss of competitive position, disgrace, and even death. All of that and more may be tallied against ignorance.

The organizational cost of not knowing was described by Graham Allison, professor at Harvard's Kennedy School of Government and a leading analyst of American defense policy. In a 2001 essay in the *Economist*, Allison wrote,

> Yet as the American government scrambles to pursue a war for which it was not prepared, it must, in the idiom, "go with what we've got." Assembling a coalition of very strange bedfellows, acquiring intelligence from sources and by methods it had mostly neglected, and jerry-rigging defenses around the most obvious vulnerabilities, it gallops off in all directions. It does so without a comprehensive assessment of the threats it now faces, and lacking a coherent strategy for combating mega-terrorism. In contrast, Mr.

bin Laden and his al-Qaeda network had been thinking, planning, and training for this war for most of a decade.[1]

Much of the fiscal waste attributable to a dysfunctional Congress can be traced to ignorance. Ignorance teams with narrowed partisan frames. Representatives of law, industry, agriculture, the environment, natural resources, energy, the military, education, healthcare, transportation, foreign trade, aeronautics, space, and communications show insufficient understanding of how all interests must be woven into one socioeconomic fabric. By focusing on sponsors' narrow needs, they blind themselves to broader issues of infrastructure, distribution of income and wealth, tax reform, energy policy, education, and costs of living. In the name of cost control, politicians ignore infrastructure maintenance, causing postponed repair to become wholesale replacement as budget-cutters perpetuate the folly of kicking the maintenance can down the road. The result is all clash and little cooperation, leaving the nation and its people poorer. The fault lies with narrowness of interests when practical solutions require input from generalists' minds. Instead, actors choose to dwell within *ism*-atic frames that exclude vital concerns lying outside their sponsors' interests. Great wrongs are done when the actors compartmentalize knowledge into two bodies: what they know and suppress vs. what they know and profess.

With the zeal of NFL teams, each *ism* struggles to be a winner, even though winning can't help but unbalance and fracture the nation. Cooperation yields to Darwinistic competition, in which vested interests vie for supremacy. The business sector *ism* chooses not to understand that what's narrowly good for business may not be good for the economy, the militarist *ism* refuses to acknowledge that what's good for the Pentagon may not be good for global peace, Wall Street has trouble accepting that what's good for banking and finance may not be good for the nation's gross domestic product, and what's good for large-scale agribusiness may not be good for the land. All this because narrowness of thinking and competition displace cooperation as the ruling paradigm. It comes at an appalling cost.

GASOLINE PRICING: A CASE STUDY IN NOT KNOWING

Because the price of gasoline in the United States is low by international standards, the public is lulled into accepting the price at the pump as a reflection of market-driven pricing factors. Voters' ignorance of behind-the-scenes manipulation of petroleum economics permits sponsors of veiled practices to continue enjoying hidden federal support. The price of a gallon of gasoline is something of a mystery in that it often costs more next door to refineries than it does a thousand miles away, and we don't know why. A gallon of gas cost twenty-nine cents in 1955. Adjusting the buying power of a 1955 dollar to 2012 value would inflate the price of one gallon to $1.76.[2] But the Cato Institute's accountants thought that the change in disposable per capita income should be factored in also, which would bring the price up to $5.17 per gallon. Was change in disposable income a real cost of gasoline? In 1996, when gas cost $1.20 per gallon,[3] an in-depth study of gasoline pricing was conducted by the International Center for Technological Assessment (ICTA) and published under the title "The Real Price of Gas."[4] The ICTA sought to determine direct and indirect cost factors of gasoline production to find out where petroleum money comes from and where it goes. The report broke the cost of gasoline into five areas: tax subsidies; government program subsidies; protection costs applied to oil shipment and vehicle service; environmental, health, and social costs stemming from use of gasoline; and other costs arising from motor vehicle use. The study didn't include undefined costs of diplomatic and military attempts to control or influence the international flow of petroleum.

The figures they gathered listed annual total costs drawn from different sources with differing interests. They were so different that answers to the same questions led to totals ranging from $558.7 billion to $1.69 trillion, which translates to per gallon pricing of $5.60 to $15.14.[5] The spread between low and high numbers shows how wildly figures from different sources varied, reflecting the biased lenses used to scrutinize costs according to different analysts' orientations. Beginning with the ICTA's spread of base figures and inflating the per gallon price to 2015's buying power, a gallon would have cost somewhere between $8.45 to $22.80. The only thing that can be trusted about petroleum accounting is that prices at the pump will never reflect society's total cost for fuel.

If it takes that much money to cover the seen and unseen costs of using motor fuel, how is it that the actual price can be so much lower? Furthermore, who picks up the tab for the difference between total cost and the price at the pump? Even if the figures are off by as much as 25 percent to 50 percent, the disparity between the price at the pump and the ICTA's data suggests that either a lot of money is moving under the radar or we are incurring expenses that society will have to pay later. During the years between the 1996 study and today, Big Oil regularly posted record profits while enjoying $2.4 billion in tax breaks in 2013 alone.[6] All the while, the industry's continuing benefits appeared immune to attempts to balance the federal budget. It is meaningfully odd that mainstream media didn't trumpet this questionable arrangement to the public, as though it wasn't and isn't newsworthy. Smart money will bet that the Powers That Be will continue the gag order on discussing petroleum economics during presidential debates. We are not meant to know.

MAKING A DIFFERENCE

It is people who don't practice cooperation who are most adept at climbing corporate ladders. At lower levels, normal people's punishments for careless pursuit of power or gain come in the form of not being invited to the next poker game or being shunned at a ladies' book club. Corrective hinting works best in the world of nurses, waitstaff, clerks, tradesmen, and laborers but not at the top where competitive actors insulate themselves from criticism by mixing with fellow offenders of their breed. And then B-Lab arrived on the corporate scene.

A corrective spark is being fanned by B-Lab, a nonprofit created by three entrepreneurs, Jay Cohen Gilbert, Bart Houlahan, and Andrew Kassoy, who came up with the concept of a "triple bottom line" that addresses not only profit but the needs of people and the planet.[7] The *New York Times* reported in June 2013 that, after Gilbert lost his firm to investors who dismantled his people-and-planet emphasis to maximize profit, Gilbert set out to win legal recognition for a new corporate structure that protects firms from rapacious restructuring, the result being B-Lab.[8] A recent survey listed twenty-four states that recognize B-Lab companies along with ten more that are considering it.[9] The B-Lab plan invites corporations to forego antisocial business expedients in order to lessen costs to society in general and B-Lab corporations in particular. Corporations on the fence ask, "If we choose to switch to B-Lab practices, can the costs of serving people and the planet actually be offset by sufficient profit? And if not, might the benefits to people and the planet plus the intangible benefits of doing the right thing 'balance the books' for investors?"

The B in B-Lab stands for Benefit, which accounts for businesses in the movement describing themselves as "Benefit Corporations." What separates them from other businesses is breadth of understanding. When the triple bottom line of a certified B-Corporation gives consideration to profit, people, and the planet it means more than donating to charities. According to the *New York Times*, "They have to share information and decision-making with employees. They must have environmental policies that take into account their pollution footprint."[10] Companies choosing the B-Lab route must pay a certification fee and complete extensive documentation that establishes baselines for scorecards. As might be expected, when B-Lab first floats its plan before boards of directors representing stockholders, the initial reaction is negative. Focus has to be broadened from fixation on profit to inclusion of the people who make a business possible and the planet on which the corporation exists. B-Lab's short history delivers proof that moving from the selective ignorance of profit maximizers to broader knowledge and responsibility can pay off in the real world.

THE COST TO SOCIETY

A sign that once hung above the door of a Puget Sound school board's meeting room said, "If you think education is expensive, try ignorance." That quotation, attributed to lawyer and educator Derek Bok, may be the most unheeded warning ever written. Society keeps trying ignorance only to find that, beyond not working, it leaves wreckage, confusion, and broken dreams in its wake. None of that is arguable. Though we know what ignorance is capable of doing, knowledge seems incapable of keeping it from constraining debate when serious situations call for deep thinking.

Just as prisons are schools for crime, the federal government has become a school for irresponsible budgeting, or budgeting in support of wrong purposes. Congresspersons stand beholden to corporate sponsors who fund their reelection campaigns, which obligates them to discourage independent-minded legislators from opposing the Powers' interests. Two major penalties for opposition are (a) that no bill backed by an independent sponsor would ever see its way out of committee and (b) facing insurmountable opposition should they seek reelection. The way things stand, officeholders are obliged to dance with whoever finances their election, which means that the Powers' interests are served first. The nation isn't ignorant of what's going on: enough knowledge of impropriety floats about to demand a housecleaning, yet little gets done. That will continue as long as the public's mind is distracted by a diet of misdirecting infotainment that keeps essential issues from the forefront of public thought. And the cost continues to rise.

No thinking person is ignorant of what political pork is or how it is used. The proverbial "pork barrel" was named for the pre–Civil War practice of giving slaves large barrels of salt pork, with each slave trying to get as much of it as possible.[11] In pork's current application, favored constituents are thanked for campaign donations with gifts of federal support for pet projects. Once conducted under the table, pork has become so embedded in Congress that few alarms go off at porkish taps into federal funds, which brings up an interesting twist on knowledge: what good is it if it lacks potency? When impropriety and even criminality become so commonplace that they can operate in the open, it means that cultural standards have been corrupted. When people know but don't act, for all practical purposes knowledge becomes the functional equivalent of ignorance. Citizens Against Government Waste (CAGW) listed characteristics of pork that accurately describe the situation: a federal expenditure is pork when it is requested by only one chamber of Congress, is not specifically authorized, is not competitively awarded, is not requested by the president, greatly exceeds the president's budget request, is not the subject of congressional hearings, and serves only a local or special interest.[12]

The reasons that needful situations fail to get helpful attention were examined in Robert Proctor's study of causes of ignorance, which became the starting point of the new science of agnotology, from the Greek *agnosis* ("not knowing").[13] Factors that keep the public complacent in the face of outrageous offenses hadn't been adequately inspected before, leaving the Powers free to mold public opinion to their purposes with little consideration for the effects of their agendas on general welfare. For example, the Powers' rationalization for the Reagan era's rush to deregulate was that unrestrained capitalism would put more money into the hands of job providers. Voters who were led to support deregulation failed to foresee that corporate backers of that legislation would ship profits to offshore accounts to avoid the civic responsibility of taxation. They also failed to anticipate the bloated executive salaries that sucked lifeblood from corporate treasuries. *Bloomberg News* reported that corporate directors' pay had hit $251,000 for 250 hours of work.[14] Nabors Oil's 2009 three-day retreat to Bermuda's Fairmont Hotel earned board members $430,000 after expenses. Intuitive Surgical paid its board members $139,000 for each of five meetings.[15] Fast-forward to 2012 when Hewlett Packard's board members were awarded $941,802, topping Apple's $898,993 compensation.[16] Corporations' failure to reverse the increasing disparity between production line and executive pay demonstrates ignorance of the dire effects of unrestrained wage disparity. Yet knowledge of the numbers appears powerless to put a dent in the Powers' acquisitive excess.

Awareness of wrongdoing becomes more common as transparency thins the fog of misinformation. Even some conservatives, having taken note of Main Street America's slide into economic serfdom, are questioning whether everything that's good for business is necessarily good for the economy that supports it. But consumers have yet to recognize that, along with the advantages of big-box merchandising, local businesses close their doors, average wages drop, and profit generated in local big-box stores is shipped off to distant corporate headquarters. The community is drained of locally generated and spent profit, eliminating the economic fertilizer that otherwise keeps local economies healthy. The nation as a whole suffers as big-box accountants employ tax dodges unavailable to local merchants.

A cost that cannot be measured in dollars is incurred when people are rudely awakened from ignorance to discover they have been duped. Reduced buying power, underwater mortgages, and loss of retirement benefits jar them from the intellectual slumber that allowed them to be taken in. As they awaken to understand how they have been victimized, the government that allowed it to happen suffers a loss of trust that undercuts public approval for tax-supported institutions and government in general. Today's emotional demand for smaller government is the result of a government that isn't serving the needs of its people. The cost is felt everywhere, from support for schools to low voter turnouts. It expresses itself in heated discussions as members of opposing *isms* demonize their opposite numbers' characters, tactics, goals, and rightness with God.

CRAB TRAPS AND PEOPLE TRAPS

The casual type of ignorance reflected by not caring enough exacts a cost from shellfish populations in the coastal waters of the Pacific Northwest when crab traps come untied from their buoy lines and become lost on the bottom. When traps' too-hasty owners tie bad knots in frayed lines to secure traps to buoys, they aren't thinking of what happens when one of their knots works loose. They know, but not at a level that polices behavior. If a knot slips or a frayed line breaks, as they sometimes do, a lost crab trap becomes an unstoppable fishing machine. Crabs attracted to the original bait enter the traps but cannot exit. They die there, and when they do they become a second round of bait that attracts more crabs that become food for still more, setting off a continuous cycle. Once the metal of the trap rusts away, the spot is marked by a midden of shells where hundreds of crabs died. Insufficient consciousness of the outcomes of culpably unconscientious work results in aircraft engines failing in flight, homes flooded due to bad plumbing, and food poisoning from poorly maintained restaurant kitchens. Simply knowing isn't enough; knowing has to be hardwired to behavior.

Though cruel fate may be the cause of much financial disaster, crippling debt more often results from bad personal choices, such as weekly visits to casinos. When funds are short, unwillingness to pass up golf invitations, fishing trips, spa treatments, recreational shopping, smoking, daily stops at Starbucks, and payments on a new car transfer control over a family's finances to possibly predatory lenders. For those who are married, the cost of overspending is measurable in guilt, high debt service charges, damage to family well-being and opportunity, and unavoidable domestic strife. It happens whenever spenders choose ignorance of financial reality over disciplined financial planning. A great amount of consumer debt results from lazy minds that find ignorance of consequences comfortably undemanding.

A friend who knows a thing or two about economics keeps

reminding me that debt never sleeps, suggesting that a writer ought to do something on the topic. He might be on to something. Count the places in any town of over twenty thousand inhabitants that, along with providing worthwhile services, profit from helping to put people into debt. First come payday loan shops. Next are vendors of goods and services that accept credit cards. Add businesses that offer discounts on your first purchase if you'll take a few moments to fill out a credit card application. Last but not least are vendors of big-ticket items that require no payments for the first six months or longer. And don't forget banks.

If it weren't for offering too much credit to those least able to handle it, financial services could be seen in a better light. No one checks for credit worthiness when customers fill out credit card applications at check stands. Shakespeare's Polonius was on the right track when he advised, "Neither a borrower nor a lender be," but that advice doesn't fit in a credit economy.[17] If high school students were required to take consumer economics classes, at least they would be warned about the dark side of credit that enslaves more than it enables. When wages are budgeted to cover the bills, one is still in control; when bills and out-of-pocket spending exceed wages, lenders take control.

Once control is lost, lenders bind borrowers into life-limiting positions. The payday loan business isn't catch-and-release financing; they have you till debt do you part. Once in the hole, down goes the credit rating and up go credit charges. In many cases, debt is a clear statement of the difference between knowledge and ignorance. Lenders know what's happening, that borrowers borrow while not knowing what they're doing. Lending is a knowledge-driven industry, while borrowing is too often an ignorance-driven activity. The lowest bottom-feeders operate at the nether fringes of the debt consolidation and settlement industry where they trust that applicants for their services are too ignorant to read the fine print.

Debtors compound their misery through poor money management, like blowing a week's pay at the casino on the way home from work. Like junkies putting it up their noses, like enjoying pricey but unaffordable vacations, once spenders tumble into debt spirals they find they are stuck with the twin burdens of living under a load of debt and knowing they are guilty of putting their families' futures squarely behind the eight ball. J. Reuben Clark, a professor at George Washington University Law School, wrote,

> Interest never sleeps nor sickens nor dies. . . . Once in debt, interest is your companion every minute of the day and night; you cannot shun it or slip away from it; you cannot dismiss it; it yields neither to entreaties, demands or orders; and whenever you get in its way or cross its course or fail to meet its demands, it crushes you.[18]

CONSUMER IGNORANCE

Society's most pervasive program of education is advertising. By turning on a TV or radio, opening a newspaper or magazine, reading the backside of a cash register receipt, or looking at store window displays, we are educated to want to make life more fulfilling and beautiful by imitating the lifestyles of fulfilled and beautiful people. Once led to identify with advertising's beautiful people, places, and activities, it is a small step to wanting their cars, homes, gadgets, cosmetics, and ask-your-doctor-today performance enhancers. No one is there to caution, "Can you afford this?" The system works because desire trumps reason. Selling and buying should be a win-win transaction, but when buying is an emotional response instead of an informed choice, marketers win and buyers lose. Of course, the buyers get something, but before each transaction they should ask themselves, "Am I giving up a measure of control over my finances and future?" If a seller or lender gains control while a buyer loses control, the cost is too steep.

Effective advertising teaches consumers to react, not think. Thoughtful consideration isn't encouraged by "Ask your doctor today," "This one-time offer expires tonight," or "We have only one in stock at this price." You will never hear a time-share sales person say, "Take the information home and think about it." Consumers' desires are more easily shaped when economic defenses are methodically dismantled and replaced by desire. Not content with tapping into the public's income day by day or week by week, marketers convince buyers to commit next month's and next year's income toward satisfying wants. Consumer ignorance is exploited when personal desires or preferences are manipulated. An excellent defense was described in a bumper sticker that read, "How to get more of what you want? Want less."

Advertisements that inform the public of the features of new products and their advantages over competing products provide useful education. When ads tell where products can be purchased at temporary discounts and special terms of purchase, they deliver more useful education. Ads serve as buyers' guides, and that is good and useful, but low-aiming advertising targets consumers who lack the buying power to provide necessities and got that way by making unwise decisions. Understanding that consumers who have little but dreams to sustain them are especially vulnerable to emotion-stirring sales pitches spurs unscrupulous sellers and lenders to further undermine their meager lives, for it is the financially ignorant who are most easily manipulated.

A concept in law that runs almost parallel to manipulative advertising is that of attractive nuisances.[19] If a neighbor's child wanders onto one's property and falls into the swimming pool, the property owner is responsible for having maintained an attractive nuisance. Even with fences, locks, and No Trespassing signs in place, a measure of responsibility cannot be dodged. The idea is that children are naturally curious and lack understanding of property rights. Effective advertising is designed to cause people to become unnaturally curious about attractive things and be drawn in. When that curiosity couples with poor understanding of consumer economics, shallow thinkers are set up to make poor decisions. A series of such decisions paves the way to a life of poverty while ensuring unfunded retirement.

When the 2014 average savings of sixty-five-year-old wage earners stood at only $56,000, an amount that at 6 percent would earn $3,360 of annual retirement income, it seems probable that a great number of people are short of self-protective financial knowledge.[20]

The amount of $3,360 is clearly inadequate to meet retirement expenses, leaving the state to cover emergency expenses for much of its aging population. If traced backward, the government's staggering cost of covering basic living costs for tens of millions of unfunded seniors can be connected not only with personal ignorance of principles of consumer economy but also shortsighted national economic policy and predatory finance and marketing tactics. In supporting policies that stagnate wages, the Powers That Be demonstrate ignorance of the importance of wages to a healthy economy. The American public matches that ignorance by showing itself to be notably ignorant of fine points of budgeting, unaware that, while cash and savings live on the plus side of the ledger, debt lives on the minus side as negative money. Total American consumer debt at the time of this writing, according to the Federal Reserve Household Credit Report, stands at $11.31 trillion, while the average debt balance of each credit card is $7,194.[21]

The numbers don't matter as much as the scope and force of what's behind them. Borrowers should understand that debt is another kind of money: negative money. If I owe you money, my debt to you is your asset—you can sell the IOU. The $11.31 trillion in consumer debt is being sold back and forth, as speculators sniff out new ways to profit from trading debt instruments. Borrowers should know that, depending on the market, traders can make almost as much money from buying and selling debt as they can from dealing in the positive money market. Courses in consumer economics fail to enlighten students about the business of trading debt and why lobbyists are hired to ensure that debt will thrive.

WHERE WE STAND

People would do a better job of staying out of debt if national fiscal policy served as a role model for responsible budgeting. Instead, banks and borrowers, following the lead of Harvard economists, embrace debt as a basic tool of macroeconomics. "Debt is a global reality," they say, "with all of our trading partners except China in debt to each other." We are not expected to know that the United States is by far the biggest member of a big debtors club comprised of nations whose debts exceed gross domestic products.[22] The only other members are Lebanon, Greece, Italy, Japan, Portugal, Singapore, Jamaica, Ireland, Eritrea, and Barbados. We are not encouraged to know that the foreign debts of so-called Socialist nations such as Norway and Denmark are among the lowest. Similar to its reluctance to switch from English measures to the metric system, the United States clings to socially destructive taxation and financial practices, both of which impose costs in terms of social expense and reduced productivity. Scandinavian nations offer examples that work better, while the United States sets itself against change to protect unrestrained capitalism. The US government operates according to the book that the Powers That Be continue to write, ensuring that ignorance of the Bigger Picture will continue to be unconscionably costly to all but a few.

The cost of ignorance is amplified by 17.5 million HIV and AIDS carriers who do not know they are infected.[23] They will continue having unprotected sex and spreading the virus, adding more to the annual 1.5 million deaths from the disease. The scandal is supported by ignorant condemnation of AIDS sufferers by cultures worldwide that have thrown up walls of discrimination against the infected and the gay lifestyle, though innocent heterosexuals are infected daily by unfaithful mates and blood transfusions. Driving it underground only makes the situation worse.

According to a BBC report, homosexuality is illegal in seventy-seven nations.[24] Gays will not come forward for testing since, by doing so, they risk prosecution and notations will be entered into personal records that surface during job applications. Russia, Uganda, and Nigeria are among the most rigid. Societies in which young gay men and women are ostracized and rejected by their families form the worst possible backdrop for attempts to control the spread of AIDS. It is only one example of how the hardcore ignorance of head-in-the-sand righteousness serves to advance the very conditions the persecutors abhor. Aside from personal tragedies, the cost is measured in wasted human resources and the spread of disease. Crippled by the inertia of tradition, closed-minded leaders persist in honoring flawed pasts across the world.

While each year's new knowledge causes the curious to become more knowledge-driven than before, stubborn ignorance leaves the incurious behind to battle against threats of change. Issue by issue, society suffers rifts between knowers and not-knowers that frustrate solutions. Examples range from trivial to global, from not respecting what diet does to the body to Islamic radicals destroying antiquities of vanished cultures, a cost measured in loss of lore, poetry, art, and clues to hidden chapters of the past. On one horrible day 1,600 years ago, the combined wisdom of many cultures went up in flames when the Library of Alexandria was burned down. It was reported that the Muslim conqueror said of the loss, "If it agrees with the Koran, we know it. If it doesn't, who needs it."

Whenever Big meets Little, the folklore of fragile cultures is put at risk as cultural juggernauts of the Western world impact remote pockets of tribal wisdom with arrogant assertiveness. The memories of a dwindling number of aging healers, fishermen, hunters, and shamans from the estimated fifteen thousand cultures remaining on the earth are at risk.[25] Half of what they know will all but disappear with the passing of the current generation of elders, since the young lose track of tribal languages and lore when they move to cities. They forget how to weave fishing weirs and extract a living from the forest. Knowledge that took thousands of years to perfect is disappearing as though it never was. This is a special tragedy since what is being lost is precisely what is most needed at this critical point: knowledge of how to live in balance with nature. While knowledge gained from the great unknown is hard won, the knowledge of remaining primitive cultures is here, ready to be understood by those with a heart for natural simplicity, which excludes many sophisticated multi-degreed analysts. The ongoing extinction of primitive peoples' cultures as documented in Art Davidson's book *Endangered Peoples* stands in judgment of the ignorance and insensitivity of power. As to cost, how can anyone estimate the value of lost cultures that will never be reclaimed?

CHAPTER 15

WORKING FROM AND WITH IGNORANCE

My greatest strength as a consultant is to be ignorant and ask a few questions.

—Peter Drucker

Peter Drucker, a twentieth-century management consultant, looked beyond the limits of small personal universes. His approach rejected scope-limiting frames, and his comments indicated an insight that some treasured beliefs might best be upended. He would have understood that thought processing in the digital age is a new game and that, ready or not, the reality we must deal with is today's reality, not yesterday's. Drucker saw how ignorance may be joined with need, knowledge, and vision to do wonderful things. Ignorance in the hands of ignorors is manipulative, but in the hands of creative thinkers, ignorance becomes a launching pad, a base camp, a foundation for thought and discovery.

Some biographies record the struggles of people who survived in the wilderness by conquering overwhelming odds. Others trace the lives of thinkers whose intellectual struggles threw off ignorant traditions to uncover secrets of nature. Whether high born or humble, their habits of early questioning linked with experiences in school and the world to open their minds. And they displayed courage, for it is never comfortable to be a questioner of tradition or orthodoxy. From time to time they made significant progress over not knowing but nothing on the scale of Stephen Hawking's pursuit of the universal constant. The usual goal is to make a measure of progress, but even accomplishing that requires acknowledging ignorance and facing up to doubts. Far more discovery is granted to the humble than to those who are certain of what they know.

RICHARD P. FEYNMAN, NOBEL LAUREATE IN PHYSICS

Feynman combined zest for life with mathematical genius, which made him one of science's most interesting characters. From his involvement with the Manhattan Project to through his Cal Tech years, Feynman's mind sparkled. Among his few critics was his second wife, who said, "He begins working calculus problems as soon as he awakens. He did calculus while driving in his car, while sitting in the living room and while lying in bed at night."[1] Feynman wrote,

> It is in the admission of ignorance and the admission of uncertainty that there is hope for the continuous motion of human beings in some direction that doesn't get confined, permanently blocked, as it has so many times before in various periods in the history of man.[2]

STUART FIRESTEIN, RESEARCHER IN BIOLOGY

Firestein offers what is likely the clearest understanding of positive ignorance. His book *Ignorance: How It Drives Science* is widely read by philosophers and researchers in every field. He asks the right questions for any time: "Are we too enthralled with the answers these days? Are we afraid of questions, especially those that linger too long?" And then he lays out our current informational situation: "We seem to have come to a phase in civilization marked by a voracious appetite for knowledge in which the growth of information is exponential and perhaps more important, its availability easier and faster than ever."[3]

As chair of the Department of Biological Sciences at Columbia University, Firestein promotes science as a process of perpetual revision that proceeds in fits and starts from one stage of ignorance to another. Or as Jonah Lehrer put it, "The only way to be creative over time—not to be undone by our expertise—is to experiment with ignorance, to stare at things we don't fully understand."[4] Firestein has a knack for bringing the hazy concept of creative ignorance into focus: "Being a scientist requires having faith in uncertainty, finding pleasure in mystery and learning to cultivate doubt. There is no surer way to screw up an experiment than to be certain of its outcome."[5] While many scientists deal in facts, Firestein wrestles with concepts, as illustrated by his descriptive metaphor for science:

> Science, then, is not like the often-used onion analogy of stripping away layer after layer to get at some core, central, fundamental truth. Rather it's like the magic well: no matter how many buckets of water you remove there's always another one to be had. Or even better, it's like the widening ripples on the surface of a pond, the ever larger circumference in touch with more and more of what's outside the circle of the unknown. This growing forefront is where science occurs. . . . It is a mistake to bob around in the circle of the facts instead of riding the wave to the great expanse lying outside the circle.[6]

HANS AND OLA ROSLING, GLOBAL HEALTH ACTIVISTS OF THE KAROLINSKA INSTITUTE, STOCKHOLM

The Roslings are a father and son team who spearheaded the development of Gapminder, a new analytical discipline that gathers and analyzes global data to correct faulty conclusions about the state and direction of health and environmental issues.[7] Gapminder feeds Ola Rosling's Trendalyzer software with statistical content that it converts to ignorance-dispelling analyses. The project is the third anti-ignorance thrust under the Roslings' direction, with Gapminder on track to straighten out misunderstanding of statistics and information about social, economic, and environmental issues at local, national, and global levels. Ola Rosling's Trendalyzer software turns mountains of Gapminder's confirmed data into easy-to-interpret animated graphics.

In a TED presentation, Hans Rosling gave his audience the same test he had recently given to an assembly of world leaders at Davos, Switzerland.[8] The poor results for both groups demonstrated the profound ignorance of highly educated participants to important world issues, illustrating how sensational news reporting skews attitudes toward the negative, leading to a sense of hopelessness that hijacks the will to make a difference.[9] Thanks to the Roslings' efforts, the world has a growing and accessible fact tank of digestible, ready-to-apply information that helps override ignorance born of misinformation and irrational fear.

PETER DRUCKER, LEADING MANAGEMENT CONSULTANT OF THE TWENTIETH CENTURY

Drucker taught about the positive impact an outsider's objectivity can have on companies where management is simply too close to issues and too linked to the traditional practices they attempt to apply to the present. He believed that only an outsider can be equipped to appreciate their specialized blindnesses. Drucker taught managers to recognize that, in spite of their years of experience, they often didn't know what they should do to fix things because they had never learned to ask the right questions. When students asked him about his success in reviving industries, he told them the same: "There is no secret. You just need to ask the right questions."[10]

A student once tossed Drucker three rapid-fire challenges: "How do you know the right questions to ask? Aren't your questions based on your knowledge of the industries in which you consult? How did you have the knowledge and expertise to do this when you were first starting out with no experience?"[11] The student had unwittingly fed Drucker the perfect straight lines to frame his approach. He said,

> I never ask these questions or approach these assignments based on my knowledge and experience in these industries. It is exactly the opposite. I do not use my knowledge and experience at all. I bring my ignorance to the situation. Ignorance is the most impor-

tant component for helping others to solve any problem in any industry. . . . Ignorance is not such a bad thing if one knows how to use it, and all managers must learn to do this. You must frequently approach problems with your ignorance; not what you think you know from past experience, because not infrequently, what you think you know is wrong.[12]

HENRY J. KAISER, AMERICAN INDUSTRIALIST

When Nazi U-boats were decimating British cargo fleets during WWII, England hatched a plan to mill out cheap ships that, while not durable, would be capable of transporting needed war materiel from America. With all the nation's able-bodied in uniform, England's plan was crippled by a shortage of manpower. Further, the eight months it took for England's shipyards to complete a ship was too long. They turned to the United States, which had built only two ocean-going cargo ships over the previous decade. Their hope was that with British designs and advisors, America might be able to complete a large number of ships within a year.

When he was called in as a consultant, Henry Kaiser knew next to nothing about shipbuilding in general and even less about cargo ships in particular. He took charge of the British designs and sent the English experts that had brought them packing, preferring to be guided by his own creative ignorance. He had no experienced shipwrights on his staff, and he knew little about shipyard procedure. He got around the shortage of shipwrights by reinvented shipbuilding according to a scheme that assigned workers to special tasks for which they could be quickly trained.[13] Then he abandoned the traditional from-the-keel-up shipyard tradition, replacing it with the assembly-line method of constructing sections separately and scheduling assembly once he knew how long each task would take.

Kaiser's shipyards lacked the heavy cutting machinery needed to precisely trim marine plates, so he attacked the cutting job with oxyacetylene torches. He departed from the standard practice of connecting plates with rivets by welding them. Kaiser's cutting and welding proved to be faster and cheaper, reducing the eight months it took to produce a freighter in England to one ship per month in Kaiser's yards and trimming days from that schedule.[14] Encouraged by their progress, Kaiser's team set a record by assembling an entire ship in four and a half days.

The Kaiser yards built 1,500 Liberty ships in two-thirds the time thought possible and at one-fourth the estimated cost of work done in competing shipyards.[15] The savings in time and money would not have been possible had Kaiser relied on established shipbuilding knowledge. Instead, he dared to explore the unknown, armed mainly with an absence of certitude about how things should be done. And it worked.

ANTOINE DE SAINT EXUPERY, FRENCH AVIATOR AND PHILOSOPHER

The example set by Antoine de Saint Exupery's openness of mind and vast personal universe will live forever through his literary classic *Wind, Sand and Stars*. Saint Exupery pioneered air routes across the Sahara in the 1920s. The fabric-covered biplanes of his time were unreliable, but crashes were more frequent than fatal because pilots brought troubled biplanes down like obedient kites. It was when Saint Exupery crash-landed a crippled plane on a remote Saharan mesa that his open mind reached to sense his place in the universe:[16]

> A minor accident had forced me down in the Rio de Oro region, in Spanish Africa. Landing on one of those table-lands of the Sahara which fall away steeply at the sides, I found myself on the flat top of the frustrum of a cone, an isolated vestige of a plateau that had crumbled round the edges. In this part of the Sahara such trun-cated cones are visible from the air every hundred miles or so, their smooth surfaces always at about the same altitude above the desert and their geologic substance always identical. The surface sand is composed of minute and distinct shells; but progressively as you dig along a vertical section, the shells become more fragmentary,

tend to cohere, and at the base of the cone form a pure calcareous deposit.

Without question, I was the first human being ever to wander over this . . . this iceberg: its sides were remarkably steep, no Arab could have climbed them, and no European had as yet ventured into this wild region.

I was thrilled by the virginity of a soil which no step of man or beast had sullied. I lingered there, startled by this silence that never had been broken. The first star began to shine, and I said to myself that this pure surface had lain here thousands of years in sight only of the stars.

But suddenly my musings on this white sheet and these shining stars were endowed with a singular significance. I had kicked against a hard, black stone, the size of a man's fist, a sort of moulded rock of lava incredibly present on the surface of a bed of shells a thousand feet deep. A sheet spread beneath an apple tree can receive only apples; a sheet spread beneath the stars can receive only star dust. Never had a stone fallen from the skies made known its origin so unmistakably.

And very naturally, raising my eyes, I said to myself that from the height of this celestial apple tree there must have dropped other fruits, and that I should find them exactly where they fell, since never from the beginning of time had anything been present to displace them.

Excited by my adventure, I picked up one and then a second and then a third of these stones, finding them at about the rate of one stone to the acre. And here is where my adventure became magical, for in a striking foreshortening of time that embraced thousands of years, I had become the witness of this miserly rain from the stars. The marvel of marvels was that there, on the rounded back of the planet, between this magnetic sheet and those stars, a human consciousness was present in which, as in a mirror, that rain could be reflected.[17]

Saint Exupery had picked up some knowledge of Saharan geology and topography that helped to unleash his imagination into the powerful *aha* moment that helped him define his place in the universe. When he picked up his first alien stone, it was no more than an oddity of which he knew nothing other than that it didn't fit its surroundings. He was faced with a mystery, which was just the thing to distract him from the uncomfortable possibility that searchers might not find him. So he set his mental tools to work on it: logic, probability, scraps of science, a curiosity that knew no limits. His concept of cosmic rain was a natural result of reluctance to work with conventional limits for thought and a perfect example of what can happen when humbly creative ignorance mates with knowledge in an open mind.

MARTIN BUBER, AUSTRIAN-ISRAELI PHILOSOPHER (1878–1965)

Martin Buber, a German-Jewish theologian of the early twentieth century, recognized that when it comes to human interactions, bits of knowledge can impose barriers against a higher and more complete level of knowing. He described a level of knowing that swallows details of knowledge into concepts that, in their wholeness, exist above and beyond details of description. He offered a test to prove this. Bring two people to mind. One is a much-loved spouse or friend. The other is an acquaintance: someone with whom you shared an interesting conversation, or the person in a shop who regularly prepares your coffee. One after the other, try to call their faces to mind. More often than not, your mental image of the casual acquaintance will be in sharper focus than your image of the person you know better. The reason is that the person you know best is known to you in relationship, while the other is known to you as an underweight person with dark hair, a birthmark on the right side of the neck, lean features, and heavy eyebrows. That's what you see; that's how you recognize her. In fact, as you get to know the coffee server over months or years, details of her description, while still being there, may melt into relationship. As long as awareness of details dominates meetings, it stands in the way of the type of relationship Buber describes as a meeting of the essential I and Thou.[18] It happens when the small knowledges of detail, from a pimple to disease-disfigured face, are overshadowed by big knowledges of spirit. Allowing details of knowledge to lose significance for the sake of relationship may be the noblest manifestation of ignorance.

THE ESSAYISTS AND PRESENTERS

The human response to discovery is to share it, albeit sometimes unwisely ("Look everybody, I just discovered gold in my backyard!"). Written history is rich in descriptions of discoveries by Archimedes, Galileo, Newton, Einstein, and thousands of others who found it hard to stay mum about new ideas that blossomed when provocative ignorance of something stirred their minds into activity. Each was a case of natural cause and effect, the cause being ignorance, the result, knowledge. The editors of the *Saturday Evening Post* once thought that discoveries of thinkers were of such lasting importance that they funded a series of essays in the magazine that would be printed later by Alfred A. Knopf Publishers in 1960 under the title *Adventures of the Mind*.[19] Though this took place during the early years of television and long before the Internet, its intent was similar to dreamers' plans that resulted in TED Talks. Many TED lectures open with statements of not knowing and progress to enlightenment, which highlights how little would be known were it not for someone's recognition of ignorance.

CONCLUSIONS

IGNORANCE: THE HUMAN CONDITION

The digital age brought an accelerating pace of change that hardened tensions between traditionalists and knowledge seekers. That tension fed the increasingly strident voice of anti-intellectualism, which fueled polarization on the political scene. At the same time, hostility, suspicion, and stagnation crippled dialogue when burning issues called for open-minded cooperation. Crippling ignorance associated with small personal universes and cultured fears worked to marginalize millions who found themselves left behind educationally, technologically, and financially. Much of their plight resulted from their own incurious minds, limited exposure to knowledge, and adverse fate, the rest because of their vulnerability to manipulation by interests that stand to gain from managing thoughts.

Ignorance surrounds us and fills us. It is everywhere, in all of us all the time because it is impossible to know everything about anything or anyone. Ignorance is the wild card dealt to every hand: we are born ignorant, blank slates. It is why eight out of ten new businesses fail in their first eighteen months.[1] It cannot be eliminated, only acknowledged and conquered bit by bit as problem solvers unearth new information and reengineer old knowledge to serve new needs. Ignorance plays an enabling role by teasing searchers to explore beyond conventional limits. Though the entirety of ignorance is impossible to grasp or define, four things about it are certain: we are all profoundly ignorant; we will always be ignorant of more than we know; we can be hurt by what we don't know; and the most effective way of reducing involvement in ignorance's mischief-making potential is by rehearsing the mantra, "I don't know."

Ignorance stunts development of thoughts and formation of opinions as surely as insects and infertility afflict plants. It takes root where information is absent, withheld, or bent. Like high priests of antiquity, today's high priests of politics and industry use knowledge control to advance their agendas, aided by the human tendency to choose the easier path of groupthink. With the health and wealth of society dependent on unhampered access to knowledge, and the Powers that Be dependent on control of knowledge, the spirit of society will always be locked in conflict with the Powers.

A significant reduction of ignorance's destructive potential requires the humbling of the ambitious opportunists who, in an age of change, seize control of corporations, nations, and even non-national forces. Recent history has recorded how they blind themselves to general welfare in defending their precarious new positions. Moreover, they act without adequate knowledge of the consequences, as when Mao Tse-tung ordered nationwide programs to exterminate flies, mosquitoes, and other pests, killing off all honey bees in the process.[2] Or when US forces in Iraq used depleted uranium to harden projectile tips and, as a result, poisoned the countryside, sending cancer and birth defect rates skyrocketing and making the land inhospitable for tens of thousands of years.[3] Blind applications of technology have a tendency to turn on us whenever there has not been enough thought about their effects, just as planners stand a good chance of failure when their vision extends no further than their careers or next quarter's profits. Whenever schemes produce failure, damage, pollution, disappointment, tension, waste, bloodshed, poverty, divorce, or bankruptcy, ignorance surely played a role.

MANAGING IGNORANCE

It is important that people come to understand how their opinions, desires, and fears come to be, and, if they come uninvited, to study what it takes to break free of the mind controls that allowed them access. It takes habitual vetting of information sources to form and hold a mind-set that denies access to subversive influences that promote favored knowledge by suppressing other knowledge.

How big is ignorance? Not as big as one might think because things and places not yet studied are made of the same atoms and stony stuff found on Earth, and the physical laws that govern our small solar system apply to the rest of the universe as well. Though much of what's true here is true there, we still find that details of what we "know" need amending, proving that, while we know it all or know it well enough, we don't know it all. Our understanding is incomplete and imperfect and always will be.

Ignorance should not be written off as categorically evil but should be welcomed at planning tables where enlightened thinkers show proper respect for the trouble they might get into by not properly considering known unknowns.[4] Otherwise, ignorance provides the shaky foundation for unfounded guesswork and wishful thinking. When planners hold ignorance in its proper place they come closer to assuring that buildings will stand, ventures will succeed, rockets will fly, and investors won't be duped.

Education's potential for correcting societal ignorance deserves more support. It was because of education that society came to accept that seat belts save lives and that smoking causes cancer, examples that show people they can truly improve their lives by changing their minds. But seat belts and cigarettes are concrete, material things while ignorance is a poorly understood state of mind that is more difficult to come to grips with. Yet its significance is such that it deserves a prominent place in everyone's everyday considerations. Its fingerprints are found on loss of opportunity and hope, lovelessness, environmental issues, dysfunctional relationships, and financial disasters.

Discerning minds come to realize how thoughts are shaped to determine who one should vote for and how to feel about a nearby development, HMO policies, or news from the war front. As Hitler proved
by repeating lies so often that he had Germans muttering them in
their sleep, artfully spread falsehoods can be made to change any
society's dominant beliefs.

I offer as a tool for personal or educational use six forms of awareness that help protect minds from thought-skewing influences:

1. Recognizing that the misdeeds and antics of public figures
   routinely making the news tend to make selfish, violent,
   greedy, and discriminatory behaviors appear normal and
   therefore acceptable, lulling people into ignorance of what
   really counts.
2. Understanding that elements of thought and opinion aren't
   produced in individuals' minds but are placed there by media,
   people, and events.
3. Studying the histories of despots and dictators to gain an
   appreciation for the power of ideologies to enslave minds.
4. Understanding that application of yesterday's answers to
   today's questions will often end in failure to resolve today's or
   tomorrow's issues.
5. Accepting that the perceptions of contestants on every side of
   issues will be incomplete and flawed and that one must understand an opposition's position before one can properly understand one's own.
6. Coming to understand that breadth of knowledge is the best
   defense against arrogant ignorance that spawns concepts like
   American exceptionalism and Aryan supremacy.

A NEW MIND

An industry staffed with ignorors exists to misinform people about everything from genetically modified foods to the future of national energy policy. They lie, bend truth, and vandalize language by employing professional propagandists who satisfy their masters' ambitions by trashing the characters of political opponents and promoting lifestyles that threaten health and welfare. Ignorors' record of knowledge-control activities is undeniable proof that what we don't know *can* hurt us.

So we work to improve our chances of a better life by sorting out the useful stuff from the surplus of information of a knowledge-rich extelligence. Becoming tangled in thickets of fact, belief, and supposition is unavoidable because everything, in its act of being, presents itself, its dynamics, and relationships in a flurry of informational ways. As world travelers come to realize, you can't see it all, for space and time are filled with too much for anyone to experience, let alone comprehend, in a dozen lifetimes. We are destined to be ignorant of most of it. The challenge then is to learn how to discern what of it we should take hold of or allow to stick to us and what we should avoid or brush away. At this point in time, our future and that of most other species depends on how we handle that. It's a heavy responsibility but one that cannot be dodged, maybe because someone was once talked into biting into the wrong piece of metaphoric fruit.

The people who seek intellectual security by marking their territory, like wolves, and then living within marked perimeters may never come to know that living without change isn't all it's cracked up to be—at least in this world, and this applies especially to conservative believers. It is only Christians, Jews, and Muslims who dare to adventure beyond the myths of their orthodoxies that sense their shared deity's habit of hanging his choicest fruits from the scary ends of precarious branches. Risk is involved when straying from the secure realm of knowing into not knowing, but, as our mythical ancestors Adam and Eve saw, that seems to be where life's compellingly attractive fruits are hung.

Since truth is elusive, it is not easy to find intellectual security. This discomforting fact divides society: one branch adopting the fiction that the fixed body of knowledge it lives by is complete and beyond criticism and correction, and the other understanding that life involves working with incomplete knowledge that is not entirely trustworthy. Those in the latter group grudgingly accept that even their own knowledge may be tainted by inaccurate sensing and testing, insufficient experiences, and a host of other reasons and excuses. Being realists they accept that limitations in the process of searching will likely leave them not with knowledge but clues to knowledge. One group behaves as though life is a matter of navigating a placid storm-free sea: planning is easy, but the surprises are many. The other group anticipates having to deal with reality. The open mind accepts ignorance as a reality that cannot be ignored. When the trusted equations of mathematicians who explore science's fringes don't balance it is because bits of the unknown reveal themselves. Medical doctors suspect that ignorance might play a role when they lose patients. Ignorance and failure are prods to learn. Were it not for becoming aware of ignorance we would never have left the Dark Ages. It is burden, threat, enemy, and friend.

Just as different texts are studied to understand different subjects, different types of minds are needed to deal with the challenges of radically different times. The challenges of the digital age require that society's leaders work from open minds with broad horizons and not be hampered by the tunnel vision of vested ideologies. A new type of mind is needed to replace a trio of squabbling mindsets that can't get their act together: critics who support yesterday's status quo, revolutionaries who condemn it, and reformers who call for transforming it into something better. The new mind is a blend of all three that supports existing systems, condemns their flaws, and transforms them into something better. The blended mind frees itself of bickering, biasing memes, and hostility toward whatever is incompletely understood or seems foreign. Educators encourage the new mind by broadening their focus from simply filling minds to opening them. The media is called to support it by returning to unbiased, investigative journalism committed to serve the highest needs of its audiences. The Church is called to revitalize its commitment to social ministries, while recognizing that its appeal to the masses might grow by encouraging a proper appreciation of the great spiritual mysteries of the unknown.

Too idealistic? Of course, but pursuit of ideals is certainly preferable to following the leads of power brokers, propagandists, and hucksters. What is at risk is nothing less than the soul of society and the health of the nation. Though the Powers That Be have come under increased scrutiny, scrutiny doesn't ensure reform of flawed leadership cultures. That takes time—decades at the least, and possibly longer—for the most promising cure for ideological ignorance is the rise of a more enlightened generation.

For that change to come about, society must first recognize how it has been trained to bow to the Powers' agendas, and it must be constantly reminded through education and reform politics that open minds, consumers' choices, ballots, unbiased news sources, weight of public opinion, and civil disobedience are the tools to set things right. But that only sets the stage for a plan. Carrying it out requires leadership from blended and open minds that hold cooperation in higher esteem than competition. That new mind is one that listens to opposing voices and learns from them. It is not fractured into *isms* that keep the Grand Social Organism that is us from coming together to work for our own welfare. The new mind cannot emerge while knowledge controllers divide us by carving off blocks of society to serve venal purposes. There is a body of operational truths that, if commonly understood, could serve society's highest purposes. This is not arguable, though propagandists and narrow-minded critics might leap to link commonly held understandings with Communism and represent them as attacks on freedom.

Our best chance to minimize the tension, conflict, and waste that accompanies ignorance is to choose leaders who best demonstrate the new mind in their personal lives and professional conduct. That mind is more likely to possess the intellectual openness necessary to bridge the rift separating anti-intellectualists and their targets. Not thinking cannot be an option for the common mind, and if one chooses not to think, one should not expect to affect others any more than the reluctant learners in that math classroom were allowed to interrupt the education of their classmates.[5] Ideally, presidents, senators, representatives, governors, mayors, pastors, priests, educators, and parents would share a visceral aversion to the divisive practice of managing others' knowledge.

It is time to think big—global peace and the health of the planet are at stake. Whether wars or environmental degradation, major problems spring from actions that aren't sufficiently preceded by understanding. The mammoth issue of ignorance is too big to tackle head-on, but its roots aren't. The media, corporate offenders, congressional stonewallers, radical bloggers, and supporters of destructive attitudes and practices stand before the court of public opinion. If humankind can be roused to recognize that openness is crucial, that minds are routinely invaded by foreign thoughts, that popular notions are often hostile to peace and well-being, and that we can live better by simply inspecting the messages that come to us before swallowing them, there is hope.

Owning up to personal ignorance is humbling, and humility is essential if we are to grow into the new mind that will improve our ability to deal with whatever lies in the future. Preparing for it requires that our efforts be seated in humble wonderment as much as knowledge because not only do we not know the answers, but we sometimes don't even have the right questions. We can, however, improve our strategies for discovering that which we must come to know by setting sophistication aside and replacing it with the openness of children. Egos, frames, and certitude must be dismissed from planning tables so that tomorrow's problem solvers might become creatively, personally, emotionally, spiritually, and intellectually humbled. Only then will the devil-may-care arrogance that propelled our kind into a history of ignorant misdeeds give way to much-needed course corrections for the good of our species and the health of our environment.

EXPLANATION OF TERMS

Since people accumulate different collections of words, each collection conditioned by personal experience, we speak differently colored versions of the same language. Should you and I have identical vocabularies, my experience with words and concepts will still be different from yours. When you say something to me, I am able to catch what you have in mind but am incapable of duplicating your exact thought because the same words came to me through different experiences. I might come close, but I can't own your thought, and that difference shapes the most innocent form of ignorance that separates us, one from the other. Because words are our basis for understanding and misunderstanding, it is necessary to not only lay words out in context but to explain pivotal words used throughout this book.

AGNOTOLOGY:

Agnotology is the study of culturally induced ignorance or doubt, particularly through publication or spreading of misleading data with the intent of rendering the recipient ignorant or at least uncertain of that which they thought they knew. The concept, toyed with by essayists for centuries, was given definition by Robert Proctor in his 2008 book *Agnotology: The Making and Unmaking of Ignorance.* The book opens with a quotation from Thomas Pynchon:

> We are often unaware of the scope of our ignorance. Ignorance is not just a blank space on a person's mental map. It has contours and coherence, and for all I know rules of operation as well. So as a corollary to writing about what we know, maybe we should add getting familiar with our ignorance.[1]

Just as debits and credits in personal ledgers differ, individuals' profiles of ignorance and knowledge differ. Proctor's question was, "How is an individual's ignorance shaped to be what it is?"[2] In other words, what external forces or agendas work to keep a person blind to processes of reality? He questioned why no one had seriously studied the processes that hold populations ignorant, going on to explore the means by which propagandists control and subvert knowledge, feeding minds with misinformation or removing knowledge from public debate. A new science was born, albeit a rather soft science since it isn't easy to get a definitive grasp on the unknown components of ignorance. However, it is not so difficult to identify the invented processes that keep people ignorant. Proctor saw understanding of those processes as doable and necessary, hence agnotology.

APATHY

Apathy is characterized by lack of emotion, lack of interest, listlessness, and indifference. Apathy has been said to be a first cousin of ignorance, but, upon inspection, the two seem so twinned that they operate more like close siblings. It was recognition of how ignorance links with apathetic hesitance to become involved that gave rise to a Q and A couplet that mocks the relationship: "What's the difference between ignorance and apathy? I don't know and I don't care."

Minds that seek knowledge and are alive to questions of the times simply cannot be apathetic. Active thinkers cannot be as disinterested, disengaged, and apathetic as intellectual dropouts. Since human brains carry not just a lively potential for thought but an inclination toward chewing on provocative questions or ideas, it seems odd that, in this fractious world, some brains choose not to chew.

BELIEF

Belief is "an assent to anything proposed or declared, and its acceptance as fact by reason of the authority from whence it proceeds, apart from personal knowledge."[3] After childhood, observations grow into notions that swell up to become opinions that then mature into beliefs. They creep up on us, gaining strength to modify our thinking and dominate our actions. One should be cautious to ensure that the *authorities* that deliver the information from which beliefs are formed are, themselves, worthy of belief.

DEFENSE

The word "defense" has been used alternately to protect the nation and ramp up fear of foreign aggressors, with the two World Wars and the ISIS challenge standing as rare instances of inarguable reason for mounting military campaigns. When confronted with the words "in defense of United States' interests," the public is routinely misinformed as to what those interests might be. At the time America was ramping up to invade Iraq, tactical plans were framed as "matters of national interests," but given a history of warring for resources, there was room for suspicion that Iraq's oil figured into the calculus, especially after petrochemical executives gathered in the White House before the invasion. Details of the meeting were leaked. A map was displayed that showed how Big Oil intended to divide Iraq's oil assets after the victory.[4] With the media aware that war planners were in collusion with Big Oil, many believed that mobilization would stop or at least be reconsidered. It didn't happen, in part because of the media's reluctance to inform the nation of confirmed links between the administration's energy policy, the oil lobby, and war planning. When a sitting president, vice president, secretary of state, and secretary of commerce were all former oil executives, a probable conflict of interest was left uninvestigated. The coupling of "US interests" with the Iraq adventure displayed a reckless misuse of language that held the nation ignorant of commercial interest in the enterprise.

Until the real and present danger of radical Islamists attacking the homeland arose, the Department of Defense would have had difficulty justifying many of its operations as "defensive." A history of such non-defensive actions were brought to light by General Smedley Butler, erstwhile commandant of the US Marine Corps, who led US military incursions into Central America and China during the early decades of the twentieth century. Butler knew what was going on because he helped to make it happen. What follows is excerpted from Butler's book *War is a Racket*:

> The trouble with America is that when the dollar only earns 6 percent over here, then it gets restless and goes overseas to get 100 percent. The flag follows the dollar and the soldiers follow the flag.
>
> For a great many years, as a soldier, I had a suspicion that war was a racket; not until I retired to civil life did I fully realize it. . . . I helped purify Nicaragua for the international banking house of Brown Brothers in 1909–1912. I brought light to the Dominican Republic for the American sugar interests in 1916. In China, I helped to see to it that Standard Oil went its way unmolested. . . . I helped make Mexico, especially Tampico, safe for American oil interests in 1914. I helped make Haiti and Cuba a decent place for the National City Bank boys to collect revenues in.
>
> The normal profits of a business concern in the United States are six, eight, ten, and sometimes twelve percent. But war-time profits—ah! That is another matter—twenty, sixty, one hundred, three hundred, and even eighteen hundred percent—the sky is the limit. . . . We must take the profit out of war.[5]

If language is to be trusted, words must convey precise meanings that may be similarly interpreted by all readers or hearers. Euphemistic dressing of unacceptable practices with acceptable words masks defense's dark doings, as in "extreme rendition," the practice of delivering suspected terrorists to foreign torture venues governed by lax human rights codes. Extreme rendition is an example of language being engineered to give unwarranted latitude to practices that would be better constrained by precise definition. American foreign policy plays loose with language in classifying nations as "moderate" or "radical," moderate nations being those that behave in a friendly manner toward the United States, though their internal policies might be brutally oppressive, Indonesia being a case in point. Nations classified as radical insist on charting their own courses without "guidance" from the United States.

We communicate through the medium of words. To the degree to which we cannot trust words to convey what they are intended to convey it becomes impossible to trust that original meanings are transmitted without flaw. Words and thoughts become hybridized and bastardized in shadowy environments where Pentagon planners and congressional committee members are forced to doubt "knowledge" and what others hold as truth. Frustrated, they find freedom from doubt in fixed codes that infect them with certitude, the enemy of reason and the friend of propagandists.

EXTELLIGENCE

Ian Stewart and Jack Cohen defined extelligence as all the cultural capital available from folklore, tribal legends, nursery rhymes, video tapes, books, CD-ROMs, libraries, and everything else that a mind might access.[6] *Ex*telligence is distinguished from *in*telligence by being "out there," ready to be accessed by active intellects, while intelligence refers to the brain and memory, all of which resides within the skull. A person can think without touching extelligence but only by reprocessing concepts and data that reside in the mind. Driven by a mind-boggling explosion of information and knowledge, the expanding scope of what is not known humbles scientists as never before. The top priority becomes establishing bases of informed ignorance as launching pads for reaching into extelligence and beyond. It is only through admission of ignorance that thinkers properly position themselves for probing the unknown from the forward fringe of knowledge, the cambium or growth layer of knowledge, the interface between known and unknown.

The new ease of calling up knowledge to dispel ignorance amazes even professional researchers. While writing *Bicycling to Amersfoort,* the biography of a friend who spent his teenage years under the Nazi occupation of the Netherlands during WWII, I was able to trace the military career of his uncle who had been apprenticed to a German piano factory during Hitler's rise to power. The uncle joined the Hitler Youth organization and later became a colonel in the feared Nazi SS. The Internet revealed clues to his unit's movements and why it was recalled to Holland from the eastern front. The growing potential of online searching increases the intellectual distance between those who take advantage of it and others who, for one reason or another, choose not to use it. That difference adds to the tension between open and closed minds to polarize positions in education, finance, diplomacy, religion, communication, and other information-driven fields.

FRAMES

Before George Lakoff published *Don't Think of an Elephant,* analysts of the political scene lacked a practical mental model for comparing the various *isms* that populate the Beltway. Lakoff used the term "frames" to describe the bounds of information that partisan minds choose to accept. A frame functions as a thought-screening aperture that rejects anything that cannot pass through it. We all have frames. Being a Prius driver, I'm not turned on by ads that romanticize muscle cars. Organic farmers won't be sympathetic to shop talk among crop dusters. Knowledge and ignorance relate directly to frames in that the makeup of one's functional knowledge-base and its system of beliefs may be identified by what makes it through a personal frame and what is deflected away.

The unpredictable nature of the great unknown poses special problems for interests that hope to shape the frames of consumers and voters. The great unknown, being indescribable and unpredictable, is impossible to manage. That being the case, frame-shaping propagandists find it easier to form and firm up frames by cherry-picking building blocks for their *isms* from history. While true intellectuals include the great unknown as part of their home court frames, they are less friendly to conservative frame-shapers and the people whose frames they manipulate. That is indeed unfortunate because whenever students of any age awaken *aha* moments by questioning the great unknown, it is because their intellects break free of prejudicial bonds and limiting personal frames to make ignorance more a friend and less a problem.

IGNORANCE

As with the words "apple," "grass," and "cougar," the word "ignorance" has accumulated too many meanings for listeners or readers to assume they understand its sense here. *Webster's New World Dictionary of the American Language,* a middleweight among dictionaries, lists only three: (1) lacking knowledge, education or experience, (2) caused by lack of knowledge, education or experience, and (3) uninformed or unaware.[7] Because that venerable dictionary carries a publication date of 1980, it should be disqualified from modern use, since it is only in recent decades that a more thorough understanding of ignorance has become more necessary and available. Yet even *Wikipedia* offers little more.

In the academic climate of the digital age, people cannot be left unsure of what a speaker intends to convey with words. The pace and content of communications have been ramped up to where a higher level of verbal discipline is required to ensure that every word's precise meaning is sent like an arrow to a bull's-eye. Yet the standard of communication remains so imprecise that hearers and readers are left unsure of what speakers and writers intend. This leaves them, to some degree, ignorant. And because knowledge is cast in language, "ignorant" also describes one who has never read or heard certain knowledge, who rejects knowledge, who has been kept from accessing knowledge, or whose knowledge has been subversively shaped. The complete list of ignorance-inducing language issues is long.

The condition of not knowing is universal, and everyone is a member in particular ways. Pretenders posing as know-it-alls are portrayed as tragic blowhards or comic figures—the cartoon character of Mr. Peabody from *The Rocky and Bullwinkle Show*, for example. The glasses-wearing mutt and his pet boy, Sherman, parodied false intellectualism for the anti-intellectual audience of the times. With his snobbish bearing and fancy vocabulary, the know-it-all pooch laid claim to intellectual high ground from where he spouted outrageous fictions that impressed his cartoon listeners. The Mr. Peabody skits, intentionally or not, characterized the ideological rift between blowhard academics and nonacademics.

Ignorance is a natural state. Much of what differentiates us is the specifics of what isn't known. It is the differences between individual ignorance that makes it so difficult to work through contentious issues. Depending upon the profile of each individual's ignorance, one's reaction may be cast as defensive, aggressive, passive, or creative, aside from the last, these do not suggest a promising program for progress. As things move along, it helps no one to rank others as ignorant when, if all corners of knowledge are considered, everyone falls short. We are afflicted by ignorance as certainly as we are afflicted by aging.

When appropriate, "not knowing" is substituted herein as a gentler label for ignorance. Perhaps a comparison of ignorance with its more physical counterpart, unpreparedness, might add perspective. Should a person be unable to respond to challenges within his or her job description it is not the same as when a person finds him- or herself in a foreign situation that renders that person unable to cope. That person too is unprepared but in a more forgivable way. In the first case, the person knows what is expected but doesn't prepare. In the second, that person is blindsided by the unknown. Is a person ignorant by virtue of not choosing to prepare or because the person was impacted by unforeseen challenges? Given the range of possibilities, my dictionary is in error for resting on only three interpretations of ignorance.

MEME

Richard Dawkins called the word up from the ancient Greek, *minema*, which meant "something imitated."[8] It was soon adopted by programmers as the digital equivalent of genes in biology: a unit of meaning that can spread. The capacity of memes to sweep through bodies of digitized information opened a parallel line of thought in sociology wherever no word was yet available to express a similar concept that infects society to produce cultural ignorance. The *Urban Dictionary* describes meme as "an idea, belief or belief system or pattern of behavior that spreads either vertically by cultural inheritance (as parents to children) or horizontally by cultural acquisition as by peers, information media, and entertainment media . . . a pervasive thought or thought pattern that replicates itself via cultural means; a parasitic code, a virus of the mind especially contagious to children and the impressionable."[9]

Memes of cultural ignorance cause society to ignore harsh realities, such as the incapacity of our planet to sustain present levels of consumption and pollution, a system where the labor of a nation benefits the few, and dysfunctional government. Though these and other offenses are intolerable, their memes allow them to be tolerated.

NATIONAL INTEREST

The national interest, often referred to by the French expression raison d'etat ("reason of state"), is a country's goals and ambitions, whether economic, military, or cultural. The definition broadens when preceded by "vital."

Samuel Huntington adds, "Without a sure sense of national identity, Americans have become unable to define their national interests, and as a result, national commercial interests and transnational and non-national ethnic interests have come to dominate foreign policy."[10]

PROPAGANDA

When seats of power work to extend their influence and enhance their images by selectively controlling or censoring information, they become propagandists of a sort. The label "propaganda" has been reserved for information-controlling acts of powers with the potential to conduct press-worthy damage, though smaller actors are just as guilty. Tradition allows political wrongdoings by spreading lies, engaging in character assassination, and demonizing opposition. Propaganda greases debate, allowing offenses to slip by with no one calling foul. Though private citizens who lie under oath, slander others, or commit intellectual piracy may suffer punishment under the law, similar propaganda spread by agents of the Powers That Be slide through with a wink and a nod. In its broadest sense, anyone stretching language beyond its intended meaning to make a point practices propaganda.

TRUTH

Indisputable knowledge that anchors beliefs and convictions is spoken of as truth. Note that the dictionary definition of truth below speaks of experience, reality, and existence, the specifics of which are understood differently from person to person. Yet the need for truths that bind peoples of tribes and nations to common purpose requires that societies agree on the unifying history, experience, and reality that make up cultural myth. The specifics of truth differ across cultures, and a visitor's concept of truth may not pass tests of congruency with a host tribe's cultural myth. The *Webster's New World Dictionary*'s entry on truth:

> Truth: The quality or state of being true; specifically, a) formerly, loyalty; trustworthiness, b) sincerity; genuineness; honesty, c) the quality of being in accordance with experience, facts or reality; conformity with fact; d) reality, actual existence, e) agreement with a standard rule; correctness, accuracy. 2. That which is true; statement, etc. which accords with fact or reality. 3. An established or verified fact, principle, etc.[11]

In practice, truth is accepted, honored, stretched, and bent, depending on a person's degree of selflessness or self-servingness. At one end of that spectrum lies the Jesus image, at the other, collectors of wealth and power. According to the Jesus image, the altruistic pole of the spectrum, the truth code involves timeless verities that resonate with all creation for the common good. At the other pole, truth is what works best according to the many branches of the practical world. The context of the Jesus type was made clear to his followers when he said to them, "You do not belong to the world."[12] That his type of truth isn't of this world is made clear by comparing what should be done for general welfare with what is done to further the advantage of vested interests. The Machiavellian political "what works" concept of truth is very much of this world, and, right or wrong, it dictates most of what we do and are. Walter Mosely explained truth as a person's explanation of an opinion he holds at the time.

NOTES

INTRODUCTION

1. Gen. 2:16–17 (New Living Translation).
2. Hans F. Sennholz, ed., *The Wisdom of Henry Hazlitt* (Auburn, Alabama: Ludwig von Mises Institute, 1993), p. 51.

CHAPTER 1. WHAT IS IGNORANCE?

1. *The Interview,* directed by Evan Goldberg and Seth Rogen, Columbia Pictures, 2014.
2. "IT Industry Outlook 2017," CompTIA, January 2017, https://www.comptia.org/resources/it-industry-trends-analysis-2017 (accessed August 21, 2017).
3. Gavin Newsome and Lisa Dickey, Citizenville: How to Take the TownSquare Digital and Reinvent Government (New York: Penguin, 2013), p. 58.
4. Gavin Newsom, *Citizenville: How to Take the Town Square Digital and Reinvent Government* (New York: Penguin Books, 2014), p. 59. Stewart Brand (1938–), editor of *The Whole Earth Catalog* and founder of the WELL, the Global Business Network, and the Long Now Foundation.
5. Jonathan Haidt, *The Righteous Mind: Why Good People Are Divided by Politics and Religion* (New York: Pantheon, 2012), pp. 315–16.
6. *Webster's New World Dictionary of the American Language,* eds. David Guralnik et al. (Cleveland: World Publishing, 1960), s.v. "stupid," p. 1499.
7. Christopher Ingraham, "37 Percent of Americans Think a Free Press Is Overrated," *Washington Post,* September 19, 2014, https://www.washingtonpost.com/news/wonk/wp/2014/09/19/37-percent-of-americans-think-a-free-press-is-overrated/ (accessed July 2017).
8. Michael Rosansky, "Americans Know Surprisingly Little about

Their Government, Survey Finds," Annenberg Public Policy Center (University of Pennsylvania), September 17, 2014, http://www.annenberg publicpolicycenter.org/americans-know-surprisingly-little-about-their -government-survey-finds/ (accessed July 2017).

9. Neil Postman, *Amusing Ourselves to Death* (New York: Penguin, 1985), pp. 157–63.

10. Bill Vitek and Wes Jackson, eds., *The Virtues of Ignorance: Complexity, Sustainability, and the Limits of Knowledge* (Lexington: University of Kentucky Press, 2005), pp. 21–36.

11. Daniel Kahneman, *Thinking Fast and Slow* (New York: Farrar, Strauss, and Giroux, 2011).

12. Ibid., pp. 23–24.

13. Walter Wink, *The Powers That Be: Theology for a New Millennium* (New York: Doubleday, 1998), pp. 1–37.

CHAPTER 2. THE SIZE OF PERSONAL UNIVERSES

1. After twenty years in theater, Firestein earned an advanced degree in science at the age of forty. By promoting the idea that researching on the basis of what we don't know is more valuable than building on what we do know, he has become an inspiration to open-minded scientists. *See Wikipedia*, s.v. "Stuart Firestein," last edited June 17, 2017, https:// en.wikipedia.org/wiki/Stuart_Firestein.

2. Gen. 1:28 (New International Version).

3. Charles C. Mann, "Introduction," in *Material World*, ed. Peter Menzel and Charles C. Mann (San Francisco: Sierra Club, 2005), p. 9.

4. Worldometers, "How Many People Have Lived on Earth?" http:// worldometers.info/world-population/ (accessed August 21, 2017).

5. Mann, "Introduction."

6. The author's definition adopted but not admitted to by the Powers That Be.

7. Drawn from an ongoing study by the author, an ex-librarian.

8. Brian Greene, *The Hidden Reality: Parallel Universes and the Deep Laws of the Cosmos* (New York: Alfred A. Knopf, 2011).

9. Brian Greene, "Our Universe May Be a Giant Hologram," *Discover Magazine*, June 2011.

10. Robert Browning, "Andrea del Sarto," *Men and Women and Other Poems* (Lanham, MD: Rowman and Littlefield, 1975).

11. Greene, *Hidden Reality*, p. 322.

12. Ibid., p. 161.

13. Frank Herbert, *Dune* (Philadelphia: Chilton, 1965).

14. Leo Szilard (1898–1964), born in Budapest, student of Einstein and Planck, and a principal of the Manhattan project. Szilard left Germany in 1933 when persecution of Jews was ramping up.

15. Gene Dannen, "Leo Szilard the Inventor" (lecture, Leo Szilard Centenary, Budapest, Hungary, February 9, 1998).

16. Amie Kaufman and Meagan Spooner, "Why Everyone Should Read More Science Fiction," *HuffPost* (blog), updated February 8, 2014.

17. Brian Aldiss, *Billion Year Spree: The True History of Science Fiction* (New York: Doubleday, 1973).

18. Greg Bear, "Plague of Conscience," in *The Collected Stories of Greg Bear* (New York: Tor, 2002).

19. Ray Bradbury, "Introduction," in *The Circus of Dr. Lao and Other Improbable Stories* (New York: Bantam, 1956).

20. Kurt Vonnegut, *New York Times Book Review*, September 5, 1965; reprinted in *Wampeters, Foma, & Granfalloons* (New York: Delcorte, 1974).

21. William Wilson, *A Little Earnest Book upon a Great Old Subject* (London: Darlton, 1851), pp. 138–39.

22. Ralph Waldo Emerson, address to the Harvard chapter of Phi Delta Kappa, 1837.

23. Jeff Nesbit, "The Earth Rotates the Sun," *US News*, February 21 2014.

24. Ignoror: this new word was invented to describe those who, for reason, manage information to keep others in ignorance.

CHAPTER 3. WHO CONTROLS KNOWLEDGE?

1. World Intellectual Property Organization, wipo.int/portal/en (accessed August 21, 2017).

2. The comment describes the author's consistent qualification of claims to control power by telling why it cannot be absolutely successful.

3. The WIPO (World Intellectual Property Organization) reported that 66 percent of their cases were standalones, of which 38 percent went to arbitration, 25 percent to expedited arbitration, and 34 percent to multitier dispute resolution followed by arbitration, indicating the indefinite state of issues and claims. Ignacio de Castro and Judith

Schallnau, "What Does It Cost to Defend Your IP Rights?" *WIPO Magazine*, no. 3 (June 2013): 24.

4. Kevin Moran, "It's Starbucks vs. Star Bock in Galveston," *Houston Chronicle*, June, 6, 2005.

5. Christopher Heath and Anselm Kamperman Sanders, *Landmark Intellectual Property Cases and Their Legacy* (New York: Kluwer Law International, 2010).

6. Ibid., pp. xvii–xviii.

7. *Wikipedia* s.v. "TESO (Austrian Hacker Group)," lasted edited July 20, 2016, http://en.wikipedia.org/wiki/TESO_(Austrian hacker_group).

8. Steve Morgan, "Cyber Crime Costs Projected to Reach $2 Trillion by 2019," *Forbes Magazine*, January 11, 2016.

9. Though publishers of printed maps and originators of map websites enjoyed equal access to government satellite mapping, increasing computer literacy captured the map market and marginalized printers of maps and atlases.

10. "Homeland Security and Public Safety Agencies to Spend $11 Billion on Big Data Surveillance by 2022," *Business Journals*, May 8, 2017, https://www.bizjournals.com/prnewswire/press_releases/2017/05/08/DC83724 (accessed August 30, 2017).

11. See foia.gov for FOIA history, grants, requests processed, and published reports.

12. "We the party control all the records, and we control all the memories. Then we control the past, do we not?" George Orwell, *1984* (San Diego: Dolphin, 2016), pp. 204–205.

13. Office of the Inspector General, *Declassifying State Department Secrets*, US Department of State, SIO/A-98-50, September 1998.

14. Alan Rusbridger, "Wikileaks: The Guardian's Role in the Biggest Leak in the History of the World," January 28, 2011.

15. John Hamre, quoted in Scott Shane, "Can the Government Keep a Secret?" in *Open Secrets: Wikileaks, War, and American Diplomacy*, ed. Alexander Star (New York: New York Times Co., 2011).

16. Since 2006, the unauthorized document archive website WikiLeaks has published anonymous submissions of documents not generally available to the public. *See Wikipedia*, s.v. "WikiLeaks," last edited July 25, 2017, https://en.wikipedia.org/wiki/WikiLeaks, for listings and redacted content.

17. *Wikipedia* s.v. "Julian Assange," last edited August 27, 2017, https://en.wikipedia.org/wiki/Julian_Assange#Early_life.

18. John F. Burns and Ravi Somaiya, "Wikileaks Founder Gets Support in Rebuking US on Whistle-Blowers," *New York Times*, October 23, 2010.

19. Ricardo Patino, Ecuadorian Foreign Minister: "Assange . . . is concerned that deportation from Sweden could lead to . . . politically motivated penalties up to the death sentence." *Aljazeera*, June 19, 2012, http:\\www.aljazeera.com/proigrammes/talktojazeera/2012/08/2012 824116129648419.html (access date unknown).

20. "A Note to Readers: The Decision to Publish Diplomatic Documents," *New York Times*, November 28, 2010.

21. Nicole Belle, "BREAKING: Wikileaks Releases US Embassy Cables—Updated," *Crooks and Liars* (blog), November 28, 2010, http://crooksandliars.com/nicole-belle/breaking-wikileaks-releases-us-embass (accessed August 20, 2017).

22. Aaron Bady, "Julian Assange and the Computer Conspiracy: 'To Destroy This Invisible Government,'" *Zunguzungu* (blog), November 29, 2010, https://zunguzungu.wordpress.com/2010/11/29/julian-assange -and-the-computer-conspiracy-%E2%80%9Cto-destroy-this-invisible -government%E2%80%9D/ (accessed August 21, 2017).

23. Ibid.

24. Bonnie Kaplan, "Selling Health Data: De-Identification, Privacy, and Speech," *Cambridge Quarterly of Healthcare Ethics* 24, no. 3 (June 2014): 256–71.

25. David E. Sanger, John Markoff, and Thom Shanker, "U.S. Steps up Effort on Digital Defenses," *New York Times*, April 27, 2009, http://www.nytimes.com/2009/04/28/us/28cyber.html?mcubz=0 (accessed July 2017).

CHAPTER 4. THE SCOPE OF IGNORANCE

1. The Dunning-Kruger Effect is a cognitive bias wherein relatively unskilled individuals suffer from illusory superiority.

2. A Seattle-based transformational leadership program. Clients include Harvard Design School, Microsoft, Mead-Johnson, Touchstone, and Alaska Airlines.

3. Julie Benezet, *The Journey of Not Knowing: How 21st Century Leaders Can Chart a Course When There Is None* (Morton Hill, 2016). See Journey Home, https://journeyofnotknowing.com/.

4. The Beginner's Mind, or Shoshin, is a concept in Zen Buddhism

referring to an attitude of openness and eagerness and lack of preconceptions.

5. Impressions by author gained during interviews with Maharishi student Lars Backstrom in Fairfield, Iowa, 2004.

6. Generally attributed to an anonymous Persian poet, though some find a (an unconfirmed) link with the thirteenth-century philosopher Omar Khayam.

7. Scott Peck, *The Road Less Traveled: A New Psychology of Love, Traditional Values, and Spiritual Growth* (New York: Touchstone, 1978), pp. 46–51.

8. *Catholic Answers*, s.v. "Mozarabic Rite," by Henry Jenner, https://www.catholic.com/encyclopedia/mozarabic-rite (accessed August 30, 2017).

9. Transubstantiation: a doctrine observed by Roman and Eastern Catholic churches that holds that the bread and wine of the Eucharist is changed into the substance of the blood and body of Christ, only the appearance of the bread and wine remaining.

10. Carol S. Dweck, *Mindset: How You Can Fulfill Your Potential* (New York: Random House, 2006).

11. Gen. 2:16–17 (New Living Translation).

12. "What angry voters want today is not change but a repeal of all the changes of the past 16 years. That's a longing no one can fulfill." Robert Samuelson, "Longing for a Golden Decade," *Week*, August 5, 2016.

13. Paul Babiak and Robert D. Hare, *Snakes in Suits: When Psychopaths Go to Work* (New York: HarperCollins, 2006), pp. 35–58.

14. Bill Vitek and Wes Jackson argue that uncritical faith in scientific knowledge has created many of the problems now threatening the planet and that our wholesale reliance on scientific progress is both untenable and myopic.

15. Wendell Berry, "The Way of Ignorance," *The Virtues of Ignorance: Complexity, Sustainability, and the Limits of Knowledge*, eds. Bill Vitek and Wes Jackson (Lexington: University Press of Kentucky), p. 46; William Vitek, "Toward an Ignorance-Based Worldview" (keynote speech, Matfield Green Campus, Kansas, 2004).

16. Ibid.

17. Stuart Firestein, *Ignorance: How It Drives Science* (Oxford: Oxford University Press, 2012).

18. Matt. 25:40 (New International Version).

CHAPTER 5. THE MANY BRANCHES OF IGNORANCE

1. Russell Baker, *New York Times Magazine*, November 9, 1980.

2. Susan Haskins and Dan Prescher, "Why Costa Rica Remains One of the World's Top Retirement Destinations," *Huffington Post*, February 5, 2013, updated April 7, 2013, http://www.huffingtonpost.com/suzan -haskins-and-dan-prescher/best-places-to-retire-why-costa-rica-remains _b_2583079.html (accessed August 30, 2017).

3. Christopher P. Baker, "The National Parks of Costa Rica," *Moon Handbooks, Costa Rica*, 2004.

4. Anonymous, *Imperial Hubris: Why the West Is Losing the War on Terrorism* (London: Brassey's, 2004), pp. 234–59.

5. Author's observations during visits to sub-Saharan towns and villages.

6. Sheldon Richman, "'Ancient History': US Conduct in the Middle East since WWII and the Folly of Intervention," *Cato Institute Policy Analysis* 159 (August 16, 1991).

7. Eduardo Galeano, *Memory of Fire*, trans. Cedric Belfrage, vol. 3, *Century of the Wind* (New York: Norton, 1998). An anecdotal history of uprisings and foreign incursions.

8. Joshua Hersh, "Extraordinary Rendition Report Finds More Than 50 Nations Involved in Global Torture Scheme," *Huffington Post*, February 5, 2013, http://www.huffingtonpost.com/2013/02/04/extraordinary -rendition-torture-report_n_2617809.html (accessed August 31, 2017).

9. Stephanie Mencimer, "The Man behind Citizens United Is Just Getting Started," *Mother Jones*, May/June 2011, http://www.motherjones.com/ politics/2011/05/james-bopp-citizens-united/ (accessed August 31, 2017).

CHAPTER 6. IGNORORS AND IGNOREES

1. Exo. 20:16 (King James Version).

2. Jeffrey Sachs, *The Price of Civilization* (New York: Random House, 2011), p. 3.

3. Samuelson's economics text had served as the basis for US economic theory and practice for more than forty years without giving critics reason to question its balancing effects.

4. Paul A. Samuelson, *Economics*, 19th ed. (New York: Irwin/McGraw-Hill, 2004).

5. Barry S. Brummett, *Uncovering Hidden Rhetorics: Social Issues in Disguise* (New York: Sage, 2008).

6. Aldous Huxley, *A Brave New World* (London: Chatto and Windus, 1932).

7. Dara O'Rourke, "Behavioural Tracking and Neuroscience Are Tools for Sustainable Innovation," *Guardian*, July 25, 2014.

8. E. L. Thorndike and Clarence Barnhart, *Scott, Foresman Advanced Dictionary* (Glenview, IL: Scott Foresman and Company, 1973), s.v. "censor."

9. David Boaz, "Censoring Ray Bradbury," Cato at Liberty (Cato Institute), June 6, 2012.

10. "The Link between Low Literacy and Crime," *Target Crime with Literacy: Literacy and Policing in Canada* (Kanata, ON: Canadian Association of Chiefs of Police, 2009), chapter 2, sheet 2.

11. Jonathan Rauch, *Kindly Inquisitors: The New Attacks on Free Thought* (Chicago: University of Chicago Press, 2013), pp. 160–71.

12. Steven S. Dubner and Steven D. Levitt, *Freakonomics: A Rogue Economist Explores the Hidden Side of Everything* (New York: HarperCollins, 2005).

13. Damla Ergun, "Majority Supports Legal Abortion but Details Indicate Ambivalence," ABC News: This Week, July 25, 2013.

14. Bobby Ross Jr., "Oklahoma's Abortion, Transgender Bills Called Political 'Smokescreen,'" *Washington Post*, May 25, 2016.

15. "Understanding Media: The Inside Story," Annenberg Learner, https://www.learner.org/courses/democracyinamerica/dia_10/dia_10_topic.html (accessed August 31, 2017).

16. "John Kerry, Flip-Flopper?" *Economist*, March 25, 2004, http://www.economist.com/node/2539128 (accessed August 31, 2017).

17. Robert Proctor and Laura Schiebinger, *Agnotology: The Making and Unmaking of Ignorance* (Palo Alto: Stanford University Press, 2008).

18. Dr. Robert Proctor is a Stanford-based specialist in interdisciplinary studies of the twentieth century and how interests impose ignorance on societies for purpose.

CHAPTER 7. ANTI-INTELLECTUALISM

1. Friend with Argentina's equivalent of EPA, in interview with author, Buenos Aires, Argentina, January 22, 1996.

2. Richard Hofstadter, *Anti-Intellectualism in American Life* (New York: Vintage, 1963).

3. Celia Wexler, "Bring Back the Office of Technological Assessment," *New York Times*, May 28, 2015.

4. See OpenSecrets.org lobbying database, 2016.

5. Sunil Iyengar, *To Read or Not to Read: A Question of National Consequence*, research report 47 (Washington, DC: National Endowment for the Arts, 2007).

6. Steven Johnson, *Everything Bad Is Good for You: How Today's Popular Culture Is Actually Making Us Smarter* (New York: Riverhead Books, 2005).

7. Thomas Sowell, *The Quest for Cosmic Justice* (New York: Simon & Schuster, 2001), p. 187.

8. "The 25 Oldest Colleges in America," Niche, https://articles.niche.com/the-25-oldest-colleges-in-america/ (accessed August 26, 2017); *Wikipedia*, s.v. "Colonial Colleges," last edited August 15, 2017, https://en.wikipedia.org/wiki/Colonial_colleges#cite_note-21 (accessed July 2017).

9. Bayard Hall, *The New Purchase, or Seven and a Half Years in the Far West* (Princeton: Princeton University, 1916), p. 207.

10. *Wikipedia*, s.v. "Anti-Intellectualism," last edited August 21, 2017, https://en.wikipedia.org/wiki/Anti-intellectualism (accessed July 2017).

11. Paul Johnson, *Intellectuals: From Marx and Tolstoy to Sarte and Chomsky* (New York: Harper and Row, 1985).

12. La noche de los batones largos. On June 28, 1966, Argentine police wielding long batons drove students and faculty from public universities and destroyed laboratories and libraries. *Wikipedia*, s.v. "La Noche de los Bastones Largos," last edited June 22, 2017, https://en.wikipedia.org/wiki/La_Noche_de_los_Bastones_Largos (accessed July 2017).

13. *Wikipedia*, s.v. "Anti-Intellectualism."

14. Ibid.

15. Ibid.

16. Stanislav Andreski, *Social Sciences as Sorcery* (Harmondsworth, UK: Penguin, 1974). A biting conservative critique on social sciences and their reliance on questionable data.

17. William L. Riordon, *Plunkitt of Tammany Hall* (New York: A. A. Knopf, 1948), chapter 2. Available online at: http://www.gutenberg.org/files/2810/2810-h/2810-h.htm (accessed July 2017). George Plunkitt (1842–1924), an unapologetic machine politician, served 12 different districts in the New York State Assembly between 1884 and 1904.

18. Alia Wong, "The Governor Who (Maybe) Tried to Kill Liberal-Arts Education," *Atlantic*, February 11, 2015, https://www.theatlantic.com/education/archive/2015/02/the-governor-who-maybe-tried-to-kill-liberal-arts-education/385366/ (accessed August 31, 2017).

19. Russell Banks, *Dreaming Up America* (New York: Seven Stories, 2009), p. 192.

20. Paul Bedard, "Pew Media Survey: 47% of Conservatives Call Fox News Their Main News Source," *Washington Examiner*, October 21, 2014.

21. Drawn from comments to the author in "spirited" discussions during the 1994 North American Association for Environmental Education Annual Conference.

22. Paul Trout, "Anti-Intellectualism and the Dumbing Down of the University" (essay, Montana State University-Bozeman, 1997), http://mtprof.msun.edu/Spr1997/TROUT-ST.html (accessed August 31, 2017).

23. K. A. F. Knepp, "Understanding Student and Faculty Incivility in Higher Education," *Journal of Effective Teaching* 12, no. 1 (2012).

24. United States Department of Labor, "College Enrollment and Work Activity of 2016 High School Graduates," Bureau of Labor Statistics, April 27, 2017, https://www.bls.gov/news.release/hsgec.nr0.htm (accessed August 26, 2017).

25. Laurence Steinberg and Sanford Dornbusch, "Negative Correlates of Part-Time Employment during Adolescence," *Developmental Psychology* 27 (1991): 304–13.

26. National Association of Scholars (NAS), *The Dissolution of General Education: 1914–1993* (Princeton: National Association of Scholars, 1996), p. 8, https://www.nas.org/images/documents/report_the_dissolution_of_general_education_1914_1993.pdf (accessed July 2017).

27. Ibid., p. 59.

28. Ibid., p. 27.

29. Ibid., p. 29.

30. Henry Bauer, *Students Who Don't Study* (essay, Baton Rouge, LA: Society for Return to Academic Standards, November 1997), http://www.bus.lsu.edu/accounting/faculty/lcrumbley/study.htm (accessed July 2017).

31. Peter Sacks, *Generation X Goes to College: An Eye-Opening Account of Teaching in Postmodern America* (Chicago: Open Court, 1996).

32. Susan Jacoby, *The Age of American Unreason* (New York: Vintage, 2009).

33. Jacoby is overreaching in inferring that figurative lessons from the Bible are nothing more than supernatural fantasy.

34. Jacoby, *Age of American Unreason*, p. 21.

CHAPTER 8. IGNORANCE IN EDUCATION

1. Howard Gardner, *Five Minds for the Future* (Brighton, Boston, MA: Harvard Business School, 2006). *See* back cover.

2. John Taylor Gatto, *Dumbing Us Down: The Hidden Curriculum of Compulsory Schooling* (Gabriola Island, BC: New Society, 1992).

3. Ibid.

4. Victoria Rideout, *Children, Teens, and Entertainment Media: The View from the Classroom* (San Francisco: Common Sense Media, November 1, 2012).

5. Gatto, *Dumbing Us Down.*

6. M. G. Siegler, "Eric Schmidt: Every Two Days We Create as Much Information as We Did up to 2003," TechCrunch.com, August 4, 2010, https://techcrunch.com/2010/08/04/schmidt-data/ (accessed August 31, 2017).

7. Alvin Toffler, *Future Shock* (New York: Random House, 1970).

8. Ignoree: one who is put into or held in ignorance by ignorors.

9. Michel Foucault, *Power/Knowledge: Selected Interviews and Other Writings* (New York: Pantheon, 1977).

10. "Stolen History: The Great Texas Textbook War (a Reader's Guide)," *Explore Journal of Science and Healing,* July–August 2011.

11. Emma Brown, "Texas Officials: Schools Should Teach That Slavery Was a 'Side-Issue' to Civil War," *Washington Post,* July 5, 2015.

12. *The High Cost of Textbooks: Options and Alternatives for Students* (Madison: University of Wisconsin-Madison, June 2008), https://www.library.wisc.edu/wp-content/uploads/2014/07/Textbooks2008.pdf (accessed July 2017).

13. "Gates, Hewlett Foundations Partner on $60 million Global Education Initiative," *Philanthropy News Digest,* December 19, 2006.

14. OER Commons, 2017, http://www.oercommons.org. A comprehensive listing of Open Educational Resources, maintained by the Institution for the Study of Knowledge Management in Education.

15. Anya Kamanetz, "Testing: How Much Is Too Much?" NPREd: How Learning Happens, November 17, 2014, http://www.npr.org/sections/ed/2014/11/17/362339421/testing-how-much-is-too-much (accessed July 2017).

16. Janet Bass, "AFT Report Shows the High Cost of Overtesting," press release, American Federation of Teachers, July 23, 2013.

17. Ibid.

18. "Bill Gates Admits That Small Schools Are Not the Answer," Scharget Consulting Group, January 27, 2009.

19. Mozert v. Hawkins County Board of Education, 827 F.2d 1058 (6th Cir. 1987), http://uscivilliberties.org/cases/4173-mozert-v-hawkins-county-board-of-education-827-f-2d-1058-1987.html.

20. Rebecca Huval, "Revising the Revisionists: The Texas Board of Ed Loses Power Over Textbooks," *Education*, January 24, 2013.

CHAPTER 9. IGNORANCE IN THE MEDIA

1. Media Research Center (MRC) is a politically conservative organization based in Reston, Virginia. Its stated mission is to prove that liberal bias in media exists and undermines traditional American values. *See Wikipedia* s.v. "Media Research Center," last edited July 24, 2017, https://en.wikipedia.org/wiki/Media_Research_Center.

2. Oscar Wilde, "The Soul of Man under Socialism," *Fortnightly Review* 49, no. 290 (February 1891): 292–319.

3. A. J. Liebling, *New Yorker*, May 14, 1960.

4. Bill Moyers, "Buying the War," *Bill Moyers Journal*, aired April 25, 2007 (New York: PBS, 2007).

5. Noam Chomsky, *Media Control: The Spectacular Achievements of Propaganda*, 2nd ed. (New York: Seven Stories, 1991).

6. Author's interpretation of Burke's text.

7. Quote attributed to Hearst.

8. Ellen Goodman, *Boston Globe*, 1993.

9. Timothy Noah, "Did Nixon Really Order the Watergate Break-In?" MSNBC, August 9, 2014, http://www.msnbc.com/msnbc/nixon-40th-anniversary-order-the-watergate-break (accessed August 31, 2017).

10. Catherine Taibi, "There Are Far Fewer Reporters in America than Ten Years Ago," *Huffington Post*, April 14, 2014, http://www.huffington post.com/2014/04/14/reporters-america_n_5147244.html (accessed July 2017).

11. Brent Baker, "Four Times More Journalists Identify as Liberal Than Conservative," *MRC NewsBusters*, March 19, 2008, https://www.newsbusters.org/blogs/nb/brent-baker/2008/03/19/four-times-more-journalists-identify-liberal-conservative (accessed August 24, 2017).

12. William Blake, "Auguries of Innocence," lines 53–54.

13. Chomsky, *Media Control*.

14. Herbert Aptheker, "Walter Lippmann and Democracy," in *History and Reality* (New York: Cameron and Associates, 1955), pp. 49–72; Chomsky, *Media Control*, in which Chomsky quoted Lippmann's ideas about democracy.

15. Aptheker, "Walter Lippmann and Democracy."

16. "Hermann Goering: War Games," Snopes, last updated April 18, 2017, http://www.snopes.com/quotes/goering.asp (accessed July 2017). Comments made in private to Gustaf Gilbert, a German-speaking American intelligence officer during Goering's incarceration at Nuremberg.

17. Theodore Roosevelt, editorial, May 1918.

18. Letter from James Madison to W. T. Barry, August 4, 1822, Library of Congress, https://www.loc.gov/resource/mjm.20_0155_0159/?st=text (accessed August 26, 2017).

19. Howard Zinn, interview by David Barsamian, "Critical Thinking," *International Socialist Review*, February 1, 2005, http://www.howardzinn .org/critical-thinking/ (accessed July 2017).

20. Ibid.

21. Staff, "33 Internal FOX Editorial Memos Reviewed by MMFA Reveal FOX News Channel's Inner Workings," Media Matters, July 14, 2004.

22. Greg Mitchell, *So Wrong for So Long: How the Press, the Pundits, and the President Failed on Iraq* (New York: Union Square, 2008), p. 119.

23. Jason DeParle, "After the War; Long Series of Military Decisions Led to Gulf War News Censorship," *New York Times*, May 5, 1991. For death toll see John Tirman, *The Deaths of Others: The Fate of Civilians in America's Wars* (Oxford: Oxford University Press, July 2011).

24. Mitchell, *So Wrong for So Long*, p. 119.

25. Paul Reikoff, *Chasing Ghosts: A Soldier's Fight for America from Baghdad to Washington* (New York: Penguin, 2006).

26. Richard Seymour, "Middle East Bloggers Set Cat among Pigeons," *Middle East*, April 1, 2008.

27. International Commission for the Study of Communication Problems, *Many Voices, One World* (New York: Rowman & Littlefield, 2004), p. 111. The McBride Report was so aimed at US-centered news agencies that it stirred thoughts among some of withdrawing support from UNESCO.

28. Over time, Hartmann's delivery has taken a sharper tone, just as drivers must exceed speed limits to keep their pace in hyper-traffic.

29. "Silvio Berlusconi Net Worth," *Richest*, http://www.therichest.com/ celebnetworth/politician/minister/silvio-berlusconi-net-worth/ (accessed August 24, 2017).

30. "Clear Channel," Federal Communications Center, https://www.fcc.gov/proceedings-actions/mergers-transactions/clear-channel (accessed August 26, 2017).

31. The FCC eliminated the *per se* limit on the aggregation of Commercial Mobile Radio Services (CMRS) effective January 1, 2003. The FCC's spectrum cap rule restricted the amount of broadband spectrum an entity could hold or have attributed to itself in a particular geographic area. In short, restrictions were eased in 2003 and after.

32. FCC Notice of Proposed Rulemaking, MB docket no. 13-236.

33. Color of Change, colorofchange.org/campaign/victories/glennbeck (access date unknown).

34. Douglas Brinkley, "Ink Will the Real Uncle Duke Please Stand Up?" *New Yorker*, May 15, 2000, http://www.newyorker.com/magazine/2000/05/15/ink-will-the-real-uncle-duke-please-stand-up (accessed August 26, 2017).

35. Hunter S. Thompson, *Fear and Loathing on the Campaign Trail '72* (New York: Simon & Schuster, 1973), p. 33.

36. Toni Morrison, ed., Burn This Book: PEN Writers Speak Out on the Power of the Word (New York: Harper, 2009), p. vi.

37. Poynter.org offers a detailed history of sales and acquisitions of newspapers.

38. William Launder et al., "Bezos Buys *Washington Post* for $250 Million," *Wall Street Journal*, August 5, 2013.

39. William Launder and Russell Adams, "Philadelphia Newspapers Sold Yet Again," *Wall Street Journal*, April 2, 2012.

40. Christine Henry, "*New York Times* Sells *Boston Globe*," *New York Times*, August 3, 2013.

41. Jeff Bezos, "Jeff Bezos on Post Purchase," *Washington Post*, August 5, 2013.

42. Ravi Somaiya, "Sheldon Adelson's Purchase of Los Vegas Paper Seen as a Power Play," *New York Times*, Jan 2, 2016.

43. "Bush Administration Documents on Secrecy Policy," *Prairie Weather* (blog), http://fas.org/sgp/bush/index.html (access date unknown).

44. Michael Cohen, "The Proliferation of the 'Parallel State,'" (working paper, Democracy Arsenal, October 2008), http://fride.org/descarga/WP71_Paralell_state_ENG_oct08.pdf (accessed July 2017).

45. Andrew Sullivan, "Why I Blog," *Atlantic*, November 2008, https://www.theatlantic.com/magazine/archive/2008/11/why-i-blog/307060/ (accessed July 2017).

46. Ibid.

47. Law professor Glen Reynolds's experimental site, *Instapundit*, soared to millions of hits following the 9/11 attacks. It became a favorite among conservatives. *See Wikipedia* s.v. "Instapundit," last edited April 20, 2017, https://en.wikipedia.org/wiki/Instapundit.

48. David Brin, *Transparent Society* (Cambridge, MA: Perseus Books, 1998).

CHAPTER 10. IGNORANCE IN POLITICS

1. *Network*, directed by Sidney Lumet (New York: MGM and United Artists Studios, November 1976).

2. George Farah, *No Debate: How the Republican and Democratic Parties Secretly Control the Presidential Debates* (New York: Seven Stories, 2004), p. 17.

3. Ibid., p. 33. All control positions regarding debates were redefined with the 2016 election.

4. "Fixing the Presidential Debates," *New York Times*, September 18, 1996, http://www.nytimes.com/1996/09/18/opinion/fixing-the-presidential-debates.html?mcubz=0 (accessed August 24, 2017).

5. *Merriam-Webster* s.v. "Certitude," https://www.merriam-webster.com/dictionary/certitude (accessed August 26, 2017).

6. Robert Ringer, *Restoring the American Dream: The Defining Voice in the Movement for Liberty* (Hoboken, NJ: John Wiley and Sons, 2010).

7. Richard Nixon, Presidential Address No. 271, "Special Message to Congress on the Problems of Population Growth" (July 18, 1969).

8. Ibid. Nixon's comment demonstrated acceptance of the Rockefeller Commission's opposition to his position on population and immigration.

9. Quote attributed to Edward R. Murrow and also attributed to French philosopher Bertrand de Jouvenel.

10. Louis Jacobson, "Congress Has 11% Approval Ratings but 96% Incumbent Reelection Rate, Meme Says," PolitiFact, November 11, 2014, http://www.politifact.com/truth-o-meter/statements/2014/nov/11/facebook-posts/congress-has-11-approval-ratings-96-incumbent-re-e/ (accessed July 2017).

11. Ambrose Bierce, *The Devil's Dictionary* (Neale, 1911).

12. "Language: A Key Mechanism of Control—Newt Gingrich's 1996 GOPAC Memo," http://www.informationclearinghouse.info/article4443.htm (accessed August 25, 2017).

13. Ibid.

14. Ibid.

15. See James I. Matray, "Revisiting Korea: Exposing Myths of the Forgotten War, Part 1," *Prologue Magazine* 34, no. 2 (Summer 2002).

16. Jonathan Kwitny, *Endless Enemies: How America's Worldwide Interventions Destroy Democracy and Free Enterprise and Defeat Our Own Best Interests* (New York: Congdon and Weed, 1984), pp. 104–109.

17. Winston Churchill, *My Early Life* (New York: Charles Scribner's Sons, 1930).

18. Richmond Lloyd and Timothy Castle, *Strategy and Force Planning*, 2nd ed. (Newport, RI: Naval War College Press, 1998), p.122.

19. Ibid., p. 123.

20. Walter Wink, *The Powers That Be: Theology for a New Millennium* (New York: Doubleday, 1998). Walter Wink (1935–2012), American theologian and activist within progressive Christianity. He served as professor emeritus of Auburn Theological Seminary, NYC.

21. Debra Bruno, "Repatriation Blues: Expats Struggle with the Dark Side of Coming Home," *Wall Street Journal*, April 5, 2015.

22. Billy Graham, *Our Greatest Need* (daily devotion), aired June 23, 2014, https://billygraham.org/devotion/our-greatest-need/ (accessed September 1, 2017).

CHAPTER 11. INSTITUTIONAL IGNORANCE

1. Robert Grudin (1938–), American writer and philosopher who wrote *Time and the Art of Living, Book: A Novel,* and other works in which he addressed psychology, politics, communications, and creative endeavor. For more information, see the Foresight Institute's page about Grudin: "Robert Grudin," Foresight Institute, http://foresight.org/about/Grudin .html (accessed July 2017).

2. Rooted at least as far back as Greek philosophy, universal reason is that something at the bottom of a thinking system that allows it to understand natural things that are generally complex.

3. America's Founding Documents, *Declaration of Independence, Constitution, Bill of Rights,* National Archives, page reviewed June 26, 2017.

4. Owen Edwards, "How Thomas Jefferson Created His Own Bible," *Smithsonian Magazine,* January 2012, http://www.smithsonianmag.com/ arts-culture/how-thomas-jefferson-created-his-own-bible-5659505/ (accessed August 28, 2017).

5. Chris Parker, "How Monsanto Is Terrifying the Farming World," *Miami New Times,* July 25, 2013.

6. Margaret Heffernan, *Willful Blindness: Why We Ignore the Obvious at Our Peril* (New York: Bloomsbury, 2011), p. 56; *The Fog of War,* directed by Errol Morris (Brighton, MA: Sony Pictures Classics, 2003).

7. The sum could include trends, vogues, architectural schools, styles, social permissions, marketing data, political polls, budgets, tolerance of behaviors, etc.

8. Ayn Rand was a Russian-born writer and philosopher known for her championing of individual rights, pursuit of rational self-interest, and laissez-faire capitalism. Her thinking finds favor among libertarians and extreme conservatives.

9. Andrea Seabrook, "On Capitol Hill, Rand's 'Atlas' Can't Be Shrugged Off," NPR Morning Edition, November 14, 2011.

10. John Carney, "The Warning: Brooksley Born's Battle with Alan Greenspan, Robert Rubin and Larry Summers," *Business Insider,* October 21, 2009, http://www.businessinsider.com/the-warning-brooksley-borns-battle-with-alan-greenspan-robert-rubin-and-larry-summers-2009-10 (accessed August 25, 2017). Brooksley Born, chairperson of the Commodity Futures Trading Commission (CFTC). Muriel Siebert, superintendent of banks for the state of New York.

11. "Waxman Questions Greenspan about Ideology," C-SPAN video, 1:40, from hearing of the House Committee on Oversight and Government Reform regarding the financial crisis and the role of federal regulators on October 23, 2008, https://www.c-span.org/video/?c4480230/waxman-questions-greenspan-ideology (accessed September 1, 2017).

12. *Wikipedia* s.v., "Movement for the Restoration of the Ten Commandments of God," last edited February 19, 2017, https://en.wikipedia.org/wiki/Movement_for_the_Restoration_of_the_Ten_Commandments_of_God.

13. John 10:10.

14. The current Christian Coalition (CCA) is successor to the original CC created in 1989 by Pat Robertson. Its priorities include rolling back Obamacare, standing with Israel, reducing government spending, promoting peace through military strength, championing the right to bear arms, opposing abortions, and defending traditional marriage. Christian Coalition, "Our Agenda," http://www.cc.org/our_agenda (accessed September 1, 2017).

15. Paul Babiak and Robert D. Hare, *Snakes in Suits: When Psychopaths Go to Work* (New York: HarperCollins, 2006).

16. According to psychologytoday.com, sociopaths lie coolly, cannot be consistently truthful, are extremely convincing, change image as needed, cannot perceive that there is anything wrong with them, and believe in their own powers.

17. M. E. Thomas, *Confessions of a Sociopath: A Life Spent Hiding in Plain Sight* (New York: Crown, 2013), pp. 25–58.

18. Disproportionally high percentages are found among CEOs, lawyers, and media leaders. See Jon Ronson's *The Psychopath Test* (New York: Riverhead, 2012) and Kali Halloway's publications for Alternet.

19. Stanley Bing, *What Would Machiavelli Do?* (New York: HarperCollins, 2000).

20. *Wall Street*, directed by Oliver Stone (New York: 20th Century Fox, 1987).

21. George Lakoff, *Don't Think of an Elephant: Know Your Values and Frame the Debate* (White River Junction, VT: Chelsea Green, 2004).

22. James Wilson, *Bureaucracy: What Government Agencies Do and Why They Do It* (New York: Basic Books, 1989), p. 317.

23. George F. Will, *The Leveling Wind: Politics, The Culture, and Other News, 1990–1994* (New York: Viking, 1994), p. xvi.

24. *The World Factbook* (Washington, DC: Central Intelligence Agency, 2010). Available for downloading, not browsing.

25. Arnie Cooper, "Environmental Heretic: Stewart Brand on Nuclear Energy, Genetically Modified Foods, and Climate Engineering," *Sun Magazine*, September 2011. Stewart Brand, TED lecturer, creator and editor of the *Whole Earth Catalog*, and cofounder of the Global Business Network.

26. John Allen Paulos, "Why Don't Americans Elect Scientists?" *New York Times*, February 13, 2012.

27. Dickens's satirical description of a case that lasted until the lawyers it supported drained the estate they represented of all funds.

28. See codeforamerica.com home page for mission and activities.

29. Gavin Newsom, *Citizenville: How to Take the Town Square Digital and Reinvent Government* (New York: Penguin, 2013), pp. 79–82.

30. From notes taken by the author from broadcast TV content on the night before the election.

31. Harry Enten, FiveThirtyEight, April 1, 2014, https://fivethirtyeight .com/datalab/poll-shows-record-obamacare-support-but-that-doesnt-mean -much/ (accessed July 2017).

32. Ibid.

33. Nathaniel Frank, "Gary Troops and the Trouble with Polls," *Huffington Post*, May 25, 2011, http://www.huffingtonpost.com/nathaniel-frank/gay-troops-and-the-troubl_b_460291.html (accessed August 28, 2017).

34. Sam Rogers, *Opinions of Military Personnel on Sexual Minorities in the Military* (Utica, NY: Zogby International, December 2006).

35. Michael Cohen, "Obama's Understated Policy Gains," *New York Times*, July 9, 2014.

36. "Study Finds Fox News Viewers Least Informed of All Viewers," *Huffington Post*, May 23, 2012, updated July 23, 2012, http://www.huffingtonpost.com/2012/05/23/fox-news-less-informed-new-study_n_1538914.html (accessed August 29, 2017).

37. Rom. 12:2 (New King James Version).

38. Hal Marcovitz, *Religious Fundamentalism* (San Diego: ReferencePoint Press, 2009).

39. *Submission*, directed by Theo van Gogh (2004).

40. Jason Burke, "The Murder That Shattered Holland's Liberal Dream," *Guardian*, November 7, 2004, https://www.theguardian.com/world/2004/nov/07/terrorism.religion (accessed August 31, 2017).

41. Footsteps, "About Us," https://www.footstepsorg.org/about-us/ (accessed August 28, 2017).

CHAPTER 12. FAITH, SCIENCE, AND IGNORANCE

1. Bill Moyers, *Genesis: A Living Conversation* (New York: Doubleday, 1996).

2. Roland H. Bainton, *Here I Stand: A Life of Martin Luther* (West Midlands, UK: Meridian, 1955), pp. 118–19.

3. St. Ignatius of Loyola, *The Spiritual Exercises*, 1548.

4. Jorge Mario Bergoglio and Abraham Skorka, *On Heaven and Earth: Pope Francis on Faith, Family, and the Church in the Twenty-First Century*, trans. Alejandro Bermudez and Howard Goodman (New York: Image Books, 2013).

5. Donald Cupitt set forth the events and milestones of his career in his web homepage doncupitt.com/don-cupitt.

6. Soren Kierkegaard, *The Portable Kierkegaard* (Lulu, 2009), pp. 225–26.

7. Tori Rodriguez, "How Science Mimics Faith: People May Use

Trust in Science as Others Use Religious Faith to Cope with Life's Uncertainties," *Scientific American*, March 4, 2014.

8. E. B. White, *Charlotte's Web* (New York: Harper and Brothers, 1952).

9. Bryan Appleyard, *Understanding the Present: An Alternative History of Science* (London, UK: Taurus Parke, 2004), p. xi.

10. Peggy Lee, "If That's All There Is," written by Jerry Leiber and Mike Stoller, released 1969, on *If That's All There Is*, Capitol Records.

11. Steven Hawking, *A Brief History of Time* (New York: Bantam Books, 1998).

12. Appleyard, *Understanding the Present*, p. 9.

13. Ibid., p. 249.

14. Quote attributed to Sir Thomas More.

15. Michel Foucault, *Power/Knowledge: Selected Interviews and Other Writings* (New York: Pantheon, 1977).

16. Walter Brueggemann, address, Atlanta, GA: Emergent Convention, September 16, 2004.

17. Karl Paul Polanyi (1886–1964) was born in Vienna and died in Pickering, Ontario. Polanyi was known for his cultural approach to economics that emphasized how economics is embedded in society and culture. *Wikipedia* s.v. "Karl Polanyi," last edited July 30, 2017, https://en.wikipedia.org/wiki/Karl_Polanyi.

18. *Academic Kids*, s.v. "Apalachicola, Florida," https://www.academic kids.com/encyclopedia/index.php/Apalachicola%2C_Florida (accessed August 31, 2017); Yellow Pages, "Apalachicola, FL Churches Places of Worship," https://www.yellowpages.com/apalachicola-fl/churches-places -of-worship (accessed August 31, 2017).

CHAPTER 13. PROPAGANDA

1. Guy Collender, "Education in Nigeria: The Impact of Bad Politics and a Blueprint for Progress," London International Develop Centre, 2014.

2. William Blake, "Auguries of Innocence," lines 53–54.

3. Edward Bernays, *Propaganda* (Abingdon: Routledge, 1928).

4. Ellen Rolfes, "Internet Advertising Revenue Surpasses Broadcast TV for the First Time," PBS NewsHour: The Rundown, April 11, 2014.

5. Chris Smith, "The Price of Super Bowl Commercials May Be About to Stall," *Forbes*, February 2, 2017.

6. Anthony Crups, "In Their Prime: Broadcasts Spots Costs Soar," *Adweek*, June 22, 2011.

7. Michele Simon, "All Eyes on Washington State for Genetically Engineered Food Labeling," Food Democracy Now! August 8, 2013.

8. Melissa Allison, "Initiative 522: Familiar Groups Lead Fight on GMO Labeling," *Seattle Times*, September 22, 2013.

9. Quote attributed to Adolf Hitler.

10. Stephanie Strom, "Connecticut Approves Labeling Genetically Modified Foods," *New York Times*, June 3, 2013, http://www.nytimes.com/2013/06/04/business/connecticut-approves-qualified-genetic-labeling.html?mcubz=0; "Connecticut Is First State to Pass GMO-Labeling Law; Maine Close Behind," Lexology, June 18, 2013, https://www.lexology.com/library/detail.aspx?g=d09961b1-0ad9-4823-92ea-f13bd640cf82; Maggie Caldwell, "Maine Is Second State to Pass GMO Labeling Law," *Mother Jones*, June 14, 2013, http://www.motherjones.com/food/2013/06/maine-gmo-labeling/ (accessed August 31, 2017).

11. Zach Kaldveer, "13 Lies about GMOs and GMO Labeling," *Wake Up World*, July 28, 2013, https://wakeup-world.com/2013/08/28/13-lies-about-gmos-and-gmo-labeling/ (accessed August 31, 2017).

12. Bob Graef, "Liar, Liar, Pants on Fire," *Marysville Globe*, November 2, 2013.

13. Elizabeth Weise, "Washington State Voters Reject Labeling of GMO Foods," *USA Today*, November 6, 2013, https://www.usatoday.com/story/news/nation/2013/11/06/washington-state-voters-reject-gmo-labeing/3450705/ (accessed August 28, 2017).

14. Alex Epstein is the author of *The Moral Case for Fossil Fuels* and founder and president of the Center for Industrial Progress, a for-profit think tank.

15. "Objectivists Are Not 'Conservatives,' We Are Radicals for Capitalism," Ayn Rand Lexicon, aynrandlexicon.com/lexicon/conservatives.html (accessed August 30, 2017).

16. Alex Epstein, "Why You Shouldn't Keep an Open Mind," *Capitalism Magazine*, November 2, 2000.

17. Ibid.

18. Ibid.

19. The Garn-St. Germaine Depository Institutions Act enabled banks and savings institutions to compete more readily in the money market; got rid of the existing interest ceiling; authorized the making of commercial loans; allowed federal agencies to approve bank acquisitions. Investopedia,

"Garn-St. Germain Depository Institutions Act," http://www.investopedia
.com/terms/g/garn-st-germain-depository-institutions-act.asp.

20. Pat Tillman left a successful football career with the Arizona
Cardinals to join the US Army. He was killed in Afghanistan in 2004, a
victim of an awkwardly planned expedition. Only minutes after his death,
people were turning him and the incident into things they weren't. Sara
Vizcarrondo, "The Legend of Pat Tillman: Deconstructing a Military
Myth," International Documentary Association, http://www.documentary
.org/magazine/legend-pat-tillman-deconstructing-military-myth (accessed
September 1, 2017).

21. Benjamin Zycher, "The President's Broken Window Fallacy:
Carbon Policies and Jobs," *American*, July 10, 2013, http://www.aei.org/
publication/the-presidents-broken-window-fallacy-carbon-policies-and
-jobs-2/ (accessed August 29, 2017).

22. Jonah Goldberg, "Inhospitable Earth," *National Review*, July 3,
2013, http://www.nationalreview.com/article/352591/inhospitable-earth
-jonah-goldberg (accessed August 29, 2017).

23. Stephen Moore and Richard Vedder, "The Blue-State Path to
Inequality," *Wall Street Journal*, June 4, 2014, https://www.wsj.com/articles/
stephen-moore-and-richard-vedder-liberal-blue-states-have-greater-income
-inequality-than-conservative-red-states-1401923793 (accessed August 31,
2017).

24. "Al Gore," http://www.aei.org/tag/al-gore/ (accessed August 29,
2017).

25. Jonah Goldberg, "America's 'Green' Quagmire," *Los Angeles Times*,
August 23, 2011, http://articles.latimes.com/2011/aug/23/opinion/
la-oe-goldberg-green-20110823 (accessed August 29, 2017).

26. Jonah Goldberg, "Cooling on Global Warming," *Los Angeles Times*,
April 26, 2011, http://www.latimes.com/opinion/opinion-la/la-oe
-goldberg-climate-change-20110426-column.html (accessed August 29,
2017).

27. Quote attributed to Joseph Goebbels.

28. Quotes attributed to Adolf Hitler.

29. Niccolo Machiavelli, *The Prince*, N. H. Thomson, trans. (Mineola,
NY: Dover, 1992). Views on the importance of being a strong ruler.

30. Adolf Hitler, *Mein Kampf* (New York: Houghton Mifflin, 1998).

31. Quotes attributed to Benito Mussolini.

32. Hitler was able to instill a national desire for "blood purity" that,
in 1935, forbade marriages between Germans and Jews, German or not.

This was extended to include members of other races under penalties for "blood treason."

33. Randal Marlin, *Propaganda and the Ethics of Persuasion* (Peterborough, ON: Broadview Press, 2003), p. 66.

34. Journalist George Creel was selected to head the Creel Commission, aka the Committee on Public Information. Created on April 3, 1917, the commission was tasked with building support for participating in WWI. Christopher B. Daly, "How Woodrow Wilson's Propaganda Machine Changed American Journalism," *Smithsonian Magazine*, April 28, 2017, http://www.smithsonianmag.com/history/how-woodrow-wilsons -propaganda-machine-changed-american-journalism-180963082/ (accessed September 1, 2017).

35. *Wikipedia*, s.v. "Walter Lippmann," last edited August 17, 2017, https://en.wikipedia.org/wiki/Walter_Lippmann.

36. Herbert Aptheker, "Walter Lippmann and Democracy," in *History and Reality* (New York: Cameron and Associates, 1955), pp. 49–72.

37. Dennis Thompson, *Ethics in Congress: From Individual to Institutional Corruption* (Washington: Brookings Institution, 1995).

38. Chris C., "Definition of Terrorism," US Department of Defense, April 8, 2014, http://www.secbrief.org/2014/04/definition-of-terrorism.

39. Dahr Jamail, "Fallujah Babies and Depleted Uranium-America's Toxic Legacy in Iraq," Alternet, March 18, 2013.

40. Ibid.

41. Noam Chomsky, *Media Control: The Spectacular Achievements of Propaganda*, 2nd ed. (New York: Seven Stories, 1991).

42. Dorie E. Apollonio and Lisa A. Bero, "The Creation of Industry Front Groups: The Tobacco Industry and 'Get Government off Our Back,'" *American Journal of Public Health* 97, no. 3 (March 2007): 419–27.

43. Ibid.

44. The US Chamber of Commerce is the largest lobbying organization in the nation in terms of spending. It was created by President Taft to counter the labor movement.

45. Apollonio and Bero, "Creation of Industry."

46. Extracted from the DCI Group's home page: "providing all the services—coalition and third party work, media relations, digital services, and field work—that clients need for a fully developed 'outside game' to support public policy campaigns." DCI Group, http://www.dcigroup.com/ (accessed July 2017).

CHAPTER 14. COSTS AND CONSEQUENCES OF IGNORANCE

1. Graham Allison, "Could Worse Be Yet To Come?" *Economist*, November 1, 2001.

2. Carrie Ching et al., "The Real Price of Gas," Center for Investigative Reporting, June 13, 2011, http://cironline.org/reports/price-gas-2447.

3. Ibid.

4. Ibid. The International Center for Technological Assessment (ICTA) is "devoted to fully exploring the economic, ethical, social, environmental and political impacts that can result from the applications of technology or technological systems." ICTA, 2017, http://www.icta.org/# (accessed July 2017).

5. Numbers derived from Ching et al., "Real Price."

6. Daniel Weiss, "Big Oil, Big Profits, Big Tax Breaks," Real Clear Politics, January 17, 2014, https://www.realclearpolitics.com/articles/2014/01/17/big_oil_big_profits_big_tax_breaks_121262.html (accessed July 2017).

7. The B-Lab mission is to use innovative corporate structures to align the interests of business with those of society. "About B Lab," 2017, https://www.bcorporation.net/what-are-b-corps/about-b-lab (accessed July 2017).

8. Jessica Bruder, "For 'B-Corps' a New Corporate Structure and a Triple Bottom Line," *New York Times*, March 14, 2012.

9. B-Corporations, "2014 Annual Report," https://www.bcorporation.net/news-media/annual-report-2014 (accessed August 31, 2017).

10. Bruder, "For 'B-Corps.'"

11. Chester Collins Maxey, "A Little History of Pork," *National Municipal Review*, 1919, p. 693.

12. Citizens Against Government Waste, "2006 Pig Book Summary," https://web.archive.org/web/20080714103840/http://www.cagw.org/site/PageServer?pagename=reports_pigbook2006 (accessed August 29, 2017). Citizens Against Government Waste is a nonprofit conservative watchdog group whose stated mission is to eliminate waste, mismanagement, and inefficiency. Its dependence on financial support from industries it then supports has brought its purpose into question.

13. Robert N. Proctor and Londa Schiebinger, *Agnotology: The Making & Unmaking of Ignorance* (Palo Alto, CA: Stanford University Press, 2008). Robert Proctor's career as science historian at Stanford took a turn when

he recognized how Big Tobacco was holding smokers ignorant of the threat to their health.

14. Jeff Green and Hideki Suzuki, "Board Director Pay Hits Record $251,000 for 250 Hours," *Bloomberg Technology,* May 29, 2013, http://www .bloomberg.com/news/artiles/2013-05-30/board-director-pay-hits-record (accessed July 2017).

15. Steve Eider, "Director's Cut: Best-Paid US Corporate Boards," *Business News,* December 16, 2009.

16. Douglas McIntyre and Samuel Wergley, "The 12 Companies with the Highest Paid Boards of Directors," 24/7 Wall Street, June 7, 2012, http://247wallst.com/special-report/2012/06/07/the-12-companies-with -the-highest-paid-boards-of-directors/ (accessed July 2017).

17. Polonius lectures his son, "Neither a borrower now a lender be, for loan oft loses both itself and friend, and borrowing dulls the edge of husbandry." William Shakespeare, *Hamlet,* act I, scene 3.

18. J. Reuben Clark, Conference Report, April 1938, p. 103.

19. Attractive nuisance is a defense to trespass by children used in tort law. The doctrine of attractive nuisance is premised on the belief that one who maintains a dangerous condition that is likely to attract children on their property is under a duty to post a warning or take affirmative action to protect children from dangers of that attraction. "Attractive Nuisance Law and Legal Definition," USLegal.com, 2016, https://definitions .uslegal.com/a/attractive-nuisance/ (accessed July 2017).

20. Rex Nutting, "The Typical American Couple Has Only $5,000 Saved for Retirement," Marketwatch, June 15, 2016, http://www.market watch.com/story/the-typical-american-couple-has-only-5000-saved-for -retirement-2016-04-28 (accessed July 2017).

21. "Consumer Debt Statistics (Federal Reserve) 1952–2016," Money-Zine, last reviewed June 30, 2016, http://www.money-zine.com/financial -planning/debt-consolidation/consumer-debt-statistics/ (accessed July 2017).

22. Dan Alexander, "World's Largest Debtor Governments," *Forbes Magazine,* November 8, 2013.

23. *Aids Epidemic Update: Special Report on HIV Prevention* (Geneva, CH: World Health Organization/UNAIDS, December 2005).

24. "Where Is It Illegal to be Gay?" BBC News, February 10, 2014, http://www.bbc.com/news/world-25927595 (accessed August 31, 2017).

25. Art Davidson and Art Wolfe, *Endangered Peoples* (San Francisco: Sierra Club, 1993); Jason Nowaczyk, "Cultural Assimilation and Extinction:

Definition & Examples," GACE Behavioral Science, 2017, http://study
.com/academy/lesson/cultural-assimilation-extinction-definition
-examples.html (accessed July 2017).

CHAPTER 15. WORKING FROM AND WITH IGNORANCE

1. Lawrence M. Krauss, *Quantum Man: Richard Feynman's Life in Science* (New York: W. W. Norton, 2011), p. 168.

2. David Lane, *The Mystical: Exploring the Transcendent* (Walnut, CA: Mt. San Antonio College, 2014), p. 54.

3. Stuart Firestein, *Ignorance: How It Drives Science* (Oxford; New York; Auckland: Oxford University Press, 2012), p. 11.

4. Jonah Lehrer, *Imagine: How Creativity Works* (Boston: Houghton Mifflin Harcourt, 2012).

5. Firestein, *Ignorance*.

6. Ibid.

7. "Trendalyzer Becomes Motion Charts: Global Health Measurements from Gapminder Are Seen as Change through Trendalyzer," http://blogstats.wordpress.com/2008/04/13/trendalyzer-becomes -motion (accessed August 30, 2017).

8. "Hans Rosling: How Much Do You Know about the World?" *BBC News Magazine*, November 7, 2013, http://www.bbc.com/news/ magazine-24836917 (accessed August 31, 2017). A version of the test given to world leaders at Davos, Switzerland, (which they failed) is open for everyone to try.

9. Readers are encouraged to take that test. A web search for "Davos Rosling test" will lead to the test on a number of sites.

10. William A. Cohen, *A Class with Drucker: The Lost Lessons of the World's Greatest Management Teacher* (New York: AMACOM, 2009), p. 58.

11. Ibid.

12. Ibid., p. 59.

13. Dwight Jon Zimmerman, "Henry J. Kaiser and the Liberty Ships," *Defense Media Network*, June 7, 2012, http://www.defensemedianetwork .com/stories/henry-j-kaiser-and-the-liberty-ships/ (accessed August 31, 2017).

14. Ibid.

15. Arthur Herman, *Freedom's Forge: How American Business Produced Victory in World War II* (New York: Random House); Patricia Keefe, "Ugly

Ducklings & Steaming the Way to Victory in WWII," *Marine Link,* January 28, 2014, https://www.marinelink.com/news/ducklings-steaming363512 (accessed September 1, 2017).

16. It was this and other solitary experiences that inspired St. Exupery to write the children's classic, *The Little Prince.* Lily Rothman, "The True Events That Inspired *The Little Prince,*" *Time,* August 4, 2016, http://time .com/4255854/little-prince-1943-history/ (accessed August 29, 2017).

17. Saint Exupery, *Antoine de, Wind, Sand, and Stars* (Cornwall-on-Hudson, NY: Cornwall, 1940), pp. 103–104.

18. Martin Buber, *I and Thou* (New York: Charles Scribner's Sons, 1957), pp. 11–13.

19. Richard Thruelsen and John Kobler, eds., *Adventures of the Mind from the Saturday Evening Post* (New York: Alfred A. Knopf, 1960). *Adventures of the Mind* was a collection of essays from such luminaries as C. S. Lewis. Edited by Richard Thruelsen and John Kobler, it served its time as windows into the unknown.

CONCLUSIONS

1. Eric T. Wagner, "Five Reasons 8 out of 10 Businesses Fail," *Forbes,* September 12, 2013, https://www.forbes.com/sites/ericwagner/ 2013/09/12/five-reasons-8-out-of-10-businesses-fail/#3813f5986978 (accessed July 2017).

2. Mao's Four Pests Campaign targeted sparrows, flies, mosquitoes, and rats. Sadly, honeybees were caught in the chemical attack on flies and exterminated. Wikipedia: Four Pests Campaign. *Wikipedia,* s.v. "Four Pests Campaign," last edited August 28, 2017, https://en.wikipedia.org/wiki/ Four_Pests_Campaign.

3. Dahr Jamail, "Fallujah Babies and Depleted Uranium—America's Toxic Legacy in Iraq," Alternet, March 18, 2013.

4. Attributed to Donald Rumsfeld in response to a question at a Department of Defense briefing on February 12, 2002. "There are known knowns. There are things we know we know. There are known unknowns. That is to say, there are things that we know that we don't know. But there are also unknown unknowns. These are things we don't know we don't know."

5. See chapter 2.

APPENDIX. EXPLANATION OF TERMS

1. Robert Proctor, *Agnotology: The Making and Unmaking of Ignorance* (Palo Alto: Stanford University Press, 2008). Introduction by Thomas Pynchon.

2. Ibid.

3. *Webster's Dictionary*, s.v. "Belief," 1828, online edition, http://webstersdictionary1828.com/Dictionary/belief (accessed July 27, 2017).

4. Paul Sperry, "White House Energy Task Force Papers Reveal Iraqi Oil Maps," *World Net Daily*, July 18, 2003, http://www.wnd.com/2003/07/19844/ (accessed August 29, 2017); Antonia Juhasz, "Are U.S. Oil Companies Going to 'Win' the Iraq War?" *Huffington Post*, May 25, 2011, http://www.huffingtonpost.com/antonia-juhasz/are-us-oil-companies-goin_b_42426.html (accessed August 29, 2017).

5. Smedley Butler, *War Is a Racket* (Port Townsend, WA: Feral House, 1935), p. 3.

6. Jack Cohen and Ian Stewart, *Figments of Reality: Evolution of the Curious Mind* (Cambridge: Cambridge University Press, 1997), p. 243.

7. *Webster's New World Dictionary of the American Language*, eds. David Guralnik et al. (Cleveland: World Publishing, 1960), s.v. "ignorance," p. 722.

8. Richard Dawkins, *The Selfish Gene*, 30th anniversary ed. (Oxford: Oxford University Press, 2006); Maria Popova, "How Richard Dawkins Coined the Word Meme: The Legendary Atheist's Surprising Inspiration," Brain Pickings, https://www.brainpickings.org/2013/10/02/richard-dawkins-meme-appetite-for-wonder/ (accessed September 1, 2017).

9. *Urban Dictionary*, s.v. "meme," by Emme December 10, 2003, http://www.urbandictionary.com/define.php?term=meme.

10. Samuel Huntington, *Who Are We? The Challenges to America's National Identity* (New York: Simon & Schuster, 2004).

11. *Webster's New World Dictionary*, eds. Guralnik et al., s.v. "truth."

12. John 15:19 (New International Version).

REFERENCES

Many thanks to the writers and editors whose published works helped to flesh out the content of *Ignorance*. The text is also colored by posts from bloggers and their fans, whose credible and incredible outpourings reflect the mood and direction of popular thought. The words of thinkers whose ponderings bear directly on the issue of ignorance are embedded in the text, a more useful place than footnotes or endnotes. The following titles that lent content and perspective to this work are recommended as excellent pasture for hungry minds.

Achenbach, Joel. "The War on Science." *National Geographic* (2015): 35–47.

Allison, Graham. "Could Worse Be Yet to Come?" *Economist*, 2001.

Anonymous. *Imperial Hubris: Why the West Is Losing the War on Terror.* London: Brassey's, 2004.

Appleyard, Bryan. *Understanding the Present: An Alternative History of Science.* New York: Tauris Parke, 2004.

Babiak, Paul and Robert D. Hare. *Snakes in Suits: When Psychopaths Go to Work.* New York: Harper Business, 2006.

Barbour, Scott, ed. *Censorship.* Farmington Hills, MI: Greenhaven, 2010.

Barrow, John D. *The Infinite Book: A Short Guide to the Boundless and Endless.* New York: Pantheon, 2005.

Bloom, Allan. *The Closing of the American Mind.* New York: Simon & Schuster, 1987.

Brummett, Barry S. *Uncovering Hidden Rhetorics: Social Issues in Disguise.* New York: Sage, 2008.

Bruno, Debra. "Repatriation Blues: Expats Struggle with the Dark Side of Coming Home." *Wall Street Journal*, 2015.

Buber, Martin. *I and Thou.* New York: Charles Scribner's Sons, 1957.

Brynjolffson, Eric and Andrew McAfee. *The Second Machine Age: Work,*

Progress, and Prosperity in a Time of Brilliant Technologies. New York: Norton, 2014.

Campbell, Jeremy. *The Many Faces of God: Science's 400 Year Quest for Images of the Divine.* New York: Norton, 2006.

Canine, Craig. "35 Who Made a Difference: Wes Jackson." *Smithsonian Magazine,* 2005.

Capra, Fritjof. *The Turning Point: Science, Society, and the Rising Culture.* New York: Bantam, 1988.

Chabris, Christopher and Daniel Simmons. *The Invisible Gorilla: How Our Intuitions Deceive Us.* New York: Harmony, 2010.

Chomsky, Noam. *Media Control: The Spectacular Achievements of Propaganda,* 2nd ed. New York: Seven Stories, 1991.

Close, Ellis, *The End of Anger: A New Generation's Take on Race and Rage.* New York: HarperCollins, 2011.

Cohen, Jack and Ian Stewart. *Figments of Reality: Evolution of the Curious Mind.* Cambridge: Cambridge University Press, 1997.

Cooper, George. *The Origin of Financial Crises: Central Banks, Credit Bubbles, and the Efficient Market Fallacy.* New York: Vintage, 2008.

Downes, Larry and Paul Nunes. *Big Bang Disruption: Strategy in the Age of Devastating Innovation.* New York: Portfolio/Penguin, 2014.

Drahos, Peter. *Information Feudalism: Who Owns the Knowledge Economy?* Abingdon: Earthscan, 2002.

Dubner, Steven S. and Steven D. Levitt. *Freakonomics: A Rogue Economist Explores the Hidden Side of Everything.* New York: HarperCollins, 2005.

Dunbar, Robert E. *How to Debate,* rev. ed. London: Franklin Watts, 1991.

Dweck, Carol S. *Mindset: How You Can Fulfill Your Potential and Who Has Accurate Views of Their Assets and Limitations.* New York: Ballantine, 2006.

Ellenberg, Jordan, I. *The Power of Mathematical Thinking.* New York: Penguin, 2014.

Ely, Katie. "Pass it on: On the Importance of Owning Knowledge in the Digital Age." *Teachermom* (blog).

Englehart, Tom. *The American Way of War: How Bush's Wars Became Obama's.* Chicago: Haymarket, 2010.

Farah, George. *No Debate: How the Republican and Democratic Parties Secretly Control the Presidential Debates.* New York: Seven Stories, 2004.

Feldman, Jeffrey. *Outright Barbarous: How the Violent Language of the Right Poisons American Democracy.* New York: IG, 2008.

Firestein, Stuart. *Ignorance: How It Drives Science.* Oxford: Oxford University Press, 2012.

Foucault, Michel. *The Government of Self and Others*. London: Palgrave MacMillan, 2008.

———. *Power/Knowledge: Selected Interviews and Other Writings*. New York: Pantheon, 1977.

Frankfurt, Harry G. *On Bullshit*. Princeton: Princeton University Press, 1986.

Galeano, Eduardo. *Memory of Fire*, trans. Cedric Belfrage, vol. 3, *Century of the Wind*. New York: Norton, 1998.

Gatto, John Taylor. *Dumbing Us Down: The Hidden Curriculum of Compulsory Schooling*. Gabriola Island, BC: New Society, 1992.

Gerken, Heather. *The Democracy Index: Why Our Election System Is Failing and How to Fix It*. Princeton: Princeton University Press, 2009.

Goldman, Benjamin A. *The Truth about Where You Live: An Atlas for Action on Toxins and Mortality*. New York: Random House, 1991.

Gross, Matthias and Linsey McGoey. *Routledge International Handbook of Ignorance Studies*. Abingdon: Routledge, 2015.

Grudin, Robert. *American Vulgar: The Politics of Manipulation versus the Culture of Awareness*. Berkeley: Shoemaker Hoard, 2006.

Haerens, Margaret and Lynn M. Zott, eds. *Internet Censorship*. Farmington Hills, MI: Greenhaven Press, 2014.

Haidt, Jonathan. *The Righteous Mind: Why Good People Are Divided by Politics and Religion*. New York: Pantheon, 2012.

Hallinan, Joseph T. *Kidding Ourselves: The Hidden Power of Self-Deception*. New York: Crown, 2014.

Harris, Lee. *The Suicide of Reason: Radical Islam's Threat to the West*. New York: Basic, 2007.

Heath, Christopher and Anselm Sanders. *Landmark Intellectual Property Cases and Their Legacy*. New York: Kluwer Law International, 2010.

Heffernan, Margaret. *Willful Blindness: Why We Ignore the Obvious at Our Peril*. London: Walker, 2011.

Hentoff, Nat. *Free Speech for Me But Not for Thee: How the American Right and Left Relentlessly Censor Each Other*. New York: HarperCollins, 1992.

Hofstadter, Richard. *Anti-Intellectualism in American Life*. New York: Vintage, 1963.

Holmes, Jamie. *Nonsense: The Power of Not Knowing*. New York: Crown, 2015.

Horton, Scott. *Lords of Secrecy: The National Security Elite and America's Stealth Warfare*. New York: Nation, 2015.

Hoyle, Russ. *Going to War: How Misinformation, Disinformation, and Arrogance Led America into Iraq*. New York: Thomas Dunne, 2008.

Huntington, Samuel P. *The Third Wave: Democratization in the Late Twentieth Century*. New York: Simon & Schuster, 1991.

Huxley, Aldous. *The Doors of Perception*. London: Chatto & Windus, 1954.

Icke, David. *The Perception Deception*. David Icke Books, 2014.

Jacoby, Susan. *The Age of American Unreason*. New York: Vintage, 2008.

Jennings, Brian. *Censorship: The Threat to Silence Talk Radio*. New York: Simon & Schuster, 2009.

Kahneman, Daniel. *Thinking Fast and Slow*. New York: Farrar, Strauss and Giroux, 2011.

Kaufman, Amie and Meagan Spooner. "Why Everyone Should Read More Science Fiction." *Huffington Post*, 2014.

Kenner, Robert. *Merchants of Doubt*. Sony Pictures, 2014.

Kerry, John and Teresa Heinz Kerry. *This Moment on Earth: Today's New Environmentalists and Their Vision for the Future*. New York: Public Affairs, 2007.

Krass, Peter. *Ignorance, Confidence, and Filthy Rich Friends: The Business Adventures of Mark Twain*. Hoboken, NJ: John Wiley & Sons, 2007.

Kwitney, Jonathan. *Endless Enemies: How America's Interventions Destroy Democracy and Free Enterprise and Defeat Our Own Best Interests*. New York: Congdon and Weed, 1984.

Lakoff, George. *Don't Think of an Elephant: Know Your Values and Frame the Debate*. White River Junction, VT: Chelsea Green, 2004.

———. *The Political Mind: Why You Can't Understand 21st Century American Politics with an 18th Century Mind*. New York: Viking, 2008.

Leigh, David and Luke Harding. "WikiLeaks: Julian Assange's War on Secrecy." *Guardian*, 2011.

Lloyd, John and John Mitchison. "Introduction," in *The Second Book of General Ignorance: Everything You Think You Know Is (Still) Wrong*. New York: Crown, 2010.

Lloyd, Mark. "Forget the Fairness Doctrine." Center for American Progress, 2007.

Lynd, Robert. "The Pleasures of Ignorance." *New Statesman*, 1921.

Manjoo, Farhad. *True Enough: Learning to Live in a Post-Fact Society*. New York: John Wiley and Sons, 2008.

Marcovitz, Hal. *Religious Fundamentalism*. San Diego: Reference Point, 2010.

Marlin-Bennett, Renee. *Knowledge Power: Intellectual Property, Information, and Privacy*. Boulder, CO: Lynne Rienner, 2004.

McIntosh, Steve. *Integral Consciousness and the Future of Evolution: How the Integral Worldview Is Transforming Politics, Culture and Spirituality*. St. Paul, MN: Paragon House, 2007.

McMaster, George and Clifford Trafzer, eds. *Native Universe: Voices of Indian America.* Washington, DC: National Geographic, 2004.

Menzel, Peter. *Material World: A Global Family Portrait.* San Francisco: Sierra Club Books, 1994.

Milbank, Dana. *Tears of a Clown: Glenn Beck and the Tea Bagging of America.* New York: Doubleday, 2010.

Mitchell, Greg. *So Wrong for So Long: How the Press, the Pundits, and the President Failed on Iraq.* Somerville, MA: Union Square, 2008.

Mitchell, Peter R. and John Schoefel, eds. *Understanding Power: The Indispensable Chomsky.* New York: New Press, 2002.

Morris, Dick and Eileen McGann. *Outrage.* New York: HarperCollins, 2007.

Morrison, Toni, ed. *Burn This Book: PEN Writers Speak Out on the Power of the Word.* New York: Harper, 2009.

Moyers, Bill. *Genesis: A Living Conversation.* New York: Doubleday, 1996.

Murawiec, Laurent. *The Mind of Jihad.* Cambridge: Cambridge University Press, 2008.

Nisbett, Richard E. *Mindware: Tools for Smart Thinking.* Toronto, ON: Doubleday, 2015.

Ortberg, John. *Know Doubt: Embracing Uncertainty in Your Faith.* Grand Rapids: Zondervan, 2008.

Otfinski, Steven. *Classic Books.* New York: Chelsea House, 2009.

Peck, M. Scott. *The Road Less Traveled: A New Psychology of Love, Traditional Values and Spiritual Growth.* New York: Simon & Schuster, 1978.

Perkins, John. *Confessions of an Economic Hit Man.* New York: Plume, 2006.

Polk, James. *The Triumph of Ignorance and Bliss: Pathologies of Public America.* Montreal, QC: Black Rose, 2005.

Postman, Neil. *Amusing Ourselves to Death: Public Discourse in the Age of Show Business.* New York: Viking, 1985.

Proctor, Robert N. and Londa Schiebinger. *Agnotology: The Making & Unmaking of Ignorance.* Palo Alto, CA: Stanford University Press, 2008.

Putnam, Robert D. and David Campbell. *American Grace: How Religion Divides and Unites Us.* New York: Simon & Schuster, 2010.

Ralston, Peter. *The Book of Not Knowing: Exploring the True Nature of Self, Mind, and Consciousness.* Berkeley, CA: North Atlantic, 2010.

Rauch, Jonathan. *Kindly Inquisitors: The New Attacks on Free Thought.* Chicago: University of Chicago Press, 1993.

Ravitch, Diane. *The Language Police: How Pressure Groups Restrict What Students Learn.* New York: Alfred A. Knopf, 2003.

Richman, Sheldon. "'Ancient History': US Conduct in the Middle East since WWII and the Folly of Intervention." *Policy Analysis* 159 (1991).

Rodriguez, Tori. "How Science Mimics Faith: People May Use Science as Others Use Faith." *Scientific American*, 2014.

Ronson, Jon. *The Psychopath Test: A Journey through the Madness Industry.* New York: Riverhead, 2011.

Rose, Gideon. *How Wars End: Why We Always Fight the Last Battle.* New York: Simon & Schuster, 2010.

Russo, Edward et al. "Identifying Misleading Advertising." *Journal of Consumer Research* 8 (1981).

Sachs, Jeffrey D. *Common Wealth: Economics for a Crowded Planet.* New York: Penguin Press, 2008.

Samuelson, Paul A. *Economics*, 19th ed. New York: Irwin/McGraw, 2004.

Sanger, David E. *The Inheritance: The World Obama Confronts and the Challenges to American Power.* New York: Crown, 2009.

Schweitzer, Peter. *Do As I Say, Not As I Do: Profiles in Liberal Hypocrisy.* New York: Doubleday, 2005.

Seymour, Richard. "Middle East Bloggers Set Cat among the Pigeons." *Middle East* 388 (2008): 62–63.

Richmond Lloyd and Timothy Castle. *Strategy and Force Planning*, 2nd ed. Newport, RI: Naval War College, 1998.

Suskind, Ron. *Confidence Men: Wall Street, Washington, and the Education of a President.* New York: HarperCollins, 2011.

Thompson, Clive. "Manufacturing Confusion: How More Information Leads to Less Knowledge." *Conde Nast*, 2009.

Thompson, Dennis. *Ethics in Congress: From Individual to Institutional Corruption.* Washington: Brookings Institution, 1995.

Tirman, John. *The Deaths of Others: The Fate of Civilians in America's Wars.* Oxford: Oxford University Press, 2011.

Tocqueville, Alexis de. *Democracy in America.* New York: Literary Classics of the United States, 2004.

Toffler, Alvin. *Future Shock.* New York: Random House, 1970.

Tomasello, Michael et al. "Two Key Steps in the Evolution of Human Cooperation: The Interdependence Hypothesis." *Current Anthropology* 53, no. 6 (2012).

Tosh, Nick. "Review of: *Agnotology: The Making and Unmaking of Ignorance. British Journal for the History of Science.*" Cambridge University Press, 2009.

Van Doren, Mark, ed. *Adventures of the Mind.* New York: Alfred A Knopf, 1960.

Vitek, Bill and Wes Jackson, eds. *The Virtues of Ignorance: Complexity, Sustainability, and the Limits of Knowledge.* Lexington, KY: University of Kentucky Press, 2008.

Watkins, Jan S. et al. *Intellectual Freedom for Children: The Censor Is Coming.* Chicago: American Library Association, 2000.

Weisberg, Herbert I. *Willful Ignorance: The Mismeasure of Uncertainty.* Hoboken, NJ: Wiley & Sons, 2014.

Williams, Mary E., ed. *Discrimination.* Farmington Hills, MI: Greenhaven Press, 2003.

Wink, Walter. *The Powers That Be: Theology for a New Millennium.* New York: Galilee Doubleday, 1998.

Wright, Micah Ian. *You Back the Attack! We'll Bomb Who We Want: Remixed War Propaganda.* New York: Seven Stories, 2003.

Zaitchik, Alexander. *Common Nonsense: Glenn Beck and the Triumph of Ignorance.* New York: John Wiley & Sons, 2010.

Zinn, Howard. *The Indispensable Zinn: The Essential Writings of the "People's Historian."* New York: New Press, 2012.

———. *The Zinn Reader: Writings on Disobedience and Democracy.* New York: Seven Stories, 1997.

Zinn, Howard, with David Barsamian. *Original Zinn: Conversations on History and Politics.* New York: Harper Perennial, 2006.

INDEX